Honourable Members

HONOURABLE MEMBERS

A Study of the British Backbencher

PETER G. RICHARDS

Lecturer in Government
University of Southampton

FREDERICK A. PRAEGER

New York, N.Y.

BOOKS THAT MATTER

*Published in the United States of America
in 1959 by Frederick A. Praeger, Inc.,
Publishers, 15 West 47 Street,
New York 36, N.Y.*

© Peter G. Richards

Printed in Great Britain

To
ANN LESLEY

Preface

This book is offered as a general examination of the role of the backbench Member of the House of Commons in the British system of government. It is concerned to argue that the individual Member is something more than a pawn in the game of party politics; that his services are essential to a democratic society; that, collectively, backbenchers can exercise significant influence over public policy. It also reviews the limitations within which Members must work. Many of the following pages are related to the parliamentary scene, but no attempt is made to provide a description of parliamentary procedure which is admirably covered elsewhere. Nor is the book concerned with the past. It includes commentary on the more important developments affecting backbenchers since 1945 but, in general, historical material has been restricted to events that are of major contemporary significance. There is, as a result, no assessment of the work of backbenchers in the exceptional conditions of war-time. The last war provided a real watershed, for 1945 marked the beginning of many changes in the pattern of parliamentary life.

To assist identification, the constituency and party affiliation are given for the Members mentioned in the text. All backbenchers noticed were still Honourable Members on the 1st May, 1958, unless the contrary is indicated. These citations have sometimes been omitted to avoid undue repetition, especially in the case of Ministers, and they are not given for statesmen of the pre-war period.

I am deeply grateful to those who have assisted me to gather information. They include Members from both sides of the House and people employed by the political parties, the civil service and the press. Probably a majority of my collaborators would not wish to be named in print, so they shall all be unmentioned. This avoids any possibility of the unfair attribution of my views—or my errors—to others. But I am very conscious of what I owe to those who have discussed or corresponded with me about the activities of backbenchers.

PREFACE

British Parliamentary Papers are the major source of published material that has been used. Reference has been made also to biographies, memoirs and the books and articles of other students of public affairs.

Acknowledgements are due to Cassell and Co. for permission to reproduce an extract from Earl Winterton's *Orders of the Day*, and to the Hansard Society for permission to reproduce a passage from *Straight Fight* by S. Milne and H. C. Mackenzie, and also to use material from an article of mine which originally appeared in the Society's journal *Parliamentary Affairs*.

The staff of the Department of Economics at this University have rendered invaluable assistance: Mrs. P. E. Dunn has helped with the typing and Miss D. Marshallsay, B.A., A.L.A., the Departmental Librarian, has checked references and is responsible for the Index. On some legal matters I have had the aid of Mr. H. A. Samuels, B.A. But, as before, the greatest debt is to my wife for the sacrifice of countless hours to the improvement and preparation of the typescript.

PETER G. RICHARDS

University of Southampton
May 1958

Contents

11

CONTENTS

12

The Selection of Parliamentary Candidates

No Independent candidate has been elected to the House of Commons since 1945: to become an Honourable Member it is necessary, in practice, to have the support of a political party. A major cause of the elimination of Independents was the abolition of university constituencies by the Representation of the People Act, 1948, for although there was a considerable political flavour about university elections, eight of the twelve university Members returned in 1945 were styled 'Independent'. Labour supporters were justified, however, in arguing that some of these Independents were generally sympathetic to Conservative ideas. Four Independents were also elected for territorial constituencies in 1945.[1] It is significant that each of these Members had been first returned at a by-election and that two had taken advantage of the war-time political truce between the major parties. The failure, and usually dismal failure, of other Independent candidates in recent years gives proof of the utter inability of the unattached individual to combat the might of the established party organizations. Mass electorates are fatal to the politically unorthodox. Thus, since 1950, any Independents there may have been in the Commons are those who have quarrelled with their parties subsequently to the previous election. The power of political machines is now also demonstrated in local government, and in large towns, where the local elections are fought on party lines, it is increasingly impossible for an Independent candidate to win a seat on the town council. In the case of parliamentary elections an Independent can have no hope of arriving at Westminster unless he can persuade one

---

[1] They were Vernon Bartlett, Member for Bridgwater 1938–50; W. J. Brown, Member for Rugby 1942–50, previously Labour Member for Wolverhampton, West, 1929–31; W. D. Kendall, Member for Grantham 1942–50; and D. L. Lipson, Member for Cheltenham 1937–50.

of the major political parties to stand aside in his favour. Very occasionally the Conservative Party may be willing to do so for tactical reasons: in 1951 they gave a blessing to W. J. Brown for Fulham, West, and in 1955 W. L. Davies was given a clear run against the Labour candidate at Pembroke. But neither of these Independents was successful.

The Liberal Party is now reduced to six Members in the House of Commons. It follows that Liberal candidates have a much smaller chance of winning an election than have Labour or Conservative candidates. The Liberals, indeed, are nearly in the same position as the Independents as four of the six Liberal Members retained their seats in 1955 more or less by the permission of the Conservatives, who did not put forward candidates against them. The leader of the Liberal Party, Clement Davies (Merioneth) and J. Grimond (Orkney and Zetland) were the only Liberal Members who had to face both Labour and Conservative opponents in 1955. The two-party system is now firmly established in this country and it is essential to recognize that it has a dominating influence over the selection of Honourable Members. The choice of the individuals who become Members is not solely a matter for the electorate, but depends largely on the decisions of the local Labour and Conservative selection committees. Voters tend to cast their ballots for a party, not for a local candidate, and it is easy to over-estimate the importance of the personality of a candidate on the result of the election in a particular constituency. 'I would vote for a pig if the party put one up' is the reported comment of an ardent party supporter at the time of the 1951 Election.[1] This is an extreme view but it is frequently asserted that the personality of the candidate is not worth 500 votes. At the 1955 Election, however, the character of the individual candidate appeared to be of rather greater importance than in 1950 or 1951,[2] and it is always of more significance at by-elections when there is no flood of election propaganda at the national level and when the choice of a government is not involved. But at general elections, in seats held by large majorities, constituency organizations of the Labour and Conservative Parties can proceed to nominate candidates with but little consideration of their suitability for Parliamentary work, in the knowledge that the local result will not be materially affected by their choice. This is not to say that local associations often behave in

[1] D. E. Butler, *The British General Election of 1951*, p. 173.
[2] D. E. Butler, *The British General Election of 1955*, pp. 203–4.

an irresponsible way, for naturally they prefer to be represented by a person who can do good service for his Party and his constituents. When a local association has selected its candidate he (or she) is known as the 'prospective parliamentary candidate'. The candidature does not become formal until the official adoption meeting at the beginning of an election campaign. In each constituency the political parties, other than the one that holds the seat, frequently adopt prospective candidates well in advance of the anticipated date of the next general election in order to give the nominees the opportunity of becoming known in the locality. The appointment of a prospective candidate is binding for one election only, and after a contest the question of candidature is automatically re-opened. Prospective candidates often resign their position before a contest, sometimes in order to move away to a more favourable seat. The Wilson Report[1] urged that prospective Labour candidates should be appointed as soon as possible, and that they should establish 'surgeries' to deal with constituents' problems in the same way as sitting Members. The Report also showed concern at the high turnover of Labour candidates.

'In some cases there were three different prospective Labour candidates in a division between 1952 and 1955. This question of turnover is a serious one. In 568 constituencies (redistribution prevents us from taking a greater number) only 287 had the same candidates in 1955 as in 1951; only 237 had the same candidates in 1950, 1951 and 1955. Out of 179 constituencies scheduled as marginal only 109 of the 1955 candidates had fought there in 1951; only 90 in 1950 and 1951.'[2]

The vast majority of those who continued to stand for the same constituency were, of course, sitting Members.

It is necessary for Honourable Members to be renominated by their local associations for every election, but they do not have to compete against other potential candidates. A Member may decide to retire and if he does he may let his local party know well in advance, so that another prospective candidate may be chosen. Or it is possible that a local party will decide not to re-nominate a sitting Member, but the scales are heavily weighted in his favour. The time between the announcement of an election and the date of the contest

[1] Interim Report of the Sub-Committee on Party Organization. The Labour Party, 1955, para. 67.
[2] Ibid., para. 66.

15

gives little time in which to decide to make a change, find a new standard-bearer, and conduct an election campaign. In the Labour Party it is necessary for the constituency party to obtain a mandate from its affiliated organizations to replace a sitting Member: a mandate is defined as a motion that has been circulated to affiliated organizations beforehand so as to enable them to instruct their delegates to the general committee of the constituency party how to vote. Only one Labour Member was thus rejected in 1955,[1] but a few other elderly Members were 'encouraged' to retire. In addition, a small number of constituencies tried to replace Members who had supported German rearmament, but their efforts were disallowed by the National Executive Committee on the grounds that the mandate procedure had not been followed correctly.

It is also possible for local party enthusiasts to initiate a campaign against their own Member before an election is in prospect. In 1940 Captain Cunningham-Reid[2] was asked to resign his seat by the St. Marylebone Conservative Association but refused to do so: two years later the Association split into two in a continuation of the dispute about their Member and the section which desired to sponsor an alternative candidate achieved recognition from Conservative headquarters. At the 1945 Election E. Gandar Dower[3] pledged himself to resign and fight a by-election at the end of the war with Japan; as his majority was as low as six it is not improbable that this pledge won him the seat. When he proposed to fulfil his undertaking the local Conservative Association objected, and after three years of controversy the Association resolved to offer no support if a by-election were held. There was no by-election but Gandar Dower was not readopted. Sometimes a Member can ride out a local storm: Lord Hinchingbrooke has successfully defended himself against his critics in the South Dorset Conservative Association. The most exceptional case of this kind in recent years is that of J. H. McKie (Galloway). Shortly before the 1945 Election the local Unionist Association decided by a narrow majority not to readopt their Member because of his alleged bad attendance in the Commons and neglect of correspondence.[4] Thereupon, McKie stood as an Independent Conservative against both Labour and Conservative can-

---

[1] D. E. Butler, *The General Election of 1955*, p. 46.
[2] Member for Warrington 1922–23, 1924–29 and St. Marylebone 1932–45.
[3] Member for Caithness 1945–50.
[4] *Scotsman*, 4th June, 1945.

didates, and was re-elected. This unusual defeat for the party machine must be attributed to the strength of McKie's local connections, for both his grandfather and great-grandfather had represented the same constituency. The impact of the Suez crisis on the position of certain Members is described in Chapter 7.

When constituency boundaries are reorganized the conditions are different. New constituency parties are formed and there is no sitting Member as the constituency did not exist at the previous election. Candidates, therefore, are chosen *de novo*. In the re-shuffle caused by redistribution Honourable Members whose constituencies are affected may fail to secure nomination without moving to pastures new: three leading Labour Members suffered in this way in 1955, Dr. Summerskill,[1] Sir Frank Soskice[2] and Woodrow Wyatt.[3] Ultimately Dr. Summerskill was elected for Warrington, Woodrow Wyatt was defeated at Grantham and Sir Frank Soskice was not a candidate anywhere.

The process of selecting a new Conservative candidate is fairly uniform, but it may be varied a little by the degree of urgency. The choice of a prospective candidate shortly after a general election for a seat held by the Labour Party can be made in leisurely fashion: the need to find a candidate for an unexpected by-election demands speedy action and preliminary consultations must be cut to a minimum. The normal procedure is for a small selection committee to be appointed which contains representatives of the various sections of the Party, i.e. a Young Conservative, a trade unionist and at least one woman member. The Chairman of the constituency association will be the chairman of this committee. Names of possible candidates will be suggested by the Conservative Central Office, local Conservatives may intimate privately that they wish to be considered and it is open to the selection committee to take the initiative itself and to ask an individual if he or she is willing to stand. From these various sources a considerable number of names may be collected and of these up to a dozen people may be asked to attend for a preliminary interview by the selection committee. Male applicants, if married, are sometimes asked to bring their wives with them. It is usual for the selection committee to send three names forward to the executive council of

---

[1] Member for Fulham, West, 1938–55 and Warrington since 1955.
[2] Member for Birkenhead, East, 1945–50, Sheffield, Neepsend, 1950–55 and Newport, Mon., since 1956.
[3] Member for Birmingham, Aston, 1945–55.

B

the local association to make the final choice. The executive council consists of from sixty to a hundred people; it listens to a political speech from each of the remaining contenders, thus giving them an opportunity to show the quality of their performance before a public meeting. The applicants do not hear each other and they may be asked questions. When this ordeal is over the council deliberates and finally decides on a candidate to recommend to a general meeting of the local association: adoption of this recommendation by the general meeting is nearly always a formality, but in 1952 the Conservatives at Southport chose a local ex-mayor in preference to the name suggested to them.[1] The nomination has also to be approved by the Conservative Standing Advisory Committee on Candidates, which is presided over by the national Vice-Chairman of the Party.

The analogous procedure in the Labour Party is complicated by the nature of the constitution of the Party. Membership of a Constituency Labour Party consists of both individual members and of affiliated organizations—trade unions and co-operatives. Individual members are entitled to attend the ward or district committee for the area in which they live. In each constituency there is a general committee composed of representatives of the affiliated organizations and of the ward or district committees. The rights of these various bodies are all determined by the rules of the Labour Party, and the selection of a parliamentary candidate must be carried out on lines rigidly prescribed by the rules. In an emergency and for by-elections the National Executive Committee permit these rules to be relaxed. When it is necessary to choose a candidate, the organizations that make up the general committee are invited to submit nominations of persons who are individual members of the Labour Party or of an affiliated organization. In the Labour Party it is not possible to put forward your own name as it is in the Conservative Party. A Labour candidate must not be a person disqualified by the constitution of the Party or through membership of a 'proscribed organization'; this provision is intended to keep out Communists and their sympathizers. The nominations received from local sources have to be submitted to Transport House before they are considered by the General Committee, and the National Executive Committee may advise the local executive that certain nominees are not acceptable on personal or policy grounds. A further provision applies to any person whose name is on the panel of parliamentary candidates of an affiliated

[1] I. Bulmer-Thomas, *The Party System in Great Britain*, p. 206.

18

organization: the written consent of the executive of the organization must be submitted with the nomination. This is because the affiliated organizations give financial assistance towards election expenditure when a member of their parliamentary panel is chosen as a candidate. While the affiliated body, a trade union or a co-operative society, may be willing to pay up to fight a safe or marginal seat, it may not be willing to finance a contest in a 'hopeless' constituency. Besides the local nominations, suggestions of two or more people will be made by Party headquarters, and these may be interviewed by the local executive committee. The local executive then draws up a 'short list' of applicants who appear before the general committee and make short political speeches. A decision is made by ballot, or a series of ballots, for no candidate is chosen without an absolute majority of all the votes cast. If there are n candidates on the short list and no one gets an absolute majority on the first ballot, those with fewer than $1/_n$ of the total vote are eliminated and another ballot is held. If necessary, the process is repeated until one contender has attracted 51% of the votes. This, however, is not the end of the process. The name of the selected candidate has to be submitted to the National Executive Committee for approval, and the N.E.C. has to satisfy itself both of the suitability of the nomination, and that adequate financial arrangements have been made to support the candidature, before it can be made public.

What factors influence the decisions of local selection committees? The description of procedure gives little guide, except to indicate that parties at the national level are concerned with the activities of constituency parties. Both the Conservative and Labour Parties have a right of veto over the local selection of candidates: yet this right is used but seldom. When it is used it is open to a local association to ignore the decision, continue to sponsor the candidate who has been found objectionable, and suffer disaffiliation from the national body. In practice, such extreme steps are almost always avoided. In 1951, however, a violent dispute raged among Conservatives in Newcastle-upon-Tyne, North, over the choice of a candidate. The feud was so strong that a breakaway association was formed and adopted Major Lloyd George[1] as its candidate: rival Conservative nominees were therefore presented to the electors. The Conservative Central Office gave a blessing to Major Lloyd George who was duly elected while

[1] Now Lord Tenby. Liberal Member for Pembroke 1922–24 and 1929–50; Liberal and Conservative Member for Newcastle-upon-Tyne, North, 1951–57.

the other Conservative candidate barely saved his deposit. The original Conservative association declined into oblivion and the power of conformity was once again demonstrated.

Can Party headquarters persuade a local association to choose a particular candidate? This is a more delicate question than the ability to use a veto, for it is a matter not of power but of influence. Strong pressure may be put on a constituency to accept a prominent member of the Party who has lost his seat in the Commons. Such pressure may be unnecessary or unsuccessful. Some local associations are pleased to have the chance to adopt a candidate with a national reputation: other associations resent interference by a central office or have a strong local contender for the nomination. If a constituency says 'No' to the suggestion of party headquarters, there is nothing headquarters can do. And it is poor tactics to over-persuade a local association for, if party enthusiasts dislike their candidate, the vigour of the local campaign may be affected. Local associations are jealous of their independence, especially in the Labour Party, and Labour ex-Ministers who lost their seats, A. Creech Jones[1] and Lewis Silkin,[2] found it difficult or impossible to again become Honourable Members. In 1955 Transport House devoted much energy to securing the seat at Warrington for Dr. Edith Summerskill, then Chairman of the Labour Party, whose previous constituency had disintegrated in re-distribution. These manœuvres included an attempt to advance the date of the selection conference at Barons Court so that it should precede the selection conference at Warrington. W. T. Williams[3] was a potential candidate at both Barons Court and Warrington: if, therefore, Williams were first accommodated at Barons Court the field would have been clearer for Dr. Summerskill at Warrington. Ultimately Summerskill was chosen to contest Warrington and the following day Williams was chosen for Barons Court. Yet there is a provision in the constitution of the Labour Party that in an emergency the National Executive may advise the local Party to select a particular nomination it may submit to it.[4] In 1955 one major instance of central intervention received much publicity. The Labour Party in the Exchange division of Liverpool decided not to re-adopt Mrs. Braddock as their candidate; the National Executive of the

---

[1] Member for Shipley 1935–50 and Wakefield since 1954.
[2] Now Lord Silkin. Member for Peckham 1936–50.
[3] Member for Hammersmith, South, 1949–55 and Barons Court since 1955.
[4] R. T. Mackenzie, *British Political Parties*, pp. 552–3.

Labour Party then held a general inquiry into the affairs of the Exchange division. It found that the division had become dominated by a small group of political extremists who failed to observe correct procedures, and that the meeting which rejected Mrs. Braddock had been improperly constituted. The N.E.C. therefore decreed that Mrs. Braddock should be reinstated. A further meeting of the General Management Committee of the Exchange division was attended by the Regional Secretary of the Labour Party, who made it clear to the assembled delegates that anyone who voted against the national directive would be expelled from the Party and that, if necessary, a new constituency party would be formed from those who supported Mrs. Braddock.[1] Thereupon Mrs. Braddock was readopted, but afterwards the local Secretary issued a statement which said:

'The issue involved is much bigger than Mrs. Braddock. It is simply whether a local body representing the Labour workers of the constituency should have the right to say who should represent it publicly. The constituency will support Mrs. Braddock—with a gun at their head.'[2]

A member of the local executive did, however, resign from the Labour Party and presented himself as an Independent Labour candidate, but he lost his deposit and Mrs. Braddock was easily re-elected. Incidents such as this are worth recalling in detail because they are rare: normally, national and local party units retain a sense of outward comradeship even when complete harmony does not prevail. In 1955 Transport House also had to give succour to a number of Labour Members who had displeased their local associations by supporting the rearmament of Western Germany. Thus A. Skeffington (Hayes and Harlington) owed his renomination to the intervention of Party headquarters.

The difference between Mrs. Braddock and the Exchange Labour Party was rooted in policy, and it might be expected that questions of policy would play a great part in the choice of candidates. In 1955 the Gorton Labour Party preferred Konni Zilliacus to Sir Frank Soskice, and Hammersmith, North, chose F. Tomney rather than W. T. Williams: the former case could be cited as a victory for the left-wing of the Labour Party, the latter as a victory for the right-wing. But other similar examples are hard to find. It seems that selection committees, for the most part, pick whoever seems to them to be the best

---

[1] *Daily Telegraph*, 29th April 1955.
[2] Ibid.

person for the job, rather than the person whose detailed views are the most acceptable. Some Labour Members are noted for their pacifist convictions while others are temperance advocates, but this is not a reflection of the views of their constituency supporters. There is no evidence to show that Members take a great deal of notice of the opinions of constituency associations; looking at the matter from the other end, the Pembroke Labour Party seemed as ready to support Desmond Donnelly when he followed Aneurin Bevan as when he opposed him. In the Conservative Party candidates are also picked on personal grounds. The belief in the stability of the two-party system has sunk deep into the consciousness of the local leaders of the major parties and this may explain why the policy aspect of choosing a particular candidate is so largely ignored.

The next factor that demands consideration is finance, which is now of greater importance in candidate selection in the Labour Party than with the Conservatives. Before Hitler's war it was commonly admitted that Conservative Members were expected to make considerable contributions towards Party and election expenses. As early as 1924, Stanley Baldwin, the newly-chosen leader of the Conservatives, was telling his supporters that few men could face the heavy financial demands made on parliamentary candidates by constituency organizations, but his warning that the Conservative Party would suffer from this limitation on its choice of representatives went unheeded.[1] In 1939 a Conservative candidate, Ian Harvey,[2] issued a memorandum to the press entitled 'A Plutocratic System'. This suggested that potential Conservative candidates could be divided into three categories—Class A whose chances of selection were excellent, Class B whose chances were reasonable and Class C who had hardly any chance at all. Class A candidates were those willing to pay all their election expenses and contribute between £500 and £1,000 p.a. to the local association: Class B could pay at least half their election expenses and subscribe between £250 and £400 p.a. to the local association: Class C could pay nothing towards election expenses and £100 p.a. or less to the association. Even if the detail of this analysis be not accepted, it is clear that in 1939 only the wealthy could become Conservative Members. The practice of 'selling seats' continued until

---

[1] G. M. Young, *Stanley Baldwin*, pp. 74, 79.

[2] Member for Harrow, East, since 1950. The important passages of his memorandum are reproduced by J. F. S. Ross in an appendix to *Parliamentary Representation*.

1948 when, following the Maxwell-Fyfe Report on Party Organization, the Conservatives adopted new rules to govern financial relationships between constituencies and prospective candidates. Election expenses are now the responsibility of the constituency association and no payment may be made towards them by the candidate. The candidate may, or may not, meet 'personal' election expenses, which are limited by law to £100, and he may not contribute more than £25 p.a. to Party funds, or £50 p.a. if elected to the Commons. Personal fortune now appears to be effectively ruled out as a determinant of Conservative candidates, and the increased financial responsibility placed on local associations has had a stimulating effect on their activities and has increased their eagerness to attract a larger membership.

Labour Party rules on this matter are complicated by the practice of allowing sympathetic organizations to sponsor candidates. A sponsor may contribute up to 80% of the election expenses incurred on behalf of its nominee. Up to £350 p.a. towards local Party funds may also be paid in a borough constituency, or £420 p.a. in a county constituency: where a full-time local agent is employed these maxima are raised to 50% of the agent's salary in boroughs and 60% of his salary in county constituencies. These arrangements, known as the 'Hastings Agreement', were first introduced in 1933 and amended in 1948 and 1957. Before 1957 an individual candidate could make payments on the same scale as a sponsoring body and in 1955 the authors of the Wilson Report were disturbed by the number of candidates who were required to make personal contributions to constituency finances. The Report recommended that 'early steps be taken to end this practice' and that at Selection Conferences 'any attempt to influence a selection by personal promises of money or any attempt to exact a financial pledge from a possible candidate shall invalidate the conference'.[1] The position now is that a candidate may pay only his personal expenses at an election—hotel bills, travelling expenses, etc.—and his annual donation to Party revenues must not exceed £50. Another new rule, dating from 1957, is that when a Labour candidate is being chosen no questions relating to the financing of the candidature may be asked until after the selection has been made; but it will still be known which, if any, of the potential candidates have the backing of wealthy organizations. Sponsoring undoubtedly weakens local Labour Parties for, by removing a large

[1] para. 68.

23

part of their monetary cares, it reduces the stimulus to increase membership. Further, it also tends to produce cash mainly in areas where Labour is strong and should be least in need of extra help. Yet no sign exists that this system will end. On the contrary, there is significant friction between the various sections of the Labour movement over the nomination of candidates; many trade unions are concerned at their falling strength in the Commons and are keen to increase it. In 1955, 128 Labour candidates were sponsored by trade unions and a further 38 by the Co-operative Party. The greatest number came from the National Union of Mineworkers with 35; second were the T. and G.W.U. with 16; others with ten or more candidates were the A.E.U., the N.U.R., the U.S.D.A.W. and the Transport Salaried Staffs Association.[1] The table below shows that the unions tend to run candidates in those seats where the chances of success are high.

TRADE UNION CANDIDATURES 1945–55

Year	T.U. candidates	T.U. candidates elected	% of T.U. candidates elected	Total Labour Members	T.U. Members as % Labour Members
1945	125	120	96	394	30
1950	140	111	79	315	35
1951	139	105	76	295	36
1955	128	96	75	277	35

There is also a slight tendency for trade union influence to be proportionately weakest in the Parliamentary Labour Party when the political climate is most favourable to Labour: had the unions sponsored as many candidates in 1955 as in 1951 or 1950 this would be much more noticeable.

The selection of a candidate for a seat that he is expected to win is necessarily a more important business than the selection of a candidate who can hope to do no more than reduce an opponent's majority. In the former case competition for the nomination will be much keener and people who have already stood unsuccessfully elsewhere, and perhaps ex-Members, will be interested in the vacancy. Potential Honourable Members often serve an apprenticeship in a 'hopeless' constituency before moving on to a constituency that offers prospects of success. The extent to which this is done is an important

[1] D. E. Butler, *The British General Election of 1955*, p. 219 (in Appendix III by M. Harrison).

SELECTION OF PARLIAMENTARY CANDIDATES

guide to the decisions of selection committees and tells something of the sense of political vocation of Members. But the personal histories of those returned at any election will depend upon the circumstances of the time. The more recent the previous election, the greater will be the number of candidates with experience of parliamentary elections. The movement of opinion is also important; if it is violent the turnover of seats is large and candidates attacking majorities thought to be safe suddenly find themselves at Westminster. Consequently, the electoral experience of new Members will be greatest when the movement of the political pendulum is small and the interval since the last election short—as in 1951. New Members will be most inexperienced politically when there is a major change in opinion and the election is the first for a long time—as in 1945.

The figures below set out some facts about the electoral experience of new Members returned at the elections of 1951 and 1955 and the by-elections in between.[1] (My definition of 'new' includes both Members elected for the first time and those returned to the House of Commons after an interval in their parliamentary service.) Some of these Members enjoy secure majorities in seats formerly held by their own party: others represent new or redistributed constituencies: others, almost all Conservatives, have small majorities in seats wrested from their opponents.

At the 1955 Election sixty-six Members were returned who had not sat in the previous Parliament; the corresponding figure for the 1951 Election was fifty-seven. The table on the following page shows how many of the newcomers were successful at their first attempt. If there is a good chance of winning a seat, selection committees in boroughs appear rather less willing to adopt a candidate unversed in the arts of electioneering. Is this because elections in towns are more keenly contested and it is thought more important for the candidate to make a favourable impression and to know how to deal with heckling? If this were true, one would expect the handful of new Members returned at their first contest by borough constituencies to represent safe seats. But this is not the case: in 1955 their percentage majorities were spread evenly between the extremes of 3·9% at Bootle and 15% at Birmingham (Selly Oak). The answer may be that county constituencies often prefer to have a local candidate.

---

[1] They are drawn from my article in *Parliamentary Affairs*, Vol. IX, No. 3, 1955, 'A Study in Political Apprenticeship', which contained the substance of the following paragraphs.

ELECTORAL EXPERIENCE OF NEW MEMBERS[1]

(Numbers of Members)

Members from	Boroughs or Burghs		Counties		Totals
	Labour	Conservative	Labour	Conservative	
1951					
First Contest	6	1	2	8	17
Previous Contest(s)	2	15	3	18	38
Totals	8	16	5	26	55
1955					
First Contest	3	3	4	12	22
Previous Contest(s)	9	18	2	15	44
Totals	12	21	6	27	66

A most useful exercise is to compare the figures on a party basis: this shows that nearly half the new Labour Members were successful at a first attempt while the corresponding proportion of Conservatives was below 30%. The Labour Party are the more willing to have untried standard-bearers in favourable seats because of trade union intervention in the process of selection. The National Union of Mineworkers usually nominates about 35 Labour candidates: these are in safe Labour seats and in 1955 all but one were elected. It follows that N.U.M. candidates normally succeed at the first attempt and this helps to explain the proportion shown in the third column of the above table. Admittedly, the N.U.M. is an extreme example, yet the potential Labour Member will gain at least as much advantage from the financial support of a trade union as he will from having fought, and possibly won, a seat at a previous election. Only three Labour ex-Members returned to the Commons at the 1955 Election: the corresponding number for 1951 was two. Nine Conservative ex-Members were returned in 1951 and two in 1955, but the figures are not comparable since scarcely any Conservatives have lost their seats

[1] Northern Ireland is excluded from this table as political conditions in Ulster are quite different from those in the United Kingdom. The new (Liberal) Member for Bolton, West, in 1951 is also omitted.

since 1945. One major difference between the two Elections is not shown by these statistics. In 1951 fourteen of the new Members had fought the same constituency at the previous general election: there was, therefore, a marked tendency for unsuccessful Conservative candidates for marginal constituencies in 1950 to stay put and fight the same territory again. In 1955 only two of the new Members had fought the same constituency in 1951 and one of these, Sidney Dye (Labour, S.W. Norfolk), had stood for this constituency at each election since 1935. The greater movement of candidates in the period 1951–55 is the result of the reorganization of constituency boundaries and also of the greater time interval between elections. In addition, the narrow majority of the Labour government in 1950 created a widespread belief that another election could not be long delayed.

Traditionally by-elections provide an opportunity for displaced Members to return to Westminster. Eight ex-Members, six Labour and two Conservative, did return in this way at the by-elections held between the general elections of 1951 and 1955. Seventeen Labour Members were returned at these by-elections, so the number re-elected was not large considering the number of Labour Members defeated in 1950 and 1951. This is a further indication of trade union influence, for many of those defeated in 1950 and 1951 had no union connections. Conservatives returned at by-elections in the counties have usually stood previously elsewhere: under the stress of having to obtain a candidate in a short time, rural Conservatives welcome experienced candidates. The table below gives an indication of the strength of this tendency.

ELECTORAL EXPERIENCE OF NEW MEMBERS
BY-ELECTIONS: 1951–55

(Numbers of Members)

Members from	Boroughs or Burghs		Counties		Totals
	Labour	Conservative	Labour	Conservative	
First contest	6	5	3	2	16
Previous contest(s)	5	8	3	12	28
Totals	11	13	6	14	44

If the figures in the above tables are aggregated it will be seen that of the 48 Labour Members concerned exactly half were successful at the first attempt, but only 31 of the 117 Conservatives were as fortunate. Forty-three of these new Members (5 Labour, 38 Conservative) had fought twice or more unsuccessfully before arriving at Westminster.

Turning from the personal history of new Members to the fate of all new candidates a similar trend can be observed. Of the 200 Conservatives standing for the first time at the 1955 Election only 17[1] were successful: of the 188 Labour 'first-timers', 7 were elected. Two hundred and nineteen of the Conservatives standing in 1955 had fought their first contest in 1945 or earlier, and of these 207 were successful: the parallel figures for the Labour Party are 294 of whom 237 were successful. It is noteworthy that unsuccessful Labour candidates are the more persistent. The general picture is remarkably clear. Most potential Members have to make their way from unfavourable to more favourable seats, and few owe their nominations to the strength of their local connections. Both the major parties have a national pool of candidates and members of the pool are expected to stand at first for a seat where their chances range from poor to non-existent. In the Labour Party this pattern is modified in some constituencies, frequently Labour strongholds, where a particular trade union has established a strong influence. Scotland, Wales and Ulster provide some regional limitation to the operation of these pools, and in rural areas distant from London the Conservatives often choose a candidate with local associations. But probably a majority of Members have no initial interest in the areas they come to represent, and political ambition demands many years of preparation for its fulfilment. Our politicians may be the more submissive to party discipline in the Commons because they are peripatetic.

It follows from the above analysis that successful candidates are older than the unsuccessful, and in 1955 the average difference was ten years. The table below shows by percentages the distribution of different categories of candidate between the different age-groups.

---

[1] The figures in this paragraph are adapted from D. E. Butler, *The General Election of 1955*, p. 39. The number of 17 successful 'first-time' Conservatives differs from that given above (p. 26) as the latter figures excluded Northern Ireland.

SELECTION OF PARLIAMENTARY CANDIDATES

AGE-DISTRIBUTION OF CANDIDATES: 1955[1]

| | Conservative | | Labour | |
	Successful	Unsuccessful	Successful	Unsuccessful
20's	1·4	11·8	—	9·6
30's	15·1	38·4	7·2	31·5
40's	36·7	29·8	26·0	33·8
50's	33·5	16·8	39·0	15·7
60's	11·6	3·2	20·9	8·2
70's	1·4	—	6·5	1·2
80's	0·3	—	0·4	—
Totals	100·0	100·0	100·0	100·0

The two octogenarians elected in 1955 were Sir Winston Churchill and David Logan, Labour Member for the Scotland division of Liverpool. The two youngest of those elected do not appear in the table above: they were Sinn Feiners serving prison sentences and were both unable and unwilling to take their seats. The youngest Members in 1955, therefore, were two Conservatives aged 27, R. Chichester-Clark (Londonderry) and P. Kirk who won unexpectedly owing to a split in the Labour vote at Gravesend.

The average age of Labour Members and candidates is higher than that of the Conservatives. In 1955 the average difference was about five years, and the same tendency has been traced since 1918.[2] Why are the Conservatives more content to have younger representatives? The Conservatives do not share the deep-seated suspicion of many Labour supporters for the young intellectual: the Young Conservative movement plays a large part in Conservative organization while the Labour League of Youth has been dissolved. Labour supporters tend to favour a person who has made his way in the world; Conservatives are more accustomed to the idea of a patrician class, the younger members of which rise early to positions of social leadership. On the Labour side the age of trade union nominees tends to be high, for unions are not willing to sponsor the candidature of any member who has not given a long period of service to the trade union movement. Then there are economic considerations other than those

[1] This information has been adapted from D. E. Butler, *The British General Election of 1955*, p. 40.
[2] For an exhaustive analysis of the ages of Members in the period 1918–51 see J. F. S. Ross, *Elections and Electors*, pp. 386–99.

relating to election expenditure. The man who wishes to build for himself some measure of financial security will not devote his early years to a political career unless he has family financial resources to fall back on: young Conservatives are clearly the more likely to have such family assistance. Thus the age differential is not merely the product of the attitudes of selection conferences, it is also a reflection on the type of potential candidate coming forward in each of the major parties.

Only a few women become Honourable Members: 24 were elected in 1955 and this equalled the record set up in 1945. How far this is the fault of women themselves cannot be precisely determined, as no adequate information exists about the number of women wishing to become parliamentary candidates. Selection committees appear to be prejudiced against women because it is easier for a woman to obtain nomination for a seat unlikely to be won than for a seat where chances are good. A comparison of the proportion of men and women candidates elected illustrates the feminine disadvantage.

SUCCESS OF CANDIDATES BY SEX: 1955

Party	% male candidates elected	% female candidates elected
Labour	45	33
Conservative	59	31

The Labour Party are less unfavourable to women than the Conservatives, and 14 of the 24 women elected in 1955 were Labour Members. This distinction is not as marked as it used to be for only one of the 24 women elected in 1945 was a Conservative—Viscountess Davidson (Hemel Hempstead). More women Members are returned from borough than from county constituencies; indeed, it is rare to find a woman representing an area that is predominantly rural in character.

There are two possible explanations for this discrimination. Either females are felt to be less suited to represent a constituency, or selection committees may fear that a woman candidate will lose votes. A survey carried out by the British Institute of Public Opinion in 1952 inquired into attitudes towards women candidates. It showed that over two-thirds of those questioned were indifferent to the sex of a candidate, and a small majority of the rest favoured men.[1] But

---

[1] The detailed results of this survey are reproduced by J. F. S. Ross in *Elections*

the question put was not phrased in such a way as to discover whether the sex of a candidate would affect actual voting. Considering the strength of the tendency to vote for parties and not for individuals, it is unlikely that a woman candidate would lose, on balance, many votes merely because of her sex. The action of selection committees is to be explained more by reference to their own attitude to women Members, and a woman is hardly ever elected in the age-group where child bearing is most common. The youngest woman elected in 1955 was 38 years of age, or eleven years older than the youngest man: she was Mrs. McLaughlin (Ulster Unionist, Belfast, West).

There are at least five other factors that may have some bearing on the choice of candidates—religion, education, occupation, connection with the peerage and experience of local government. Yet in commenting on these factors it is difficult to separate cause from effect. Let us take some examples. A large number of Conservative Members have family ties with the peerage: is this because many of those with such associations wish to become Members of the Commons, or because Conservative selection committees heavily favour those with such a background? Many Labour and Conservative candidates attended Oxford University; in 1955 they numbered 206, and the total of Labour and Conservative candidates with a University education was 597. The preponderance of Oxford is remarkable. Are Oxonians more keen to come to Westminster than the alumni of other universities? Do they make a better impression on selection committees because of their superior quality or merely because they have been to Oxford? Questions of this type cannot receive a precise answer, but the comparison of the background of successful and unsuccessful candidates is sometimes suggestive. In 1955, 56% of all Conservative candidates were elected; of those who had been to Oxford, Cambridge and other universities, 72%, 73% and 40% respectively were elected. The advantage of those attending the older Universities is clear. No parallel distinction of this magnitude can be found for the Labour Party. Even more remarkable is the success of Conservatives who are Old Etonians: in 1955, 78 out of 97 were elected.

The legal profession is the section of the community most heavily represented in the Commons. This is a traditional feature of the

and Electors, p. 468. Chapter 16 of this work also portrays in full the limited success of women at elections between 1918 and 1951.

parliamentary scene: 107 barristers were Conservative candidates in 1955 (66 successful), and Labour nominated 48 barristers (27 successful).[1] It will be seen that barristers had a rather higher chance of winning than had the average of all other candidates. No doubt barristers are chosen because of their persuasive powers of advocacy; but it is increasingly difficult to combine any considerable practice at the Bar with the full exercise of parliamentary duties, although important divisions normally take place late in the evening. Constituents demand increasing attention so it is a little surprising that barristers find it easy to secure adoption, especially by the Labour Party. A few other occupations call for special mention. As noted above, miners nominated by the Labour Party are almost always elected. Conservatives try to strengthen their connection with the trade union movement, but of the 18 wage-earners they nominated in 1955 only one was elected—R. Mawby (Totnes). It is apparent that Conservative trade unionists are offered only unfavourable seats: the same is true of Conservative members of the teaching profession, as in 1955 only 4 out of 24 were successful. The financial obligations of Conservative candidates have been lifted but in favourable seats Conservative selection tends still to be limited to some exclusive social categories.

Little needs to be said about the two remaining factors. Apart from those areas where non-conformity is most vigorous and a Roman Catholic representative would not be acceptable, religious opinions of candidates are not important. Full information about religious beliefs is not available, possibly because those who are not enthusiastic worshippers are not anxious to advertise the fact. About local government experience the main feature is that service on local authorities is more widespread among Labour candidates than their opponents. It is common for leading members of the Labour Party to have 'worked their way up' from the ranks. Membership of a local council is regarded as a useful preliminary for a future parliamentarian, and the most forceful of Labour councillors often generate parliamentary ambitions. In the Conservative Party social status is more important than past service. Even in the Labour Party it is doubtful if membership of a local authority is often a dominant factor in the choice of a candidate. But in both Glasgow and Liverpool there is a tendency for the two major parties to choose can-

[1] D. E. Butler, *The British General Election of 1955*, p. 43. This book contains a full analysis of the background of candidates at this election.

didates who are members of the City Council: this is especially the case in the Glasgow Labour Party.[1]

The choice of a parliamentary candidate is a highly personal business, and the grounds for the decision will vary with each case. The typical Labour Member and the typical Conservative Member simply do not exist. Sometimes when a sitting Member retires a local personality fills the vacancy which he has been anticipating; but chance rules more often than foresight. The preceding pages have discussed a variety of matters that influence selection conferences, and the candidate adopted will usually have a combination of these factors working in his favour. Thus a constituency Labour Party in a poor financial condition will welcome a trade unionist of about fifty, who is serving on a local authority and who has stood at a previous parliamentary election. Conservatives will often choose a man from Eton and Oxford, age nearer forty, connected with commerce or law and who has already fought a seat. Yet these are but generalities and fortunately they describe but a minority of candidates. Local associations are most jealous of their right to select the person who may become the Honourable Member for their constituency. The final decision rests with the electors, but their actions are far more predictable.

---

[1] D. E. Butler in *Public Administration*, Spring 1953, Vol. 31, p. 46.

c

2

The Election of Members

I

The right to summon a Parliament is part of the Royal prerogative. In modern times it has been used in accordance with the advice of the Prime Minister who has, in effect, the power to decide the timing of a General Election. Under the Parliament Act, 1911, the duration of a parliament is limited to a maximum of five years, but in war-time the life of parliament has been extended by a series of annual Acts and a general election postponed until the cessation of hostilities.[1] Thus the Parliament elected in December, 1910, lasted eight years and the 1935 Parliament continued for nearly ten years. In peace-time it is usual for a Prime Minister to ask for a dissolution rather before the end of the five year maximum and since 1918, excluding the 1935–45 period, only two out of nine parliaments have lasted into a fifth year. It is often asserted that the right to determine the date of an election gives an unfair advantage to the party in power, for the Prime Minister can choose a moment when he judges the political climate to be favourable. At many periods of the year, however, it is not convenient to hold an election. Christmas and the summer holiday season provide counter-attractions for the voluntary workers on whom all parties depend to conduct a campaign, and the actual numbers of people voting would also be affected: an election in January or February involves a risk of severe weather: after Easter Parliament is busy with the annual financial legislation. The most popular seasons for the hustings are the early summer and the autumn, but in 1950 Lord Attlee[2] took a successful chance on a relatively mild February.

After a Parliament has been dissolved by royal proclamation the

---

[1] In 1945 the election was held after the end of hostilities in Europe, but before the end of the war in Asia against Japan.

[2] Prime Minister 1945–51, Member for Limehouse 1922–50 and Walthamstow, West, 1950–55. Created a peer in December 1955.

new Parliament is summoned by writs issued from the Chancery—the Lord Chancellor's office. The writs for the Commons are sent to the returning officers who are, in England and Wales, the Mayors of boroughs and the Sheriffs of counties,[1] and in Scotland the Sheriffs. The date for nominations is announced in the royal proclamation and the time has come for the would-be Members to bestir themselves. To obtain nomination it is necessary to produce a deposit of £150, which is returnable to a candidate who obtains one-eighth of the total poll, and to secure a proposer, seconder and eight assentors from among the local electors. It is usual for candidates to present more than one nomination paper to show evidence of their wide support. A returning officer may declare a nomination paper to be invalid if there is any defect in the qualifications of the supporters named on it, but he is not entitled to inquire into whether candidates are qualified to become Honourable Members. The qualification of Members is a complex problem which is described in the following chapter.

Polling day is held on a Thursday and is some ten days after the last date for nominations. In urban areas the count commences shortly after the polling booths have closed and competition has developed to be first with the declaration of the poll: early announcements are expected from Cheltenham, Salford and Watford. In rural areas the count is postponed until the following day. The method of election is the essence of simplicity, for the candidate with the highest number of votes is returned to Westminster. It follows that where more than two candidates are standing the person elected may fail to have obtained a majority of the total vote. If there are three contestants who enjoy nearly equal popularity, the Member elected may have as little as 34% of the total vote. Two classic examples of this situation are shown below.

General Election 1929: Cheshire, Northwich

Lord C. Crichton-Stuart (Con.)	15,477
Mrs. B. A. Gould (Lab.)	15,473
J. D. Barlow (Lib.)	14,161
	————
Con. majority	4

[1] A few boroughs, like Southampton, are both counties and boroughs: in these places the writ is directed to the Sheriff, not to the Mayor. Such boroughs are not to be confused with county boroughs.

HONOURABLE MEMBERS

General Election 1945: Caithness and Sutherland

E. L. Gandar Dower (Con.)	5,564
R. McInnes (Lab.)	5,558
Rt. Hon. Sir A. Sinclair (Lib.)	5,503

Con. majority	6

If four candidates stand it would be possible in the extreme case for the victor to receive a fraction over one-quarter of the total poll—and so on. The larger the number of candidates in a constituency the greater is the probability that none will obtain an over-all majority. This is illustrated by the experience of recent general elections set out in the table below:

CANDIDATES AND MINORITY MEMBERS

General Election	Total of Candidates	Candidates per seat	Members elected on minority vote
1945	1,683	2·63	174
1950	1,868	2·99	187
1951	1,376	2·20	37
1955	1,409	2·24	37

As there is now virtually a two-party system in this country, one of the main parties, Conservative or Labour, is assured of a majority in the Commons, and the majority party can form a government which has a reasonable expectation of remaining in office for the duration of the parliament. Smaller groups tend to be crushed out of existence by the electoral system; a small party whose representatives normally come bottom of the poll in triangular contests may hardly ever be strong enough to win a seat, although in total it may collect a large number of votes. Such is the fate of the Liberal Party, and it is natural for Liberals to advocate change in the method of election.[1] As the present arrangements work to the advantage of the large parties they are unlikely to be altered. Certainly, if seats were distributed proportionately according to votes it would be rare for a party to win a majority in the Commons: even under the present system, with its

---

[1] Much has been written by those who advocate proportional representation or some other alternative to the present method of voting. Two recent books on this subject are J. F. S. Ross, *Elections and Electors*, and Enid Lakeman and J. S. Lambert, *Voting in Democracies*.

strong discouragement to smaller parties, no party has obtained a majority of the total vote in a general election since 1935. It is, therefore, unrealistic to argue that a government not supported by a majority of electors has a weak moral claim to rule, and a Member elected on a minority vote is not thought to be in a different position from other Members. Indeed, a seat won on a minority vote may well be more secure politically than a seat won by a narrow majority in a straight fight.

II

The role of the individual candidate in an election campaign is of little importance. Voters are swayed by national issues, not by local events. Where the political scene is dominated by two parties, the essential choice facing the electors is which of these parties they wish to see in office. This was recognized by Lord Bryce writing at the end of the nineteenth century.

'A general election is in form a choice of representatives, with reference primarily to their views upon various current questions. In substance it is often a national vote (what the French call a plebiscite), committing executive power to some one prominent statesman.'[1]

Modern science has changed the form of the election campaign, and election broadcasts and television programmes have replaced the public meeting as the chief focus of political interest. The consequence has been a further enhancement of the position of party leaders, who dominate the tone of the campaign. In comparison, the local candidate can reach but a tiny audience: his speeches will receive wide publicity only if he says something eccentric or potentially damaging to his own cause. It is a major handicap to the Liberal Party to be allowed less air and screen time than their larger rivals. And in 1955 no party with less than 50 candidates was given any facilities by the B.B.C.—which entailed the complete exclusion of the small groups.

The lack of concern with personalities, local and regional interests accounts for the remarkable uniformity in the movement of opinion throughout Britain which has been a feature of recent elections. The 'swing' is nearly the same in most constituencies. Fluctuations in the popularity of the two major parties are the most significant changes

[1] *The American Commonwealth*, p. 69.

of opinion, and the 'swing' is best measured by taking the average of the Conservative percentage gain in the total poll as compared with the previous election, and of the percentage Labour loss, similarly calculated.[1] The Macclesfield division of Cheshire provides a simple example—in 1955 the Conservative candidate won 60% of the total vote in a straight fight with Labour, and in 1951, with the same conditions, the Conservatives obtained 59% of the poll. Thus the 1955 figures showed a 1% swing to Conservative. If there are more than two candidates the arithmetic is more complicated but the same principles apply. It is true that this method will not give a useful result in any constituency where a Liberal or some other minor party candidate occupies first or second place in the poll[2] but, outside Northern Ireland, such seats are few in number. Nor is it possible to calculate the swing for any constituency that has suffered boundary changes since the previous election. Granted these limitations, the swing provides an invaluable index to the political climate and can be used to show how similar it is in the great majority of constituencies.

The median swing over the whole country in 1955 was 1·6% in favour of the Conservatives. In four-fifths of the constituencies in which comparison with 1951 is possible the size of the swing lay within the extremes of $3\frac{1}{2}\%$ and $-\frac{1}{2}\%$.[3] From this it is clear that the individual candidate is at the mercy of a national tide of opinion. A Member holding a seat by a small majority is likely to be swept away if the tide is against his party. Candidates attacking seats held by their opponents for many years will arrive at Westminster only if there is a massive surge in favour of their party, as happened for the Conservatives in 1931 and Labour in 1945.

Fortunately there are exceptions to the general picture and the individual is not deprived of all responsibility. The intervention of third and fourth candidates may affect the result in a seat held by a small majority. There are also minor variations in the success of the

---

[1] This is the method employed by D. E. Butler in the Nuffield series of election surveys. If the Labour Party were in the ascendant, the swing would be measured by taking the average of the Labour gain and the Conservative loss.

[2] The Liberal vote is still most important to the major parties. If a Liberal candidate appears in a constituency uncontested by his party at the previous election, the problem is will he attract mainly those who voted Conservative, or those who voted Labour, in the last contest? Where no Liberal candidate is forthcoming the other candidates make efforts to attract Liberal support.

[3] This figure is based on D. E. Butler, *The British General Election of 1955*, Appendix 1.

main parties in different areas: in 1955 the Labour Party improved its position in East Anglia, against the general trend, but the Conservatives did exceptionally well in Coventry and on Tees-side. In 1955, also, sitting Members had a slight advantage over other candidates. For the 13 constituencies where Labour Members retired, and in which such comparison is possible, the median swing to the Conservatives was 2·2%, or 1·0% more than where Labour Members stood again. On the other side, where Conservative Members retired the swing against Labour was 0·7%, as opposed to 1·5% in seats where Conservative Members stood again.[1] There is a small bonus of votes, therefore, to be won by a Member who gives good service to his constituency, and in a few cases the benefit may be sizeable. It is not easy to explain the swing of 2·1% in favour of G. De Freitas (Lab. Lincoln) or 6·1% in favour of H. Gower (Con. Barry) without reference to personal popularity.

As long as Members retain their old party label individual political views seem to have little effect on their chances of re-election. Members at the extremities of the spectrum of opinion in the Labour Party seem to fare equally well at elections; this is a further strong indication that votes are cast not for a person but for his party. Yet this generalization conceals its exception; in 1955 there was a swing of 5·1% against Sir William Darling,[2] one of the most unprogressive Conservative Members, in a constituency unaffected by boundary changes.

The uniformity of opinion throughout the country facilitates the forecasting of results. Before the election is held it is possible to make a guess at the result in any constituency by relating the latest public opinion poll figures to the majority of the successful candidate at the last election. For example, if the poll shows that there has been a 3% swing against the Government since the last election, any Government supporter who then obtained less than 53% of the vote in a straight fight should contemplate the possibility of defeat. The situation in a constituency may also be affected by a complicating factor such as the presence, or absence, of a Liberal candidate. In addition, public opinion polls may not be accurate, and they do seem to have a tendency to over-estimate Conservative support: this may be explained either by defects in the organization of the poll, by suggesting

---

[1] Ibid., p. 204. This tendency has not been so clear in other recent elections. The lessened interest in party warfare may explain these figures for 1955.

[2] Member for Edinburgh, South, 1945–57.

that a few of those questioned do not answer the pollsters honestly, or because wavering voters suddenly decide to vote Labour at the last minute. Using the figures published by the British Institute of Public Opinion just before the last two general elections, we find that the Conservative share of the total poll was estimated to be a little over 1% higher than they actually received. This has led Labour supporters, in particular, to decry reference to public opinion statistics.

As the results begin to be announced on the evening of election day a further attempt may be made to forecast the final outcome; from the average swing shown by (say) the first half-dozen declarations it is possible from previous calculations to assess how many seats will change hands over the whole country.[1] Again there are pitfalls. The earliest results may not be typical, or highly important marginal seats may not quite conform to the national pattern. But the fact that such forecasts can be made with reasonable accuracy is a consequence of the homogeneity of opinion.

By-elections are fought under quite different conditions and their results are less predictable.[2] At a general election the voter is choosing a government: at a by-election he is merely electing a Member, for the fate of the Cabinet is not in question. There is a tendency for the Government to fare ill at by-elections as the electors can record a vote of protest without facing the responsibility of deciding whether they really desire alternative policies. It was, therefore, a singular triumph for P. Williams (Con. Sunderland, South) to gain a seat from Labour in May, 1953, while his party was in office. By-elections are not dominated by sound and television broadcasts: when they are being fought the newspapers are not full of election news. Usually fewer people vote than at general elections. In these contests personality may be more important, minor party candidates are less unsuccessful, and the party defending the seat may be at a further disadvantage if its opponents have candidate(s) already well known to the local electors from previous contests. For a variety of reasons by-elections may produce unusual and exciting results, but they are poor guides to the course of the next general election.

Returning to general elections, it has been argued above that these tend to take the form of a plebiscite: the voters nominate one or

---

[1] In 1955 *The Economist* published a table showing the constituencies that would probably change their allegiance in given national swings.

[2] D. E. Butler, *The British Electoral System, 1918–51*, pp. 180–7, contains a detailed study of by-election results during this period.

another of the leaders of the main parties to be the next Prime Minister. How significant, therefore, is the individual candidate in an election campaign? If the election is fought and decided on a national basis, what is there left for him to do? He must ensure, with the aid of his supporters, that his name becomes firmly associated with his party in the mind of the electorate. Political parties are unknown to the law: the actual ballot paper contains the names of the candidates, their addresses and occupations, but no mention of their political allegiances. Electors must obtain this information before they go to the polling station; hence the insistent message of posters, window placards and loudspeakers—

Brown = Conservative, Smith = Labour, Jones = Liberal.

To a notable degree campaigns are dominated by tradition. Things are done because they have always been done, not because they are likely to make any effective difference to the result. Public meetings are part of the accepted pattern of an election campaign and they continue to be held in spite of diminished audiences, consisting largely of the party faithful.[1] The majority of those interested in politics are content to follow the election on the B.B.C. and the persuasive effect of election addresses and canvassing by the candidate is limited. Yet these time-honoured practices must continue for a variety of reasons. If a candidate fails to hold meetings, he presents his opponents with an opportunity for criticism. If electors are not canvassed they may be resentful and decide to stay away from the polling-booths. If a candidate fails to meet as many of his supporters as he can possibly manage, their enthusiasm may wane, and their failure to join in the election preparations of the local party may mean that less ardent sympathizers of the party will fail to vote. It follows that candidates, including Members seeking re-election, must go through a ritual, the purpose of which is not political persuasion but rather to generate sufficient excitement locally to persuade their probable adherents to turn out and vote. This is the explanation of why the individual opinions of Members have so little effect on their chances of re-election.

[1] The London School of Economics conducted a survey of the election campaign in Greenwich in 1950: roughly one-sixtieth of the electorate were questioned and none of those who changed their opinions during the campaign had attended a political meeting. Mark Benney, A. P. Grey and R. H. Pear, *How People Vote*, pp. 177–8.

The detailed arrangement of the campaign is the responsibility of the election agent, who is either a professional organizer or a local supporter who has agreed to undertake the task. The great majority of constituencies have a professional Conservative agent, and roughly 40% of Labour candidates have the benefit of a professional agent. A reasonable acquaintance with the details of the law of elections should be possessed by an agent; he controls the campaign funds and must prevent any improper or excessive expenditure. The quality of local party organization will affect the result only in marginal seats, but it is probably true that a good agent is worth as many votes as a good candidate, especially since the introduction of the postal vote. Under the Representation of the People Act, 1948, certain categories of voters are entitled to vote by post or proxy; they include service personnel, the blind and infirm, those whose occupations prevent them from voting in person, those who could only reach a polling booth by a sea or air journey and persons who have moved outside the borough, urban district or parish in which they have a right to vote. In 1955 the average number of postal votes was 2% of the total vote: the extreme variations were Fermanagh and Tyrone with 11·5% and Birmingham, Ladywood, with 0·5%. The postal vote was nearly twice as great in seats won by Conservatives as it was in Labour seats.[1] It is generally agreed that the Conservatives are much the more efficient in organizing the postal vote: the size of this advantage in terms of extra seats won is a matter for conjecture, but it may be as many as ten. Persuading supporters entitled to a postal vote to register their claim to it is, or should be, an important part of the work of an agent.

Freed from such chores, the candidate can devote himself to the field of public relations; the aim of a good candidate should be to meet as many people as possible. If the public fail to come to political meetings they must be encountered in the streets with a loud-speaker van. And there may be local organizations that wish to discuss particular questions with the candidates. In a constituency where no Liberal candidate is standing, the local Liberal Party may ask the candidates to receive deputations, but even if this is done, it is common for the deputation to fail to advise Liberal supporters to vote for a particular candidate. At the 1950 and 1951 elections the Roman Catholics attempted to put pressure on all candidates about the financing of Catholic schools. These representations had little effect,

[1] D. E. Butler, *The General Election of 1955*, p. 113.

and candidates should remember that sectional groups may not be able to deliver the votes that they are reputed to command. At Greenwich in 1950 the Conservative candidate alone expressed sympathy for Catholic demands, but it has been estimated that 70% of Catholics in Greenwich still voted Labour.[1] Candidates also receive a number of letters, mostly stating the views of a variety of sectional interests.[2] Meanwhile, the electorate thinks of the candidates as party representatives and judges them accordingly.

The chances of a Member seeking re-election are good. It was shown in the previous chapter that a Member seeking re-nomination can usually obtain it, and the vast majority of those nominated retain their seats. In a two-party system, the party in the ascendant will hold nearly all the seats it possessed in the last parliament, so its previous Members should be safely returned. The other major party will, of course, lose seats, and its Members defending marginal seats will be defeated: the number of casualties depends on the size of the swing. At the elections of 1950, 1951 and 1955 the numbers of Members defeated were 70, 25 and 20 respectively. In 1951 and 1955 well over 550 Members were re-elected; in 1950 with the bigger swing the number was near 500. Members normally fight the same seat at each successive election, but a few have changed their party or their constituency, or both. Occasionally a Member may be able to move to another constituency that is politically safer—in 1950 G. Jeger (Lab. Goole) moved from Winchester; in 1955 N. Fisher (Con. Surbiton) moved from Hitchin. It is fatal to lose party support and in 1950 five Members who had been expelled from the Labour Party were all roundly beaten: they were H. L. Hutchinson (Manchester, Rusholme),[3] J. F. Platts-Mills (Finsbury), D. N. Pritt[4] (Hammersmith,

[1] Mark Benney, A. P. Grey and R. H. Pear, *How People Vote*, pp. 94 and 111.

[2] The following is an extract from the detailed study made of the election campaign in Bristol, North-East, in 1951. *Straight-Fight* by R. S. Milne and H. C. MacKenzie, p. 14: 'Out of 57 letters sent to the two candidates, five at most were from individuals; the rest came from organizations. More than half of those were sent from a national headquarters outside Bristol; the remainder came from local branches of national organizations. Even the individual letters were perhaps only "translations" of national pressure group themes. Two were on divorce, one on firemen's pay, one on Sunday opening of theatres and one on the "excessive tax on speedway racing".'

[3] At the 1950 Election Hutchinson moved to Walthamstow, West, to fight against his party leader Clement Attlee.

[4] Pritt was expelled in 1940 and survived the 1945 Election as an Independent Labour candidate.

43

North), L. J. Solley (Thurrock) and K. Zilliacus (Gateshead, West). In 1955 Sir Richard Acland (Lab. Gravesend) withdrew from his party over the issue of the hydrogen bomb and was defeated as an Independent. Members changing from one party to another do not survive the passage as well as Sir Winston Churchill. In 1950, A. Edwards, standing as a Conservative, was defeated at Middlesbrough, East, which he had twice won with Labour support: Ivor Thomas (ex-Lab. Keighley) was the defeated Conservative candidate at Monmouth: T. L. Horabin (ex-Lib. North Cornwall) lost at Exeter as a Labour candidate. But these are all examples of the unorthodox, and a Member who remains true to his party—and who has a majority in excess of 5,000—can count himself unlucky if he fails to return to Westminster after a general election.

III

There are now 630 Honourable Members, each elected for a single-member territorial constituency: 511 represent English constituencies, Welsh Members number 36, there are 71 Scottish Members and the remaining 12 come from Ulster. The size of the Commons has varied. At the 1950 and 1951 elections there were 625 seats, in 1945, 640, and the figure was 615 in the inter-war period after the withdrawal of Members from Southern Ireland. Double-member constituencies were abolished along with the univsity seats by the Representation of the People Act, 1948. Constituencies are now, therefore, all of the same basic type, except that some are classified as borough and others as county constituencies.[1] This distinction is of importance in relation to some aspects of electoral law: candidates fighting county constituencies are permitted to spend rather more on election expenses and to use more cars on polling day, owing to the greater difficulties of political organization in rural areas. In boroughs, candidates may spend £450 plus 1½d. per elector, or, in county seats, £450 plus 2d. per elector: these figures include the agent's fee but exclude the sum of £100 allowed for the personal expenses of the candidate. In Ulster there is no basic allowance and the limit is 2d. per elector. Each candidate is permitted to provide one car to convey electors to poll-

---

[1] Smaller boroughs not entitled to a seat on their own are included with surrounding areas in a county constituency.

ing booths for each 1,500 voters in a county constituency, and a car for each 2,500 voters in a borough.

In 1944 the House of Commons (Redistribution of Seats) Act established permanent bodies of Boundary Commissioners[1] to make periodic reviews of constituency boundaries. Before this date reorganizations of constituencies had taken place at irregular intervals and were associated with Bills to extend the franchise. The unequal size of constituencies in the Victorian period was notorious, but even in 1939 there were 20 Members each representing over 100,000 electors, while over a dozen Members had less than a third of this number of constituents. Movements of population are continuous: the centres of cities become depopulated while suburbia advances at terrifying speed. In the interests of equity the case for regular re-examination of the constituency map is overwhelming. Yet the work of the Boundary Commissions has caused much disquiet and heartburning.[2]

The legislation governing the work of the Boundary Commissions was amended in 1946 and 1948, consolidated in the House of Commons (Redistribution of Seats) Act, 1949, and amended again in 1958. The Commissions carry out their task with the guidance of a series of Rules which determine the total number of constituencies, enjoin the Commissioners to respect local government boundaries as far as practicable, allow special provision for sparsely populated and inaccessible areas and lay it down that the electorate in all constituencies shall be as near as possible to the electoral quota. This quota is the average number of voters per constituency. Scotland and Wales are somewhat over-represented in comparison with England but the Commissions have instructions that their present numbers of seats shall not be reduced. Electorates in Northern Ireland average 73,000 or roughly some 17,000 more than electorates in Great Britain: the justification for this discrepancy is that domestic affairs of Ulster are dealt with in their own Parliament at Stormont. The Rules set out above have been a cause of much difficulty for they are self-contradictory. Equal electorates cannot be reconciled with respect for local government boundaries; where the two principles

---

[1] There are four Commissions: one each for England, Scotland, Wales and Northern Ireland.

[2] On this whole topic see D. E. Butler, 'The Redistribution of Seats' in *Public Administration*, Vol. XXXIII, pp. 125–47, and the Appendix to *The Electoral System in Britain* by the same author.

clash, which is to be respected? And if relaxations are allowed for some rural areas, how great shall be the concessions?

Initially the four Commissions were instructed that constituencies should not vary more than 25% from the electoral quota, but this criterion was found to be too rigid and was withdrawn in 1946. When the Commission for England produced its first recommendations in 1947 it was seen that the average electorate in Borough seats would be 6,000 greater than the corresponding figure for county seats. Acting on a protest from Dr. Dalton (Lab. Bishop Auckland),[1] the Labour Government instructed the Commission to prepare plans for an additional 17 seats for the English boroughs. At the time this was attacked by the Conservative opposition as a flagrant example of gerrymandering, but it is by no means clear that the Labour Party gained much advantage from the creation of these additional seats.[2] It must also be remembered that the Labour Party lost significantly from the redistribution, as the seats with small electorates in London and the centres of other large towns which were amalgamated or obliterated were almost all Labour strongholds. The City of London was a notable exception. But the action of the Labour Government must still be regarded as an unfortunate precedent. The whole purpose of creating independent Commissions to determine constituency boundaries was to ensure that political partiality should not creep into the decisions made. Government intervention on a matter of this kind must cause suspicion and mistrust, even when they are not well founded.

Under the pre-1958 law, reviews of constituencies were to be carried out at intervals between three and seven years in duration. Accordingly, further changes were proposed by the Commissions in 1954.[3] In 1948 the boundary revisions were included in a schedule to the Representation of the People Act, but subsequent changes are to be made by Orders in Council approved by Parliament. On 15th and 16th December, 1954, and on 26th January, 1955, the Commons had lengthy debates on the proposed Orders. Members on both sides of the House protested with vehemence against the alteration of their own constituencies, and the procedure of the Commission for England. The Government steadfastly supported the Commissioners' recommendations, but the Opposition challenged divisions on 16 of

[1] H.C. Deb., Vol. 447, col. 936 *et seq.*

[2] H. G. Nicholas, *The British General Election of 1950*, pp. 4–5.

[3] 1953–54 Cmd. 9311, Cmd. 9312, Cmd. 9313, Cmd. 9314, ix.

the Orders. A few Conservatives adversely affected by an Order abstained from voting on it, and a few went into the Opposition Lobby on a particular division. These rebels included J. J. Astor (Plymouth) and two Manchester Members, Dame Florence Horsbrugh and Mrs. E. Hill.

The method of re-defining constituencies offered many opportunities for criticism. In some areas where changes took place, local inquiries were held; elsewhere changes were made without such preliminaries. Under the 1958 Act an inquiry must be held if a Commission receives an objection to a proposed alteration from an interested organization or 100 electors—unless an inquiry was held before the proposal was announced. This should, in future, avoid the feeling that local opinion has not had a proper chance of expression. Again, the Commissions do not always give full explanations for their conclusions: the 1954 Report on English constituencies is of similar length to the contemporary report for Scotland, although the reorganization proposed for England was far more complex and extensive. There is also no means of appeal against the suggestions of the Commissions, except to the Home Secretary or to Parliament.[1] Yet, as argued above, if the Government intervenes in this matter and uses its parliamentary majority to make changes in the recommendations, allegations of political partisanship must ensue. In 1954 the Government took the proper course of supporting the Commissions. The problem, however, remains; should the decisions of the Commissions be open to review and, if so, by what kind of body?

The way in which the Commission for England applied the Rules is also open to objection. Each county receives seats in accordance with its population. This county basis of allocation means that the largest counties more frequently gain or lose seats than the smallest counties: constituencies in Middlesex, Lancashire and the West

---

[1] On 17th December, 1954, an action was heard in the High Court in which the Lord Mayor of Manchester sought an injunction to prevent the Home Secretary from submitting the draft Order for Manchester to the Queen for confirmation on the ground that it did not conform to the Rules under which the Boundary Commission had to work. Mr. Justice Roxburgh ruled that a *prima facie* case had been made out and granted an interim injunction. As Parliament had already approved the Order, this decision raised serious constitutional issues. The case was then taken to the Court of Appeal which held that the Courts had no right to intervene in the proceedings and also that the Commission for England had not infringed the Rules. *Harper and Another v. Secretary of State for the Home Department* (1955), 1 All E.R. 331.

Riding are far more likely to suffer dislocation than those in Cambridgeshire or Herefordshire. It needs less than a 2% change in the Lancashire electorate to alter the number of seats for the county; the corresponding figure for Cambridgeshire is 30%.[1] The pursuit of equality in the size of electorates has led to violations of local government boundaries. Reading was reduced from two Members to one in 1955, but the Tilehurst ward of Reading is now included in the Newbury Division and, at the other end of the town, the East ward is included in the Wokingham division. Blackburn was likewise reduced to a single Member and three of its wards are now within the Darwen constituency. Other constituencies have a peculiar shape: the new Eastleigh division of Hampshire surrounds Southampton like a horse-shoe, and Southampton itself is the only convenient centre in which constituency business can be transacted. Arbitrary constituencies are an administrative convenience devoid of any feeling of unity, and they must do some damage to the representative functions of Members.

A re-drawing of the electoral map is necessarily unpopular with Honourable Members. Those affected by redistribution fear, with or without just cause, that they will suffer politically. Some may find that their seats have disappeared entirely. In 1955 the following Members, whose constituencies suffered a major revision, were defeated in the General Election, Conservative: F. Bennett (Reading)[2] and Sir G. Braithwaite (Bristol, North-West); Labour: C. A. R. Crosland (South Gloucestershire),[3] M. Foot (Plymouth, Devonport), W. Keenan (Liverpool, Kirkdale), H. N. Smith (Nottingham, South), M. Webb (Bradford, Central), I. Winterbottom (Nottingham, Central) and W. Wyatt (Birmingham, Aston).[4] It does not follow that all these Members—the Labour supporters—would have been re-elected had their seats remained unaltered. Besides those who ultimately lost their seats, other Members suffered interim anxieties and Sir Frank Soskice (Lab. Sheffield, Neepsend) failed to obtain nomination as a candidate.[5] Sir R. Assheton (Con. Blackburn, West),

---

[1] D. E. Butler, *Public Administration*, Vol. XXXII, p. 133.

[2] Bennett was returned for Torquay at a by-election in December, 1955.

[3] Crosland chose to move from South Gloucestershire to Southampton, Test. This was a miscalculation: the Conservative majority in his old seat was less than that in the Test Division.

[4] Wyatt failed to obtain re-nomination in Birmingham and was defeated at Grantham.

[5] Sir Frank was returned for Newport (Mon.) at a by-election in July, 1956.

who retired when his constituency was abolished, had also previously 'lost' another constituency, the City of London, through redistribution.

The shock of the 1955 redistribution was the more severe as it was completed but four months before the subsequent General Election. The Commissions cannot be held responsible for this short interval, as they were not to know that the 1951 Parliament would last only three and a half years. Yet in future it would be better if the redistribution procedure commenced shortly after a General Election in order to give a maximum of warning to Members, the political parties and the public. In 1955 two main criticisms were levelled at the existing arrangements: that the reviews of boundaries were being held too frequently and that changes were made in the interests of equality which ignored other considerations of equal importance. In 1948 as few as 80 constituencies remained unchanged: in 1955 a total of 324 remained unaltered. In England electoral mathematics have demanded the transgression of many local authority boundaries and the justification for this is a matter for argument in each case. The redistribution of constituencies causes a re-shaping of local party organization, and in some areas—for example East Sussex—there was a major upheaval twice within seven years. Such disturbances are confusing to the voters and may well damage long standing relationships between Members and their constituents.

In future, the amount of disruption should be reduced. The House of Commons (Redistribution of Seats) Act, 1958, extended the period between general reviews of constituencies to a minimum of 10 and a maximum of 15 years. The Act also encourages the Commissions to be more flexible in the application of the redistribution rules in order to lessen upsets of local relationships.

IV

University representation was terminated by the decision of the Labour Government embodied in the Representation of the People Act, 1948. Since the General Election of 1950 the twelve university Members—3 from Scotland, 2 each from Oxford, Cambridge and the Combined English Universities, and one each from London, Wales and the Queen's University, Belfast—have disappeared from the Commons.[1] The abolition of these academic constituencies became

[1] The last university contests at a general election are fully described by R. McCallum and A. Readman, *The British General Election of 1945*, Ch. xii.

the major issue in the discussions on the 1948 Act. The Conservatives alleged that the Labour Government was breaking a 'bargain' made at the 1944 Speaker's Conference on electoral reform, and that the elimination of the university seats was a gross breach of faith. The Speaker's Conference, held under war-time conditions of coalition government, had considered a wide range of topics connected with the conduct of elections. Besides university representation, these included the redistribution of constituencies, the business vote, the assimilation of the local government franchise to the parliamentary franchise and the use of cars on polling day. The Conference worked in a spirit of compromise and the Conservatives, although they were the majority party, made concessions to the views of the Labour Party. Both Conservative and Labour members of the Speaker's Conference agreed to support the recommendations then made, and from this situation the concept of a 'bargain' developed. Neither the precise nature of the bargain, nor its intended duration, was set down in 1944; subsequent interpretations differed and depended on calculations of party advantage.[1] The further argument of the Conservatives that major changes in the electoral system should depend on inter-party agreement, places a remarkable limitation on the authority of the Cabinet and is not entirely supported by precedent.

It will be noticed that the debate on the abolition of university representation concentrated on constitutional ethics: less was said about the value of the university Member. For this there is a simple explanation. At by-elections in 1946 and 1947 for the Combined English Universities and the Scottish Universities two Conservative Members, H. Strauss and Walter Elliot, who had been defeated in 1945, were re-elected to the Commons. Both of these seats had previously been held by Independent Members, Eleanor Rathbone and Sir John Boyd-Orr. It was, therefore, difficult for the Conservatives to argue in 1948 that the university constituencies gave an opportunity for distinguished persons, unconnected with political parties, to serve in the House. These by-elections tended to give the controversy an unhelpful emphasis, but they did not decide the fate of university seats. Labour was strongly wedded to the 'one man, one vote' principle, and it is not easy to believe that a Labour Cabinet could have agreed to the passage of an Act that contained provision for plural voting likely to be of advantage to their opponents. Alone

[1] D. E. Butler, *The Electoral System in Britain, 1918–51*, gives a full and fair description of this controversy (pp. 109–37).

in his party T. Skeffington-Lodge[1] defended the university seats nobly, but with no avail.

The Members returned by the universities were, in general, conservative in political outlook. In this context the word conservative has a small 'c', for the description is intended to cover some Members who were nominally Independents. No Labour candidate was ever returned for a university seat, and the university electorate consistently returned a majority of Members who were either Conservatives or Independents who, although possessing unorthodox opinions on a variety of questions, could normally be relied upon to support Conservative policies. The two Independents elected in 1945 who were most left-wing in sympathy, Eleanor Rathbone and Sir John Boyd-Orr, as noted in the paragraph above, were replaced by orthodox Conservatives at by-elections. Sometimes a University Conservative Association was willing to stand aside in favour of an Independent whose political views were thought to be satisfactory. In the autumn of 1939 a by-election was in prospect for Cambridge University and the University Conservatives approached J. M. Keynes to stand as an Independent. Keynes's political views may be broadly described as Liberal; certainly he was not an orthodox Tory. He refused the invitation because membership of the Commons did not seem to him to be the best way of contributing to the development of war-time economic policies.[2] Conservative support ensured the election of an Independent, Wilson Harris, at Cambridge in 1945.[3]

Not all Independent candidates depended on Conservative goodwill. The election of Eleanor Rathbone for the Combined English Universities in 1929 was not preceded by negotiations with representatives of any of the political parties.[4] The same is also true about the election of A. P. Herbert at Oxford in 1935.[5] Indeed after Ramsay MacDonald had found a refuge in the Scottish Universities in 1936, there was some revulsion in universities against party candidates. But it still remained true in 1948 that the university seats were a source of strength to the Conservatives, and Sir Winston Churchill was particularly violent in his condemnation of their abolition.

---

[1] Member for Bedford, 1945–50.
[2] R. F. Harrod, *The Life of John Maynard Keynes*, pp. 488–9.
[3] W. Harris, *Life so Far*, p. 271–2.
[4] Mary D. Stocks, *Eleanor Rathbone*, pp. 129–30.
[5] A. P. Herbert, *Independent Member*, pp. 21–30.

51

Conservative election manifestos at the 1950 and 1951 Elections promised their restoration, and as late as November, 1952, Sir Winston again promised legislation on the subject.[1] Since then other counsels appear to have prevailed among the Conservative leadership: at present the major political parties have remarkably equal and stable strengths, and it would be intolerable for the balance of power in the Commons to rest with University Members. If university representation is ever revived, it may be as part of a reform of the composition of the House of Lords. In conclusion, it should be stressed that the end of the university seats did not deprive the nation of the services of all the University Members as five of them, all Conservative supporters, were subsequently elected by other constituencies.[2]

[1] H.C. Deb., Vol. 507, col. 1869.
[2] Walter Elliot, Member for Lanark 1918–23, Scottish Universities 1946–50 and Glasgow (Kelvingrove) 1924–45 and 1950–58. K. Pickthorn, Member for Cambridge University 1935–50 and Carlton (Notts.) since 1950. Sir Arthur Salter, Member for Oxford University 1937–50 and Ormskirk 1951–53. Professor Savory, Member for Belfast University 1940–50 and Antrim, South, 1950–55. H. Strauss, Member for Combined English Universities 1946–50 and Norwich 1935–45 and 1950–55.

3

The Qualification of Members

Who is entitled to be elected an Honourable Member? This problem has created a considerable amount of difficulty in recent years, and in 1955 the Government produced a House of Commons Disqualification Bill to clarify the legal position. The Bill was subsequently remitted to and modified by a Select Committee.[1] The House of Commons Disqualification Act, 1957, was placed on the statute book in the course of the following session and was largely concerned with three aspects of disqualification, offices of profit under the Crown, Crown pensions and Crown contracts. Other barriers to entry into the Commons were left unchanged, most of them being quite uncontroversial: briefly, these cover aliens, minors, some clergy, lunatics, peers, bankrupts, felons and those found guilty of corrupt practices at elections. There is also a legal obstacle to leaving the Commons, for no Member can resign his seat; instead he must apply for appointment to one of two sinecure offices, the Steward of the Chiltern Hundreds and the Bailiff of the Manor of Northstead, which as offices of profit automatically involve forfeiture of a seat in the Commons.[2] To prevent the forced removal from the House of an obnoxious Member through the use of the patronage weapon, no Member, or nominated candidate, can be appointed to a disqualifying office without his consent.[3]

Any query on whether a person is entitled to be a Member is settled after his election, either by a Court or by the Commons itself.

[1] Cf. Report, 1955–56 (349) ix.

[2] Holders of these offices are not barred from offering themselves for re-election. Therefore it is possible for a Member to resign his seat as an act of protest and fight the ensuing by-election. The most recent example is that of the Duchess of Atholl (Con. Kinross and Western 1923–39) who resigned over the Government's policy on Spain, but lost the by-election.

[3] House of Commons Disqualification Act, 1957, S. 8.

If a candidate is nominated in accordance with the law—if he has sufficient valid signatures on his nomination form and deposits £150 —a returning officer has no power to prevent him from standing, even if it is abundantly clear that he is not qualified to take a seat. Should a dispute arise over the conduct or result of an election, the issue will be determined by an aggrieved party presenting an election petition to a Court, and the procedure for the hearing is now governed by the Representation of the People Act, 1949, together with the Election Commissioners Act, 1949. Before the passage of the 1957 Disqualification Act a person who sat or voted in the Commons when ineligible to do so was liable to a penalty of £500 per day, payable to a common informer who brought a successful action in the Courts. The threat of heavy monetary penalty is now removed, and under new procedure an allegation that a person elected to the Commons is ineligible can be submitted to the Judicial Committee of the Privy Council.[1] But the House also retains the right to judge the fitness of its Members and may declare any seat to be vacant. Alternatively, it may direct that the previous occupancy of a disqualifying office shall be disregarded, provided that the cause of disqualification is first removed.[2] The result is some overlapping in the jurisdictions of the Courts and the Commons. A clash of authority is prevented by two stipulations in the 1957 Act: the Commons may not validate the position of a Member, as described above, if his position is subject to examination by an election court;[2] conversely, no application to the Privy Council can succeed if the Commons have already decided that the disqualification in question shall be disregarded.[3]

The alternative procedures are well illustrated by the outcome of the election of two Sinn Fein candidates in 1955. The Sinn Feiners, P. Clarke (Fermanagh and South Tyrone) and T. Mitchell (Mid-Ulster), were both at the time of the election serving a ten-year prison sentence in Belfast Gaol for their part in a raid on the depot of the Royal Inniskilling Fusiliers. Mitchell was unseated by a resolution of the Commons,[4] but Clarke was replaced, as a consequence of an election petition, by Lieut.-Colonel R. G. Grosvenor, his Ulster Unionist opponent. Events proved that Lieut.-Colonel Grosvenor

[1] House of Commons Disqualification Act, S. 7.
[2] Ibid., S. 6(2).
[3] Ibid., S. 7(5)(b).
[4] H.C. Deb., Vol. 544, cols. 33–83.

had taken a wise course, for at the subsequent by-election in Mid-Ulster between the same candidates, Sinn Fein obtained an increased majority. C. Beattie, the Ulster Unionist candidate in this constituency, changed his tactics and secured the seat by an election petition. But this triumph was short-lived. Five weeks later it was discovered that Beattie was a member of appeals tribunals under the National Insurance and National Assistance Acts which, as offices of profit under the Crown, disqualified him as well. In similar cases to that of Beattie it has been the custom to validate the election by retrospective legislation, but in the special circumstances the Select Committee on Elections felt unable to recommend this course.[1] A second by-election followed at which Beattie was not a candidate.[2]

Fermanagh and Mid-Ulster are, of course, exceptional constituencies in which the electorate consciously ignored the inability of the Sinn Fein candidates to serve at Westminster. Normally, a candidate thought to be disqualified would suffer a serious loss of electoral support and would be highly unlikely to obtain nomination by a party. Doubts about the position of Members, therefore, emerge after their election. Some aspects of the law of qualification are clear and give rise to no difficulty. Aliens are barred but they may, by naturalization, acquire the political rights and obligations of a British subject. Minors are ineligible, but before the 1832 Reform Bill it seems that this rule was sometimes not observed; Charles James Fox and Lord John Russell were both elected before attaining the age of 21.[3] Insanity is now covered by the Lunacy (Vacating of Seats) Act, 1886, under which any authority concerned with the committal or reception of a Member into any house as a lunatic must notify the Speaker. The Speaker must immediately obtain a report on the condition of the Member, and a further report after a period of six months: if the Member is then still of unsound mind, his seat is declared vacant. A bankrupt is barred from sitting in the Commons, and if a Member is adjudged a bankrupt his seat becomes vacant at the end of six months unless the bankruptcy is previously annulled or discharged and a certificate is obtained that it was not caused by misconduct. By the Forfeiture Act, 1870, persons convicted of treason or felony, for which they have been sentenced to at least twelve months'

[1] 1955–56 (145–1) vi.

[2] For further discussion of these incidents see 'The Controverted Elections in Northern Ireland' in *The Table*, Vol. 24.

[3] Anson, *Law and Custom of the Constitution*, Vol. I, p. 81.

imprisonment, cannot be Members until their punishment has been completed.[1] It remains for the House to deal with any Member convicted of a misdemeanour or sentenced to a term of less than twelve months' imprisonment; should the House decide on expulsion the Member would not be barred from offering himself for re-election.

Corrupt practices at an election are a further source of disqualification and the law on this matter is governed by the Corrupt and Illegal Practices Act, 1883. The extent of the penalty depends on whether the candidate had foreknowledge of the illegality committed on his behalf. One who had such knowledge is barred for ever from representing the place at which the offence occurred, and for seven years in the case of any other constituency; if the offence was an unauthorized act of an agent, the employer is merely barred for seven years from the particular constituency. The last Member to be unseated for an election offence was the Liberal contender at Oxford in 1923.

An English or Scottish peerage is a disqualification. Irish peers may sit in the Commons, other than those elected to the Lords as Irish representative peers before these elections ceased on the creation of the Irish Free State. One such Member was Earl Winterton[2] who represented various constituencies in West Sussex between 1904 and 1951, and was Father of the House for seven years. An heir to a peerage who is also an Honourable Member cannot escape translation to the Lords when he succeeds to the title. He is, therefore, deprived of the possibility, through circumstances beyond human control, of staying in the main centre of political life. His chances of attaining many of the highest offices of state disappear, as the political heads of the leading departments are now invariably drawn from the Commons. This is widely felt to be a hardship and some elder statesmen have refused peerages out of consideration for their sons. In recent years two Members have tried without avail to cause a change in the law. When his father, Viscount Hailsham, died in August, 1950, Quintin Hogg[3] wrote to the Prime Minister to ask if the Government would introduce legislation to obviate the need for a by-election in the City of Oxford. The request was conveyed in terms which were not wholly conducive to a favourable reply: '. . . if

[1] The most recent case of this kind was in 1954 when Captain Baker (Con. Norfolk, South, 1950–54) was convicted of forgery.

[2] Now Baron Turnour in the peerage of the United Kingdom.

[3] Conservative Member for Oxford 1937–50.

your answer is in the negative I must tell you frankly that unless you can justify the present situation as a matter of principle I shall draw the inference that you and your party prefer to continue a system which is fraught with inconvenience to my former constituents, contrary to public interests and unjust, in order to pursue a grievance rather than to pursue the public good'.[1] Such legislation would have been without precedent and the Prime Minister refused to take any action.

In 1954–55, Wedgwood Benn (Lab. Bristol S.E.) attempted to renounce his right to the peerage of his father, Lord Stansgate,[2] during the latter's lifetime. He first tried to obtain this relief by means of a Personal Bill, but a Lords Committee reported that the supplication raised questions of general importance which were not proper to be dealt with by a Personal Bill.[3] Subsequently Lord Stansgate introduced a Public Bill in similar terms, but this was rejected on the Second Reading by 52 votes to 24.[4] In the debate Lord Stansgate revealed that before accepting a peerage in 1941 he had obtained the approval of his eldest son who was later killed on active service: the second son was then still at school and had not been consulted. A letter from Sir Winston Churchill, who had ceased to be Prime Minister three weeks earlier, was also read in support of the Bill. Yet the Government was unyielding and argued that the issues raised must await a general settlement of the future constitution of the Upper House. Thus the matter rests as a blot on our system of democratic institutions: meanwhile, twelve Members[5] may at any time be removed from the Commons contrary to the wishes of the majority of their constituents. On the committee stage of the 1957 Disqualification Bill J. Parker[6] tabled a new clause which sought to

---

[1] The correspondence between the Prime Minister and Hogg was published in *The Times* on 8th September, 1950.

[2] Previously Wedgwood Benn, Liberal Member for St. George's, Tower Hamlets, 1906–18 and Leith 1918–27; Labour Member for N. Aberdeen 1928–31 and Manchester, Gorton, 1937–42.

[3] Personal Bills Committee. Report, para. 3; 1954–55 (H.L. 23) iii.

[4] Cf. H.L. Deb., Vol. 192, cols. 561–93.

[5] Lord Balniel (Con. Hertford), W. Benn (Lab. Bristol S.E.), T. G. D. Galbraith (Con. Glasgow, Hillhead), J. Grimston (Con. St. Albans), Lord Hinchingbrooke (Con. Dorset, South), L. W. Joynson-Hicks (Con. Chichester), Viscount Lambton (Con. Berwick), P. Legh (Con. Petersfield), P. Maitland (Con. Lanark), P. O'Neill (U.U. Antrim, North), D. Ormsby-Gore (Con. Oswestry), R. Stanley (Con. N. Fylde).

[6] Labour Member for Romford 1935–45 and for Dagenham since 1945.

allow a Peer to be elected to the Commons, provided that he surrendered his seat in the Upper House so long as he remained in the Commons. This clause, however, was ruled out of order and so could not be discussed.[1]

Clergy of the Church of England and the Church of Scotland are disqualified by an Act of 1801, and Roman Catholic clergy by the Catholic Relief Act, 1829. The Welsh Church Act, 1914, ended the disqualification of its clergy, and priests or deacons of the Established Church may also become Members if they have been previously divested of their orders. Other non-conformist clergy can enter the Commons. This discrimination is impossible to justify but there has been no demand for a modification of the law: the Select Committee on Offices or Places of Profit reviewed the problem and, without making any recommendation, implied that it was not dissatisfied with the existing position.[2]

In 1950 the election of the Rev. J. G. MacManaway for Belfast, West, raised the question of whether ordination in the Church of Ireland constituted a disqualification. This Church was disestablished in 1871. The Select Committee on Elections reported that it was unable to reach a decision on the legal position,[3] and subsequently the case was referred to the Judicial Committee of the Privy Council for an advisory opinion. The issue depended on the interpretation of the phrase in the House of Commons (Clergy Disqualification) Act, 1801, which disqualified a person having been ordained to the office of priest or deacon. Did this apply only to ordination in the Church of England or to other forms of episcopal ordination? The Judicial Committee could find no authority for restricting the application of the section to the Established Church and held that the Rev. MacManaway was thereby disqualified.[4] Following the MacManaway case a Select Committee nominated to consider the whole issue of clerical disability reported that the matter should not be considered in isolation but only as part of the general question of disqualification for the House.[5] The 1957 Disqualification Act specifically left the status of clergy unchanged.[6]

[1] H.C. Deb., Vol. 566, col. 355.

[2] Report, paras. 59–60; 1940–41 (120) iii.

[3] 1950 (68–1) v.

[4] 1950 Cmd. 8067, xviii.

[5] 1952–53 (200) vi.

[6] Section 14 (3). An attempt to terminate disqualification of clergy was defeated by 160 votes to 38: H.C. Deb., Vol. 565, col. 1194.

Other barriers to entry into the Commons are all connected in some way to a relationship with the Crown which may be a source of profit to the individual concerned. In the past these barriers have been regarded as a vital safeguard to the independence of the legislature. If the monarch or his Ministers could distribute at will sinecure offices, pensions or contracts, it was feared that they would be able to purchase support in the House. This attitude was fully justified in an age when every man was said to have his price. Until 1957 the basis of the law on offices of profit was the Succession to the Crown Act, 1707. The central provisions of this statute were that no one could be a Member who held a 'new' office, i.e., one created since 25th October 1705; that those holding certain other appointments could not be elected; that persons holding pensions during pleasure could not be elected; that the election of those appointed to 'old' offices—positions which existed before 25th October 1705—was void, but that such persons might stand for re-election immediately. A further section of the Act excepted commissions in the armed forces from the above limitations. The number of Ministers who could sit in the Commons was thus controlled, and legislative sanction had to be obtained to permit holders of new appointments to remain in the House by excluding them from the provisions of the 1707 Act. As the size of the Cabinet increased there has been a corresponding list of such enabling Acts.[1] The provision which forced newly nominated Ministers to seek re-election remained partly in force until 1926, when it was abolished by the Re-election of Ministers (Amendment) Act. No doubt it was highly inconvenient for Ministers to have to fight by-elections at the same time as they shouldered new responsibilities, and the results of these contests could be embarrassing to the government. On occasion, a tendency developed to appoint as Ministers only Members who held safe seats. Re-election is no longer required as a check against corruption but, while the strength of the case for its abolition is admitted, the 1926 Act did reduce the contacts between Ministers and the electorate. The present position is that not more than seventy persons holding offices in the Government may sit and vote in the Commons, including a maximum of twenty-seven with Ministerial rank.[2]

In addition to the general exclusion of office-holders by the legis-

[1] Cf. 'Ministers of the Crown and the House of Commons' in *Public Administration*, Summer 1952, Vol. XXX, pp. 159–62.

[2] House of Commons Disqualification Act, 1957, S. 2.

lation in the reign of Anne, a large number of other statutes have specifically disqualified those holding various types of appointments. Anson has listed 42 such instances.[1] These, added to the complex provisions of the Succession to the Crown Act, created a state of legal confusion which the 1957 Act sought to remedy. The growth of the machinery of public administration in modern times has brought with it a vast range of official appointments, many of which provide but occasional employment and attract but negligible remuneration, but which are technically offices of profit and constitute a disqualification. It is common knowledge that civil servants cannot enter Parliament, but a person in private employment who is occasionally summoned to serve on an appeals tribunal, and receives a fee of a couple of guineas, may fail to realize his disability. Since 1945 a number of Members have unwittingly transgressed against the law in this way. Immediately after the 1945 Election it was discovered that J. Forman (Lab. Glasgow, Springburn) and Mrs. J. Mann (Lab. Coatbridge) were both disqualified since they had been appointed to tribunals created under the Rent of Furnished Houses Control (Scotland) Act, 1943:[2] their position was regularized by the Coatbridge and Springburn Elections Validation Bill, 1945, which was the first statute ever to validate an election retrospectively in this country. Similar legislation has since been passed to cover the cases mentioned below, except that of Beattie. Doubts arose about the position of others elected in 1945 and the Select Committee on Elections decided that a further three Labour Members were disqualified:[3] S. S. Awbery (Bristol, Central) and Mrs. F. Corbet (Peckham) in respect of their appointments as part-time assessors to deal with hardship cases under the National Service (Armed Forces) Act, 1939, and J. Harrison (Nottingham, North) by virtue of his membership of a tribunal nominated under the Pensions Appeals Tribunals Act, 1943. After the 1955 Election five further cases came to light, one of which, C. Beattie (Mid-Ulster), has been described above. The other four were J. George (Con. Glasgow, Pollock) who had been nominated by the Ministry of Works as a director of Scottish Slate Industries Ltd.;[4] Sir R. Jennings (Con. Sheffield,

[1] *Law and Custom of the Constitution*, Vol. I, pp. 101–4.
[2] Cf. Elections. Select Committee Report, 1945–46 (3–1) vi.
[3] Report, 1945–46 (71–1) vi.
[4] Cf. Elections. Select Committee Report, 1955–56 (35) vi.

Hallam) who was an Approved Auditor of Friendly Societies;[1] C. Holland-Martin (Con. Ludlow) a member of the London Board of Directors of the Bank of New Zealand;[2] C. Howell (Lab. Birmingham, Perry Barr) who had belonged to two panels from which were drawn employees' representatives on local tribunals under the National Insurance and National Insurance (Industrial Injuries) Acts.[3] The minor flood of technical disqualifications in 1955 forced the introduction of the clarifying legislation which had frequently been urged in the past.

Public appointments may be thought incompatible with membership of the Commons for a variety of reasons, apart from the original fear that a legion of place-holders would undermine the independence of the legislature. It is desirable that those exercising judicial powers should not compete for political honours to prevent any possibility of judicial discretion being used to forward personal or party interests. The greatest possible separation of the judiciary from other branches of state activity is recognized to be a major safeguard of the probity of Courts of Law and the rights of the individual. There is also a problem of time. If Members, other than Ministers, were allocated a miscellany of public responsibilities they would be forced to devote less energy to the business of Parliament. Such a situation emerged during the last war when the House of Commons Disqualification (Temporary Provisions) Act, 1941, was passed to safeguard the position of Members who had received exceptional wartime appointments. Its effect was to exempt from disqualification Members who were given a certificate from the Prime Minister that their appointments were required in the public interest to assist the prosecution of the war. Some of these posts were overseas and complaints were voiced that too many Members were abroad. Duff Cooper has recorded that, when British Representative to the French Committee of Liberation in Algeria, he suggested to the Prime Minister that he should resign his seat to meet the feeling that more Members should be available at Westminster. Sir Winston's reply was brief. 'No need for Chiltern Hundreds.'[4] In 1940, however, a

[1] Ibid. Sir Roland was Member for Sedgefield 1931–35 and for Sheffield since 1939.

[2] Elections. Select Committee Second Report, 1955–56 (50–1) vi.

[3] Elections. Select Committee Report, 1955–56 (117) vi. Howell had never sat on a tribunal although he had been summoned to do so.

[4] *Old Men Forget*, pp. 323–3. Duff Cooper, later Lord Norwich, was Conservative Member for Oldham 1924–29 and Westminster, St. George's, 1931–45.

Select Committee on Offices or Places of Profit under the Crown was established to consider the problem of these extraordinary war-time appointments. The Committee agreed that, for the period of the emergency, the normal disability relating to Offices of Profit might be waived, but recommended that Members holding such positions should refrain from addressing the House and from voting on matters connected with their service under the Crown, unless convinced that their doing so would receive the general assent of the House, or was urgently necessary in the national interest.[1] It will be seen that even at the most critical stage of the war the Commons was deeply concerned to preserve its independence of Ministerial influence. The Select Committee also examined the state of the law relating to Offices of Profit and recommended that a consolidating enactment be passed, and the original form of the House of Commons Disqualification Bill when introduced in 1955 was based on the detailed proposals of the 1940 Committee.

It is possible to meet the need to bar certain office-holders from the Commons in either of two ways. As an alternative to the traditional method of disqualification of those who occupy offices of profit, the situation could be reversed so that Members once elected would be prohibited from holding any of a given range of public appointments. This latter method of 'reverse disqualification' was closely studied by the Select Committee on the 1955 Bill but was ultimately rejected.[2] Reverse disqualification has the advantage that it would open the way to the Commons for virtually the whole adult population, but the Committee feared that it might create legal difficulties for future Members. At present, if a Member is found to be technically disqualified for a trivial reason the House can hastily regularize his position. If the reverse situation existed a Member might continue to occupy, through an oversight, some official position for which he was disqualified, and should he then be involved in a lawsuit arising from his *ultra vires* actions, it would be difficult for the Commons to protect him.[3]

The 1957 Disqualification Act repealed the provisions relating to offices and places of profit which had been enacted two hundred and fifty years previously. Instead, the 1957 Act contains lists of specific

[1] Report. Para. 86, 1940–41 (120) iii.
[2] Report. Para. 4, 1955–56 (349) ix.
[3] Ibid. Cf. Evidence of the Attorney-General, Q.s 334–5.

offices which do not disqualify[1]—Ministerial posts—and lists of offices which do disqualify,[2] including judicial offices, membership of a large number of Commissions and tribunals, and a wide range of other miscellaneous positions. Some offices disqualify only for particular constituencies. A Lord Lieutenant of a county, a Sheriff, and a chairman or deputy chairman of quarter sessions may not represent any constituency within the area covered by his appointment. Similarly, a Recorder may not sit for any constituency comprising the whole or part of the borough for which he is appointed.[3] Civil servants, policemen and regular servicemen, including National Servicemen, are ineligible for membership of the Commons, but not auxiliary or reserve personnel.[4] Further amendments to the list of disqualifying offices are to be made by Orders in Council.[5]

On the advice of the Select Committee the disqualification of Crown pensioners and Crown contractors has been terminated.[6] The Crown pensioners affected were receiving sums under the Civil List; their number appears to be declining and in the financial year 1954–55 was 181.[7] Crown contracts are a more formidable problem, but the law before 1957 was both anomalous and indefensible. It had been framed in an age when trade was carried on mainly by individuals acting singly or in partnership, and not by large companies: in consequence a Member with financial interests in a large engineering firm holding many valuable state contracts could sit in the House without penalty, while another Member who supplied a small quantity of furniture or stationery to a Government department might be disqualified. No Member has been disqualified for holding a government contract since 1924 and there seems little danger in allowing this category of disability to lapse. Should it be alleged in future that a contract were offered to a Member to influence his conduct, the matter could be dealt with as a contempt of the

[1] Second Schedule.

[2] First Schedule.

[3] Except the Recorders of London, Liverpool and Manchester, who are completely disqualified. It is not uncommon for Members to become Recorders as this function occupies a limited amount of time. Between 1946 and 1956 a dozen such appointments were made at annual salaries ranging from £24 to £400: H.C. Deb., Written answer, 14th May, 1956.

[4] House of Commons Disqualification Act, 1957, S. 3.

[5] Ibid. S. 5.

[6] Ibid. S. 9. Cf. paras. 6–8; 1955–56 (349) ix.

[7] Minutes of Evidence, App. II; 1955–56 (349) ix.

Commons and a breach of parliamentary privilege.[1] Analogous to government contracts are Crown briefs, the employment of counsel to represent Government departments in lawsuits. Crown briefs are frequently allocated to Members, but have never been treated as a disqualification. In evidence before the Select Committee the Attorney-General had been able to show conclusively that no political considerations entered into his choice of Members to plead the official viewpoint.[2] There has been, however, some concern on the Labour benches about this 'secret or semi-secret patronage,'[3] and a division was forced unsuccessfully on this subject during the Committee stage of the Disqualification Bill.[4]

Since 1957 the law of parliamentary disqualification has been clear and simple. Except in relation to the heirs of peers it may be regarded as satisfactory. There is likely to be a marked reduction in the number of cases of disqualification for trivial reasons. Every parliamentary candidate should study the First Schedule to the 1957 Act, for there will be little excuse in future for Members who transgress through ignorance.

[1] Minutes of Evidence, Appendix I, para. 5.

[2] From the Michaelmas Term, 1954, to the Hilary Term, 1956, 15 Members received nominations of this kind; 8 were Conservatives, 6 Labour and 1 Liberal. Minutes of Evidence. Q.s 669–71; 1955–56 (349) ix.

[3] H.C. Deb., Vol. 545, col. 1876.

[4] H.C. Deb., Vol. 566, col. 357 *et seq.*

4

Members in Parliament

An immediate task for a newly-elected Member is to become acquainted with the buildings in which the Mother of Parliaments conducts her business. To the new arrival the Palace of Westminster may appear impressive but inconvenient. Fuller acquaintance can induce a degree of reverence for all aspects of our parliamentary tradition, and still inspire a wish for rather greater facilities in its physical home. Yet the absence of private rooms for ordinary Members may have a beneficial effect upon the parliamentary scene, for Members are forced into communal surroundings which serve to encourage the exchange of opinions and the moderation of tempers.

Official guide-books contain a full description of the Palace buildings which, therefore, will not be attempted here. A brief outline must suffice. The great fire of 16th October, 1834, destroyed the major part of the Palace of Westminster with the important exception of Westminster Hall. Designs for a new Palace were invited in a public competition: ninety-seven sets of drawings were submitted and finally those of Charles Barry were selected. The first stone of the new buildings was laid in 1840 by the architect's wife, but not until 1847 were the House of Lords and its lobbies available for use and the Commons did not finally settle in their new chamber until 1852. The Palace is thus little more than a century old. It was built in the age of the Gothic Revival and the fashion of the period is responsible for its medieval characteristics. What would the Palace be like today had the great fire taken place a quarter of a century earlier? The chance of fate has bequeathed to us a great edifice born of antiquarian enthusiasm, which is a magnificent sight on the river frontage and from a distance. At closer quarters the Palace may seem less impressive, and the wealth of decoration—largely the work of Barry's assistant, Pugin

—frequently commands respect rather than admiration. These are, of course, matters of taste. But it is certain that the Palace does not stand up well to the modern criterion of functional efficiency, for 22% of the building is occupied by two miles of corridors.

The Commons' Chamber was destroyed in an air raid on 10th May, 1941,[1] and at the end of 1943 a Select Committee was appointed to consider arrangements for rebuilding. It decided that the traditional dimensions and the essential features of the Chamber should be retained, so that the sense of intimacy and the conversational form of debate they encouraged should be preserved.[2] The short walk from the Central Lobby of the Palace to the Commons' Chamber presents a remarkable contrast. The Central Lobby, in which strangers congregate when they come to see their Members, is an octagonal vaulted apartment, 60 ft. across and 75 ft. high; it is impersonal, comfortless and unfeeling. A little more than a hundred feet away the home of the Commons manages to combine friendliness with great dignity. It is surprisingly small. The floor is 68 ft. by 45 ft. 6 in.—exactly the same as Barry's Chamber—but at gallery level the dimensions have been increased to provide more room for strangers and reporters. The modest size is achieved because seats never have been provided for all Members; they have 346 seats on the floor of the House and a further 91 in the side galleries. For important debates the House is always crammed to capacity and the sense of crush accentuates the importance of the occasion; in quiet moments the few Members present seem far less isolated than they would be if six hundred odd seats were provided on the floor. There are also no desks between the benches, making it difficult to write or read and, thereby, increasing the possibility that attention will be paid to the speeches. In the Committee rooms there are desks, and a Member sitting in an inconspicuous position may deal with his correspondence.

Sir Giles Gilbert Scott was the architect of the new Chamber. In keeping with the rest of the Palace, the style is late Gothic, although no attempt has been made to follow the details of Barry's design. The ecclesiastical form of window was abandoned in favour of a more modern domestic type: most of the windows do not open in order that the excellent system of air conditioning shall remain unaffected by nature. The woodwork, Shropshire oak, has received iron sulphate

---

[1] From then till 1950 the Commons normally met in the Lords' Chamber, while the Lords used the Queen's Robing Room.

[2] Cf. Report: 1943–44 (109) (109–1) ii.

treatment to produce a restful light grey. The benches and the carpet are a pleasant green. Under the carpet are metal panels which can be heated to warm the feet of Members. Acoustically the Chamber is not satisfactory, in spite of a discreet system of amplifiers. A decision to have a sloping roof was taken for aesthetic reasons, although it was realized that this shape reflected sound waves, and the greater simplicity of ornament in the new building is thought to diminish audibility.

There are no rooms in the Palace for individual Members, except for Ministers and the Leader of the Opposition. A room is available for the Whips in each Party. In the basement of the new Commons' Chamber a number of small interviewing rooms have been provided for Members, but these do not seem to have given satisfaction, partly because of their situation and partly because of a smell which appeared to come from the wooden flooring.[1] Communal rooms available to Members include the Library, the Smoking Room, the Writing Room, the Chess Room, a Newspaper Room, and the Members' Bar and Cafeteria. All these rooms contain bells, which summon Members to divisions, and a silent annunciator showing the name of the Member speaking in the Chamber, so that the House can assemble rapidly if it is thought that an important speech is being made. Two television rooms have been established, one for B.B.C. and one for I.T.A. programmes, but these are ill-patronized by Members except sometimes when a major sporting event is on the screen. There are also a number of committee rooms of varying size, mostly on the first floor. A stroll on the Terrace will give Members a close view of the Thames. Under St. Stephen's Hall—the meeting-place of the Commons before 1834—there is the Crypt which is used for the celebration of Holy Communion, and sometimes for the wedding of a Member or the baptism of their children. In 1924 when a Member, who did not belong to the Established Church, arranged to have his child christened in the Crypt, an attempt was made to stop the proceedings: the opinion was sought of the Law Officers who decided that the Crypt was under the sole authority of the Lord Great Chamberlain, and that no ecclesiastical jurisdiction existed in respect of the Crypt. The Library seems to suffer from troubles similar to those of other busy libraries. The Select Committee on Accommoda-

[1] House of Commons Accommodation, etc. Select Committee Report. Para. 14; 1953–54 (184) vii. Conditions in these rooms were later said to have improved, H.C. Deb. Written answer, 10th November, 1954.

tion reported in 1954 that the Library was unsuited to the constant use now made of it; upper shelves were out of reach except by climbing ladders; other books had to be drawn from inaccessible stores; volumes urgently required were sometimes missing. The Committee felt that a better check ought to be kept on books leaving the Library and the co-operation of Members should be sought to this end.[1] In 1956 G. Benson (Lab. Chesterfield), Chairman of the Commons' Library, sent a letter about its use to every Member. He commented that 'unfortunately Members are still apt to borrow books without filling in cards', and quoted the case of an ex-Member who was found after his death to have 22 volumes from the Library amongst his belongings.[2] The problems, financial and otherwise, of providing refreshment for Members and their guests are fully described in the annual Reports of the Kitchen Committee.

The Serjeant-at-Arms is the chief executive of the Commons and has to enforce its orders, in accordance with the directions of the Speaker, and also do what he can to add to the comfort of Members. He receives a warrant from the Lord Great Chamberlain which entrusts to his care those sections of the Palace allocated to the Commons while the House is sitting. The Serjeant is, then, the 'housekeeper' for the Commons. The task is doubly difficult as all expenditure on improvements must be authorized on the estimates of the Ministry of Works and is subject to the normal processes of Treasury control: further, he is hampered by lack of space and the nature of the building. Conditions of parliamentary life have changed greatly since the middle of last century. Accommodation which may have been adequate then is no longer so, now more Members are in the Palace for a larger number of hours each sitting day.

Since 1953 a series of Select Committees, presided over by R. Stokes,[3] have studied the problem of accommodation, and their Reports show there is much dissatisfaction among some Members with the facilities provided for them. One complaint is that ventilation and heating in the buildings are generally inadequate: draughts are prevalent in all rooms facing the river front.[4] Many rooms are thought to be overheated, including the Library where 'the atmosphere at times is conducive neither to the proper preservation of

---

[1] Report, para. 15.
[2] *Daily Telegraph*, 21st January 1956.
[3] Labour Member for Ipswich, 1938–57.
[4] Para. 17; 1953–54 (184) vii.

books nor to personal comfort'.[1] All Members do not agree about the level of an optimum temperature. Sir J. Lucas (Con. Portsmouth, South) has complained that, since the abolition of coal fires in the Palace, Members arriving in a chilled condition cannot get warm.[2] The more serious problem is the lack of space for individual Members to do work connected with parliamentary affairs. In days past the Houses of Parliament were said to be the best club in London: as a club the facilities may be satisfactory, but for the central workshop of a modern democracy they are absurd. No proper provision is made in the Palace for Members to file correspondence or other papers. Space is available for rather less than 150 Members' secretaries but, as only a minority of Members can afford full-time clerical help, this is not as inadequate as might be thought. The Select Committee canvassed the possibility of providing individual pedestal desks for Members themselves; these would obviate the need *inter alia* to dictate letters in the corridors. It issued a questionnaire to discover the extent of the support for this proposal. 489 Members sent replies: 295 indicated that they would make substantial use of such a desk; 177 said that they wanted provision which would enable them to work with a secretary; even if no room could be found in the Palace, 93 still wished for a desk to be provided in the near vicinity.[3] As a result of these activities of the Select Committee three desk rooms, containing a total of about forty desks, have been provided for Members. In allocating desks, preference is given to Members who have not got a secretary accommodated in the Palace. The difficulty of shortage of space at Westminster is aggravated by the competing claims of other occupants of the building. There is some feeling that Members have an unduly small share of the Palace in relation to the Lords and the Palace Officials. Various detailed schemes have been under consideration to reorganize the use made of the rooms available, but extensive building operations would be necessary to produce facilities equal to those enjoyed by Members of Parliaments elsewhere in the Commonwealth.[4]

---

[1] Ibid.
[2] H.C. Deb., Vol. 535, cols. 2588–9.
[3] Para. 5; 1953–54 (184) vii.
[4] Ibid., para. 3.

II

The first business of a newly-elected House of Commons is to choose a Speaker to preside over its debates. The Speaker embodies the authority of the House, enforces its rules of procedure and interprets them whenever necessary. He is the First Commoner in the Realm, and in the table of precedence comes immediately behind the Prime Minister and the Lord President of the Council. He receives a salary of £5,000 per annum and has a residence in the north-east corner of the Palace of Westminster. Traditionally it has been the task of the Speaker to represent the views of the Commons to the Crown and to uphold the rights and privileges of individual Members: in modern times he has ensured a fair hearing for minority opinion in the Commons. The office of Speaker is deeply respected by Members, for it is recognized as being a guardian of their own status. The Speaker has no gavel with which to call for order, but when he rises in the Chair calm falls on the most excited debate. No doubt this ascendancy is assisted psychologically by the robes of office, but the Speaker himself may seem to be a lonely figure, isolated in the Chair from the cut and thrust of party warfare. It has been well said that the moral authority of the Speaker is far greater than his power, for any motion passed by the House relating to the conduct of its business must be accepted and enforced by him. An action of the Speaker may not be criticized inferentially during the course of a speech: his conduct is open to challenge solely on a specific motion to that effect. Adverse comment about the Speaker is rare. But in his autobiography L. S. Amery did hint at partiality when he suggests that, in the debate in 1940 that led to the fall of the Chamberlain Cabinet, the Speaker decided to call him in the dinner hour, when the House was thin, because the Speaker knew 'that I was out to make trouble'.[1]

When called to the Chair a Speaker abandons all his political connections and since 1870 has not spoken in the House save on procedural questions. Since 1835 he has been re-elected by successive

[1] *My Political Life*, Vol. III, p. 355. Amery added that Clement Davies (Lib. Montgomery) went off to collect an audience from the Smoking Room and the Library. The speech was a major success and subsequently was widely quoted (H.C. Deb., Vol. 360, cols. 1140–50). Amery was Conservative Member for Birmingham, Sparkbrook, 1911–45, and held a wide variety of ministerial posts between 1919–29 and May 1940–45.

Parliaments irrespective of any change in the political complexion of the House. If a vacancy occurs through death or retirement a new Speaker is chosen from the majority party; the selection is made by the Cabinet but it is the custom for the election to be moved and seconded by backbenchers. To date, no Labour Member has become Speaker because the office has never become vacant while Labour has had a majority in the House. There are no clear conventions governing the choice. At the end of the nineteenth century it was generally accepted that Ministers were ineligible and that the traditions of the office made it appropriate to select a backbencher who had not been over-active in party controversy. Sometimes the man appointed was relatively unknown. Lord Rosebery commented that all Speakers were highly successful, deeply regretted and generally pronounced to be unreplaceable, but that a new Speaker was soon found, and found amongst the mediocrities of the House.[1] But in this century a change has taken place and the practice has developed of promoting either the Chairman of Ways and Means or the Deputy Chairman. These are the only two Members who may deputize for the Speaker, but they are Government nominees, do not abandon their party ties, and lose their positions when the Opposition comes to power. The advantage of selecting the Chairman of Ways and Means or his Deputy is that they have had much experience relevant to the duties of the Speakership: the disadvantage is that as Government nominees,[2] although not Ministers, they may be thought more susceptible to official influence. An objection on these lines was made in 1921 at the time of the election of Speaker Whitley.[3]

The election of Speaker W. S. Morrison (Cirencester) in 1951 completely failed to conform to pattern in three respects. For the first time since 1872 a Speaker with Ministerial experience was chosen: for the first time since 1895 neither the Chairman of Ways and Means nor the Deputy Chairman was chosen: for the first time since 1895 the election of the Speaker was contested and forced to a division.[4] The first of these items is the most serious break with tradition. Speaker Clifton Brown had retired at the General Election when the Labour

---

[1] *Letters of Queen Victoria*, 3rd series, II, p. 495.

[2] But they are not necessarily Government supporters. In 1950 the Labour Government nominated a Conservative, Sir Charles MacAndrew, as Deputy Chairman; in 1951 the Conservative Government nominated a Liberal as Deputy Chairman.

[3] H.C. Deb., Vol. 141, col. 310.

[4] H.C. Deb., Vol. 493, cols. 2–24.

Government was defeated; in spite of the verdict of the polls, Labour Members pressed the claims of Major Milner,[1] who had served for eight years as Chairman of Ways and Means including a period during the war-time coalition administration. To choose Major Milner would have been an act of unusual generosity and the new Cabinet were merely following precedent in preferring one of their political supporters. But this does not explain why the obvious candidate, Sir Charles MacAndrew,[2] was passed over. Nor was any excuse offered for putting forward the name of one who had occupied a wide variety of Ministerial offices in the two previous decades. This paragraph is concerned with the principles involved and is not in any way a personal criticism of Speaker Morrison. And it must be stressed that if the 1951 precedent is followed in future, there is a danger that the Speakership will be used by Prime Ministers as a means of accommodating senior ex-Ministers who, for one reason or another, are not required in the formation of a new government. No method of selection could be more contrary to the historical purpose of this office.

Because the Speaker must maintain a position of strict political neutrality, he is in difficulty if forced to defend his seat at a general election. It would be unfitting for him to praise or criticize the Government and, therefore, to campaign in the normal fashion. Until 1935 the Speaker was usually re-elected unopposed, but on the last four occasions at which the Speaker has been a candidate the election has been contested: the Speaker's opponents were Labour in 1935 and 1945, an Independent in 1950 and an Independent Labour candidate in 1955. The convention of his unopposed return is thus badly tattered. If the Speaker did not represent a fairly safe 'seat', his presence in the Commons after an election could not be guaranteed. Another unsatisfactory aspect of this situation is that the Speaker's constituency is virtually disenfranchised, for its Member is not able to represent local interests as other Members do. A Select Committee was appointed in 1938 to examine these problems, but would not accept any of the innovations proposed to it.[3] The best suggestion was that the Speaker should represent a special constituency,

[1] Labour Member for Leeds S.E. 1929–51. Created a baron in 1951.

[2] Conservative Member for Kilmarnock 1924–29, Glasgow, Partick, 1931–35 and Bute and North Ayrshire since 1935. Sir Charles was Deputy Chairman of Ways and Means in 1945 and 1950–51, and Chairman of Ways and Means since 1951.

[3] Cf. Parliamentary Elections (Mr. Speaker's Seat). Select Committee Report, 1938–39 (98) viii.

St. Stephen's, for which the only electors would be Honourable Members: this would both eliminate any disadvantages the Speaker's constituents may be thought to suffer and isolate his election from political controversy. The Select Committee rejected this idea for the peculiar reason that the Speaker would be left without a seat in the House should the House itself decide not to re-elect him. As the Commons have not refused to re-elect the Speaker since 1835, this contingency seems more unlikely than the possibility of a Speaker losing his seat if he continues to represent an ordinary constituency.

The Chairman of Ways and Means[1] has also, since 1855, acted as Deputy Speaker, and he receives a salary of £3,250 per annum. His assistant, the Deputy Chairman of Ways and Means[1] may also function as Deputy Speaker, and has a salary of £2,500 per annum. These two Members may relieve the Speaker when presiding over the House, and they also take the Chair when the House is in Committee and the Speaker may not be present. They are expected to be impartial and do not enter into party controversy, although they still retain party allegiance. The Chairman of Ways and Means has the delicate task of deciding which amendments shall be selected for discussion when a Bill goes to a Committee of the Whole House. He is also responsible for the supervision of Private and Personal Bills and for seeing, when necessary, that an opportunity is found to debate them. When the House is in Committee the Chair may also be taken by a Temporary Chairman who is on the Speaker's Panel. In 1948, Mrs. F. Paton[2] became the first woman to preside over the Whole House as Temporary Chairman.

The Speaker's Panel is a body of at least ten Members chosen by the Speaker who act as Chairmen of the Standing Committees. They are unpaid for these services and come from both sides of the House. Members on the Panel do not abstain from Party warfare, except when in the Chair, but Members with violent and extreme opinions are probably not selected by the Speaker for this purpose. The Panel meets occasionally to discuss difficult points of procedure that may arise in Committee. A Chairman may be called on to decide whether an amendment to a Bill is outside the terms of the financial resolution passed by the Whole House,[3] or if a starred amendment—one that

[1] These officials are also known respectively as the Chairman of Committees and the Deputy Chairman of Committees.

[2] Labour Member for Rushcliffe 1945–50.

[3] See p. 107.

appears on the Order Paper for the first time—should be rejected because there has been inadequate time for prior consideration. It is generally agreed that the Chairmen reach a high standard of impartiality and their judgment is accepted without question. Thus an Opposition supporter, occupying the Chair, may rule out of order a motion or a speech by a Minister, and this is indicative of the atmosphere in which parliamentary business proceeds. The Chairman and Deputy Chairman of Ways and Means are often chosen from Members who have obtained appropriate experience through service on the Panel.

The procedure of the Commons is admittedly complex. New Members returned at a general election are invited to attend lectures by the Clerk of the House to help them to master it. Intricacy arises because of attempts to achieve a compromise between conflicting requirements—the need for a Government to complete its business and the need for Honourable Members to have reasonable time for voicing their opinions and grievances. The present volume does not describe the details of procedure, but some aspects of it will be seen in the following pages which sketch the parliamentary scene and the pattern of parliamentary endeavour.

III

The Commons' Chamber is rectangular in shape and is divided lengthwise by a wide central aisle which separates the parallel benches facing each other. Thus is symbolized the division of the House between Government and Opposition. At one end of the aisle is placed the Speaker's chair, below it sit the Clerks of the House and in front again are the two dispatch boxes used by front bench spokesmen when making a major contribution to the debate. At the other end is the bar of the House, where those who have offended against the dignity or authority of the Commons may be brought for judgment. Immediately behind the bar is the seat of the Serjeant-at-Arms. The benches contain room for 346 Members and a further 91 can be accommodated in the side galleries; Members may address the House from the galleries, although this is inconvenient and never done, but they cannot speak from seats on the floor of the Chamber which are 'below the bar' and, therefore, furthest from the Speaker. In the middle of the Chamber, at right angles to the central aisle, a gangway runs up between the benches on both sides. The allocation of seating in the House is governed by ancient convention. The Treasury Bench, the front bench above the gangway on the Speaker's right hand, is occupied by Ministers: on major parliamentary occasions Junior Ministers may be crowded off and they retire to the bench immediately behind. On the front bench to the Speaker's left sit the leading Members of the Opposition—Privy Councillors, the 'Shadow Cabinet' and any Member who may have been invited to make a major speech for the Opposition on that particular day. No permanent reservation of seats is allowed, but as a matter of courtesy a few eminent backbenchers will always be allowed to occupy the place of their choice. A Member who intends to be present at prayers at the start of a sitting can place a 'prayer card' on a bench; this card has to be obtained personally from an attendant at the House at any time after eight a.m. on the same day. Only a Member who is engaged on a select committee, standing committee or departmental committee can retain a seat without attending prayers; for this purpose another special card (pink) has to be obtained.

After the election of the Speaker a new House of Commons proceeds to take the oath of allegiance. Since 1888 Members have been allowed to make an affirmation in lieu of an oath if the oath is contrary to their beliefs. A Member need not take the oath at the commencement of a Parliament, but he may take no part in business until he has done so. The House as such no longer attempts to compel the attendance of Members, for this function is undertaken by the Whips. At the opening of a Parliament those returned for the first time take the oath in the same way as other Members, but Members returned at by-elections are introduced at the end of question-time by two sponsors: in 1945 Dr. MacIntyre[1] attempted to take the oath without sponsors but the House, on a division, refused to agree.

A new Parliament meets after a general election and, therefore, may be summoned at any time of the year; it continues to sit, apart from adjournments for the recognized holiday periods, until the prorogation. Prorogation is normally in the autumn and takes place only a short time before a new session is convened. Pressure of business means that the hours of labour for Members are much longer than in the nineteenth century when it was common for the session to open in February and end in July or August. In modern times the House sits on average for 35 weeks in a session, and the burden of committee work is far greater. From Mondays to Thursdays the

[1] Scottish Nationalist Member for Motherwell for two months.

75

House meets from 2.30 p.m. to 10.30 p.m., unless the closing time is postponed for one of a number of possible reasons: on Fridays the sitting lasts usually from 11 a.m. to 4.30 p.m. Each sitting commences with prayers. Then follow items of uncontentious business which may include a reply to an address to the Crown delivered by the Vice-Chamberlain of the Household;[1] communications to the Speaker; the announcement of the death of a Member; motions for writs for by-elections[2] and unopposed private business. These items occupy but a few minutes and the remaining time until 3.30 p.m. on Monday to Thursday is devoted to questions.[3] There is no question hour on Fridays. The main business of the day due to start at 3.30 p.m. may be preceded by any of the following matters, each of which have priority. New Members are introduced to take the oath. Any Member may seek to move an emergency adjournment of the House.[4] The ballot is held to determine which Members shall move motions on private Members' Fridays.[5] Ministerial statements explaining the policy of the Government may be made; as no question is before the House when this is done, any debate thereon is irregular, but the Speaker occasionally allows a little latitude. A Member may give a personal explanation or apology arising from a previous speech in the Chamber. This is also the time for raising matters of privilege,[6] the formal introduction of public bills and for a backbencher to bring in a bill under the '10-minute rule'.[7] Finally, Government motions relating to the business or the sittings of the House may be moved; a common form of such a motion is to postpone the termination of the main business of the day from ten o'clock to eleven o'clock.

When all these items have been completed, the House proceeds to the main business—the Orders of the Day. On the majority of sitting days only one or two matters arise in the categories described in the paragraph above, and it is unusual for the House to fail to reach its main business by 4 p.m. The first days of a new session are devoted to a general discussion of ministerial policy in the debate on the

[1] A Member who acts also as a Government Whip.

[2] If a writ is opposed, consideration of it is deferred until after questions. For a recent example see *Hansard*, 9th May, 1957, H.C. Deb., Vol. 569, cols. 1149–50 and 1186–9.

[3] For a description of question time, see pp. 117–21.

[4] See pp. 122–3.

[5] See pp. 203–4.

[6] See pp. 224–5.

[7] See pp. 194–5.

Queen's Speech. The two types of business that consume most time during a session are the passage of legislation[1] and the consideration of estimates by the whole House in the Committee of Supply.[2] A number of days will also be spent in debating Government motions, approving some aspect of official policy, or on Votes of Censure proposed by the Opposition. Important debates last for two or three days and on most sitting days only one bill or motion is considered, but a number of bills of secondary importance are often advanced through one or more stages in a single day.

The normal closing hour of ten o'clock may be postponed—as already noted—by resolution of the House, and does not apply when business exempt from the ten o'clock rule is under discussion. The chief forms of 'exempted business' are bills which originate in the Committee of Ways and Means (the annual Finance Bills), and proceedings pursuant to an Act of Parliament, which covers parliamentary examination of Statutory Instruments.[3] In addition, when ordinary business is interrupted for an emergency adjournment debate, the ten o'clock closure is postponed for a period equal to that of the interruption. And however late the hour at which other business ends, the motion 'that the House do now adjourn' can be discussed for thirty minutes by a backbencher who raises a topic of which notice has been given.[4]

The whole of the time of the House is now controlled by the Government, apart from the 26 days allocated to the Committee of Supply, when the Opposition chooses the subjects for debate, and the twenty Fridays still permitted to private Members' bills and motions. It is the responsibility of the Leader of the House and the Government Chief Whip to plan the parliamentary timetable so that time is available for Government legislation and for the discussion of the most urgent matters of public policy. The Leader of the House announces the business for the coming week on a Thursday afternoon in reply to a question from the Leader of the Opposition. The parliamentary schedule has a considerable degree of flexibility and is greatly affected by informal agreements between the Whips of the main parties. If the Opposition wish to discuss a topic for which the Government can find no time, the Opposition may agree to cut short

[1] See pp. 107–16.
[2] See pp. 128–30.
[3] See pp. 125–8.
[4] See pp. 123–5.

77

the debate on a Government bill and use the time thus saved to their own desires. Such arrangements originating in the 'usual channels' are made known to Members by the Whips and constitute an unofficial timetable for the day's proceedings; they would tend to become unoperable if there were any considerable number of independent Members in the Chamber. An individual Member has little influence over the pattern of parliamentary activity, but if there is evidence of a widespread desire to debate a particular topic the Government does its best to be accommodating so far as the limited time available permits. Management of the parliamentary programme is a delicate art, and the temper and quality of debate depends to a great extent on the skill with which it is conducted.

The shortage of parliamentary time also limits severely the period for which any single Member can expect to be able to claim the attention of the House. Choice of those who are called to participate in debates rests entirely upon the discretion of the Speaker, but is also conditioned by convention. A major debate is opened by a speech from each of the front benches, and is ended in the same fashion: the normal maximum debating time for the main business of the day is $6\frac{1}{2}$ hours of which at least two will be used by front-bench speeches. It follows that backbenchers do not usually command the ear of the House for more than $4\frac{1}{2}$ hours a day or, allowing 4 hours on a Friday, for more than roughly 22 hours a week, excluding question time and the adjournment periods. This calculation can be made only in very general terms. A plethora of ministerial statements or verbosity from opening speakers will curtail the opportunities of backbenchers, but any postponement of the ten o'clock closure will increase them. On the basis that there are about 35 weeks in a session, there is an average of less than an hour and a half of debating time per backbencher each session. Most Members do not obtain even this meagre ration, for backbench Privy Councillors—ex-Ministers—have precedence over their less distinguished fellows.

Members who wish to address the House rise in their places when a speech is concluded.[1] Those who are wise will have mentioned their desire to the Whips or will have written to the Speaker. The Whips advise the Speaker informally of the names of their supporters who

---

[1] There is one exception to this rule: a Member who wishes to raise a point of order while a division is in progress must sit down and put on a hat. This is the most effective method of becoming conspicuous when other Members are moving around in the Chamber.

hope to join in a debate, but they have no control whatsoever over the Speaker's choice. Whips may also ask a Member to be prepared to speak if it is felt that he could make a useful contribution, or if a debate seems in danger of dying inconveniently. The Speaker attempts to distribute the time available in such a way as to produce the most varied discussion and Members tend to be called from alternate sides of the House. Holders of less orthodox opinions often find it easier 'to catch the Speaker's eye'. Independents and Members belonging to minor groups enjoy a generous proportion of the attention of the House: during the two-day debate in May 1957, which followed the decision that British shipping should again use the Suez Canal, three of the eight Conservatives who had resigned the Whip on this issue were called by the Speaker. Precedence is accorded to Privy Councillors, and the Speaker, being human, is more likely to favour Members known to be lively and witty debaters than those with the reputation of being tedious bores. Members who seldom wish to speak are also less likely to go to bed with their speeches unrecorded. But after most important debates there must be a number of frustrated Members who have sat through many speeches in the unrealized ambition of being asked to address the House themselves.

A verbatim record of everything said aloud in the Chamber is printed in *Hansard*, which is a daily publication when the House is sitting. There are strict rules about maintaining the accuracy of the parliamentary reports. Members frequently examine the official transcripts of their speeches and may make corrections which improve the grammar or clarity. 'But let there be no mistake about the rule of the House in these matters. It is not permissible to make alterations in the transcript which materially alter the sense of what was said.'[1] No doubt there have been occasions in the past when this principle has been applied with some flexibility. Sir Henry Morris-Jones has revealed one such example. After the landing of Hess in Scotland, he had spoken in the House 'somewhat impetuously, and perhaps unwisely',[2] and was afterwards taken by the Speaker to the latter's room to modify the sense of his speech for the official report, where it could be read by the enemy.

Hansard is an invaluable source of information regarding the interests and energies of Members, but there is no satisfactory

[1] Mr. Speaker's ruling. H.C. Deb., Vol. 536, cols. 1275–7.

[2] *Doctor in the Whips Room*, p. 158. Sir Henry was Member for Denbigh: Liberal 1929–31, Liberal National 1931–50.

method of measuring the extent to which Members participate in parliamentary business. The table below is an attempt to show variations in the amount of activity, by using the length of the entry under the name of each Member in the Index volume to *Hansard* for the session 1953–54. Members who belonged to the Commons for only part of the session are excluded, as are the Speaker, Deputy Speaker, and the Deputy Chairman of Ways and Means, all of whom take no part in debates except from the Chair. The 1953–54 session was a little longer than average and lasted from 3rd November, 1953, to 25th November, 1954; during this period the House sat for 39 weeks. Before commenting on the table it is important to stress its limitations. At best, the figures are but a rough guide to the frequency with which individuals were active in the parliamentary scene; there are roughly ten entries in a quarter of a column in the

PARLIAMENTARY ACTIVITY MEASURED FROM THE INDEX TO HANSARD:

SESSION 1953–54

Length of entry (Columns)	Ministers	Government Supporters	Opposition Members[1]
No entry	6[2]	8	6
Less than $\frac{1}{4}$	2	54 (3)[3]	52 (5)[3]
$\frac{1}{4}$–$\frac{1}{2}$	2	58	48
$\frac{1}{2}$–$\frac{3}{4}$	3	41	27
$\frac{3}{4}$–1	3	18	23
1–1$\frac{1}{2}$	5	25	47
1$\frac{1}{2}$–2	2	16	22
2–3	6	13	15
3–4	5	3	33
4–5	5	1	8
5–7$\frac{1}{2}$	17	2	9
7$\frac{1}{2}$–10	5	–	1
Over 10	11	–	–
Total	72	239	291

[1] Including Liberals and Irish Nationalists.

[2] The inaudible Ministers were Whips.

[3] The numbers in brackets refer to Members whose entries relate only to questions that received written answers and who, therefore, took no part in discussion in the Chamber.

Hansard index, and a Member with a column of references after his name has earned notice on at least forty occasions during the session. But the size of his entry is no indication of the importance of a Member's work. The putting down of a large number of questions—which may be relatively trivial—will produce a lengthy entry in the *Hansard* index, while a dozen thoughtful contributions to major debates will barely score a quarter-column. Nor can *Hansard* record attendance at committee meetings, either unofficial party gatherings or the Select or Standing Committees. Of course a Member active in committees is more likely to intervene in the Chamber when topics relevant to his committee work are under discussion, but there is no necessary correlation between activity in committee work and in the Chamber, for Members who seek publicity will concentrate on the latter. Parliamentary private secretaries, many of whom devote much energy to their duties, tend to be restrained in their comments in the House and make, therefore, a slim showing in the index.

These qualifications do not detract from the central message of the table—that Members command very uneven shares of parliamentary time. In 1953–54 it will be seen that 28 Members did not detain the House at all, and twice this number made a negligible contribution to the discussions. Ministers are, of necessity, the most heavily engaged since every question demands a ministerial reply and most debates contain at least two ministerial contributions. Opposition Members are more active than government supporters, but on this matter the figures are again a little deceptive. They do not distinguish between the frontbenchers and the rank and file on the Opposition side, where it is impossible to draw the sharp distinction that exists between Ministers and their supporters. The Labour Members with the largest entries in the index were not, however, from the Shadow Cabinet: the first prize for eight columns went to Lieut.-Colonel Lipton (Lab. Brixton) and the runners-up were other voluble back-benchers. But the table does show that government supporters are not, as is sometimes urged, little more than lobby-fodder, for a fair proportion of them have a substantial performance in the Chamber to their credit. Even so, party leaders do not smile on those who intervene frequently in debate, and few government backbenchers who became Ministers in later years had an entry of much more than half a column. The index also gives an indication of the different tactics adopted by Members. Some rarely or never ask a question; some ask questions only on policy matters and not on personal cases;

some restrict themselves to debates on a few topics and others seem willing to speak on everything. These characteristics are widely understood in the House and one of the hardest things for a Member to achieve is to surprise his friends.

Voting figures at divisions in the House are a good indication of the level of attendance of Members in the Palace of Westminster. When a question is put in the Chamber the Speaker or his Deputy proceeds to 'collect the voices'. If his verdict on the relative volumes of sound produced by the 'Ayes' and the 'Noes' is disputed, the order is given for the division lobbies to be cleared and the exit doors are locked. Division bells are rung all over the Palace,[1] and policemen shout 'Division' in the corridors. Immediately the bells ring, committee meetings, meals, interviews and a wide variety of other activities are interrupted. Members have six minutes in which to assemble before the entrances to the division lobbies are locked. Extreme measures have sometimes been taken to vote; on one occasion a Member having a bath in the Palace arrived in the lobby with a large towel swathed round his person.[2] The names of Members voting in each lobby are recorded by clerks at the entrance of each division lobby, and Members are counted at the lobby exits by tellers: the names of tellers are announced by the Speaker who is advised by the Whips. For most divisions party discipline is invoked; the 'Whips are on' and two Whips on each side act as tellers. This system of voting does, of course, take time, on average about ten minutes. But it is widely urged that the tramp through the division lobbies helps to cool the passions of debate, and the Select Committee on Procedure[3] decided against any change in the present system. The use of time in this way would become serious if the number of divisions were as large as in 1909 when 895 votes were recorded; the average number is now rather less than a quarter of the 1909 figure, but a total of 25 divisions took place in a single sitting on the 1951 Finance Bill and occupied about four hours. Standing Orders do allow the Speaker to conduct a vote by calling both sides to stand up in the Chamber and be counted without further delay, but this procedure is not used because it deprives Members of having their names and opinions registered in *Hansard*.

---

[1] It has not been unknown for Members living nearby to have had division bells, attached to the House circuit, installed in their homes.

[2] E. Taylor, *The House of Commons at Work*, p. 119.

[3] Second Report, para. 13; 1945–46 (58–1) ix.

MEMBERS IN PARLIAMENT

The table below analyses the voting records of the short parliamentary session of 1950, when 65 divisions took place, and the 100 divisions that occurred before Easter 1957 in the session 1956–57. These dates were chosen to illustrate the effect of a narrow government majority on attendance in Westminster: in 1950 the 'whipping' was sterner than ever before, but in 1956–57 an adequate majority permitted a normal amount of flexibility. When a three-line whip has been issued the total of Members voting will be near or even a little above 600. If a two-line whip is in operation Members with opposing views may 'pair' with each other and absent themselves from the House. In 1950 the three-line whip was used constantly because of the exiguous nature of the Labour majority. On one occasion the casting vote of the Chair had to be used to give the government a majority,[1] and a demand by Sir Winston Churchill for a secret session on defence matters was also defeated by a single vote.[2] The figures show how greatly the Whips affect the level of attendance; in 1957, at a free vote on a private Member's Bill, the total vote fell as low as 54. It can also be seen that the attendance of ministerial supporters in 1956–57 was rather better than that of the Opposition, since the proportion of Members in the Government lobby at any division was normally higher than their proportion of seats in the House as a whole.

MEMBERS' ATTENDANCE AT DIVISIONS:
SESSIONS 1950, 1956–57

	1950	1956–57
Number of Members[3]	622	627
Average number of Members taking part in a division	507	412
Average number of Members taking part in divisions where both parties used Whips	566	435
Average number of Members taking part in other divisions[4]	293	206
Government majority over all other parties	8	63
Average Government majority in divisions where both parties used Whips	17	50

[1] H.C. Deb., Vol. 474, col. 1549. The casting vote is always used in such a way as to allow the question under review to be reconsidered at a later date.

[2] H.C. Deb., Vol. 478, col. 695.

[3] Excluding the Speaker, Deputy Speaker and Deputy Chairman of Committees, and ignoring casual vacancies.

[4] Divisions with no Whips or Government Whips only.

As noted above, a Member who wishes to be away from the House may arrange a 'pair' with a Member of the opposing party. A 'pair' is simply a mutual agreement not to vote on a particular day; it reduces the numbers voting but leaves the size of the Government majority unaffected. Pairing arrangements are made known to the Whips, who see that they are honoured, and are very convenient for Members who have important engagements away from Westminster or who are uninterested in the day's business. Except when a three-line Whip is in operation, pairing is very common: many Members, especially those in the legal profession, have a regular 'pair' with someone on the other side of the House. When possible, pairing arrangements are also made for Members who are abroad or who are ill. This system adds to the flexibility of parliamentary life, and makes it easier for Members to travel and pursue a wider range of interests.

Those present in the Chamber itself are frequently but a small part of the numbers who will suddenly appear when division bells ring. A visitor in the public galleries may see but a thin sprinkling of Members on each side of the House if the debate is on an unexciting topic. Attendance also varies with the time of day. The Chamber is usually well filled for question-time and to hear the opening speeches in the main debate; by tea-time backbenchers are addressing the House and many of those left in the Chamber will be hoping for a chance to speak. Yet the news travels fast if a contribution of unusual interest is being made. Towards ten o'clock the Chamber will fill again to hear the closing front-bench speeches, especially if a division is anticipated. Ten o'clock is the most usual time for divisions, but voting on procedural motions takes place after question-time about 3.30 p.m. If the main business of the day is split into two, the second topic will be due to commence at 7 p.m., when a division may also be challenged on the first item of business. On the Committee or Report stages of a Bill, divisions can be more frequent and occur at any time: it is traditional that some sittings on the Committee stage of the Finance Bill go on through the night and some divisions then take place in the small hours.

The post-war increase in committee activity has had a detrimental effect on attendance in the Chamber itself. Earl Winterton, who became 'Father of the House' in 1944, has been strongly critical of this tendency.[1]

---

[1] *Orders of the Day*, pp. 317–8. Earl Winterton (created Baron Turnour in 1952) was Conservative Member for Horsham 1904–51.

MEMBERS IN PARLIAMENT

'The younger members of the Conservative Party have, in recent years, become imbued with the belief that they can best serve the interests of the Party and advance the prospects of their own careers by becoming immersed in the affairs of the numerous committees and sub-committees of the Party which meet, during the sittings of the House, in a committee room. They are in the Chamber itself only when they want to speak or are interested in the particular subject. So, all too often in the 1945 and 1950 Parliaments, the Opposition back benches were sparsely filled by a handful of M.P.s too engrossed in thinking out what they were going to say, if they were fortunate enough to be 'called', to encourage by cheers those of their own side who were actually speaking. No impression of unity or enthusiasm was created. Old hands, like myself, could get over this tepidity by deliberately picking a quarrel with the Government spokesman which almost invariably produces cheers, counter-cheers, and an exhilarating excitement.'

The problem of 'catching the Speaker's eye' has been discussed above, but there are a number of methods by which backbenchers can achieve prominence in the Chamber. Members with extreme views find that their comments have a higher news value: Sir Waldron Smithers[1] and Emrys Hughes (Lab. S. Ayrshire) would fall squarely into this category. A Member will become noted if he consistently criticizes the Government on a particular topic: examples are the attitude of Stanley Evans[2] towards farming policy, and that of G. Nabarro (Con. Kidderminster) on purchase tax. The raising of matters which are highly topical—Lieut.-Colonel Lipton (Lab. Brixton) is an expert at this—will attract publicity. A few experienced Members, like S. Silverman (Lab. Nelson and Colne), have been adept at interrupting important speeches to ask a question or put a point of order. To be successful this technique must be used with discretion and not too frequently. Earl Winterton has commented: 'If the questions are relevant, and directed by a backbencher of acumen and intelligence against some important figure on the other side of the House, they are tolerated, provided that the interrupter can hold his own in debate against similar treatment.'[3] A Member may refuse to 'give way' to an opponent who seeks to ask a question or challenge a statement of fact, but to refuse to do so savours of

[1] Conservative Member for Chislehurst 1924–45, Orpington 1945–55.
[2] Labour Member for Wednesbury 1945–56.
[3] *Orders of the Day*, p. 325.

85

cowardice unless time is short or the speech has been previously interrupted. After he has spoken it is also the custom for a Member to remain in the Chamber during the subsequent speech, partly as a matter of courtesy and partly to hear any comment that may be made about his own remarks. The Department concerned with the subject under review is always represented on the Treasury Bench, and the Minister due to reply to a debate normally sits through the greater part of the preceding discussion.

A Member's first speech, his 'maiden' speech, is heard without interruption, and earns a few words of congratulation from whoever follows him in a debate. It is generally agreed that a maiden speech is an ordeal, especially as the novice knows fairly exactly at what time he will catch the Speaker's eye. The novice receives a measure of priority for, within limits, he can choose the time at which he addresses the House; naturally the Speaker cannot allow too many first attempts on any one day, and they cannot follow in immediate succession because of the need for commendation. As they enjoy these privileges, maiden speeches are subject to limiting conventions. They should not be too long—a quarter of an hour is more than enough—and they should not be over-controversial. Frequently they contain references to the Member's constituency. But not all maiden speeches conform to this pattern. A. P. Herbert commenced his parliamentary career by protesting against the decision of the Government, which was supported by the Opposition, to restrict the amount of private Members' time, and followed his protest by forcing a vote on the issue which the Government won by 232 votes to 5. This performance was described by Winston Churchill as 'a maiden hussy of a speech'.[1] A more recent exception to the common run of maiden speeches was that of D. Keegan (Con. Nottingham, South) who, in 1956, delivered an attack on capital punishment.[2] The traditional advice given to new Members is that they should not speak too soon or before they have assimilated something of the traditions and atmosphere of parliamentary debate. It is natural for old hands to stress the value of experience and that a new Member should avoid a reputation for brash impetuosity. But not all Members delay their initiation. Apart from the desire of a new Member to get started, he

[1] A. P. Herbert, *Independent Member*, pp. 21–30. Herbert represented Oxford University as an Independent 1935–50. Nearly all the autobiographies of Members or ex-Members contain an account of their maiden speeches.

[2] H.C. Deb., Vol. 550, col. 99 *et seq.*

also feels debarred from playing a normal part in parliamentary business until the courtesies associated with his maiden speech have been completed.

The House of Commons is not an easy audience to address, and Members soon realize that the conditions are very different from those of the public platform or the lecture theatre. Unless a Member speaks from the rearmost bench at least a part of his audience will be behind him. The effect of this is lessened in so far as those behind are party colleagues; but a Member, or a Minister, who makes comments that are unwelcome to his own side, is not made more comfortable by the sense of disapproval at his back. Another distracting feature is that Members do not sit still. There is continuous movement in and out of the Chamber as Members leave to attend to other business or return from a meal, a committee or an interview with a constituent. The backbencher who speaks immediately after a Minister must expect his hearers to dwindle at the start of his speech. Then, of course, the Commons is an experienced and critical audience, and many of those listening are hoping that their own chance to speak will come next. There is no really distinctive House of Commons style of oratory, but an excess of gesticulation and synthetic emotion are frowned on. Great speeches are still made, and are appreciated on both sides of the House, but the ordinary Member should eschew anything in the nature of a grand peroration. Above all, the nature of a speech varies with the form of the business. On the committee stage of a Bill the contributions are briefer and narrower in scope; on a second reading or in a general debate Members will attempt a wider canvas.

The tone of a debate depends largely on the nature of the occasion; some issues are specialized and largely uncontroversial, while others are flashpoints of party feeling. When the political temperature is high any minor incident will produce a storm, and the House is not at its best if an election is anticipated or desired. Physical conditions in the Chamber and parliamentary tradition, enshrined in the rules of debate, are all aids to harmony. Order papers are always available to be waved in congratulation, but there are no desk-lids to bang. When addressing the House a Member may use notes, but speeches should not be read. Speeches must also be in English. One Member referring to another in debate must refer to the latter not by name but by a descriptive periphrasis in the third person, so minimizing the possibility of personal abuse. Thus a Member is described by refer-

87

ence to the name of his constituency, e.g., 'the Honourable Member for Orkney' or by some phrase as 'the Honourable Member who spoke last', 'the Honourable Member below the gangway', etc. Privy Councillors are 'Right Honourable', Queen's Counsel are 'Honourable and learned', Service officers are 'Honourable and gallant', and a peer is 'the noble lord the Member for . . .' This terminology serves to soften allusions to other Members, but how far a Member may go in personal criticism of his fellows depends to a considerable degree on the severity of the Chair: it is out of order to impute discreditable motives to other Members and to accuse them of deceit. Comments on the physical appearance of Members, or about their private lives, are not permitted. A wide variety of abusive descriptions have been disallowed through the years, including 'villains', 'hypocrites', 'murderer', 'insulting dog', 'swine', 'pecksniffian cant', 'cheat', 'stoolpigeons' and 'bastard'. While a Member is speaking other Members should remain silent or converse in under-tones in order not to interfere with the debate. Should the volume of conversation make it difficult to hear a speech, the Speaker or Chairman will call the House to order. Cries of 'hear, hear', 'question', 'divide, divide', are sanctioned by long usage and are not out of order unless they obstruct the course of business. A Member should not move from his place when addressing the House and offensive weapons should not be brought into the Chamber: Mrs. Braddock (Lab. Liverpool, Exchange) has been censured for displaying air-pistols,[1] the sale of which she was urging should be restricted.

The Commons is usually a well-behaved assembly; if the House does become extremely disorderly, the Speaker will suspend the sitting for a short period. This occurred on 1st November, 1956, during the Suez crisis. If an individual Member is guilty of grossly disorderly conduct, he is normally warned by the Speaker or Chairman and, if the warning does not have the necessary effect, the Member will be ordered to withdraw from the House. In extreme circumstances the Member is 'named' by the Chair—if the House is in Committee, the Speaker is summoned—and a motion is put, without debate, that the offending Member be suspended from the service of the House. Since 1926 the period of suspension has been five sitting days for the first offence, twenty sitting days for the second, and the remainder of the session on any subsequent occasion. It is not always possible to warn Members in advance about their

[1] H.C. Deb., Vol. 555, col. 1061.

conduct, as at the famous incident when John Beckett[1] seized the Mace. A Member can only be 'named' in this way because of misbehaviour in the House; the use of offensive expressions or the commission of an assault elsewhere in the Palace is treated as a contempt of Parliament, in accordance with the procedure described in Chapter 12. Members have been suspended, however, for obstructing the completion of a division. In 1926 a baker's dozen of Labour Members sat on the floor of the division lobby and refused to pass the tellers to attract publicity for their protest against a Conservative economy measure.[2] This did not prove to be a very effective means of delaying the business of the House for, after a short interval, the Speaker decided that adequate time had elapsed for the division to be completed and summoned the tellers, leaving the votes of those sitting on the floor uncounted. The Serjeant-at-Arms was instructed to obtain the names of the offenders who were subsequently 'named' and suspended.

In the literature of parliamentary reminiscence occasional references are to be found to the question of drink. Because the Houses of Parliament are a Royal Palace, the restrictions imposed by the Licensing Acts do not apply; unusual opportunities exist, therefore, for those so inclined to be unwise. According to Fenner Brockway, in the 1929–31 Parliament it was common for one or more Members in the Chamber to be intoxicated after nine o'clock in the evening.[3] Lord Brabazon records that there was little drunkenness in the House during his period of membership, but recalls that during the Committee stage of the Trade Disputes Bill an intoxicated Member managed to say of the Attorney General—'I can see the Rt. Hon. Gentleman pleading with all the eloquence of well-remunerated indignation.'[4] But habits have changed over the last thirty years, and the Members' Bar is only a third of the size it was when the incidents cited above took place. In a letter to the author Mr. Fenner Brockway has stressed that there is much less drinking by Members now than in the early 1930s, and that it is very rare for any Member to show signs of intoxication in the House, whether after nine o'clock or at any other time.

[1] Labour Member for Gateshead 1924–29, Peckham 1929–31.

[2] H. Dalton, *Call Back Yesterday*, pp. 160–1.

[3] *Inside the Left*, p. 222. Brockway has been Labour Member for Leyton, East, 1929–31 and for Eton and Slough since 1950.

[4] *The Brabazon Story*, p. 115. Lord (then Lt.-Col.) Brabazon was Conservative Member for Chatham 1918–29 and Wallasey 1931–42.

5

The Control of Policy and Administration

Members and Ministers

'The principle of Parliamentary sovereignty means . . . that Parliament has, under the English constitution, the right to make or unmake any law whatever; and further no person or body is recognized by the law of England as having a right to override or set aside the legislation of Parliament.'[1] This classic statement by Dicey sets out the extent of the power of Honourable Members, for the authority of Parliament is now effectively concentrated in the House of Commons. The principle of constitutional monarchy precludes royal intervention in matters of political controversy, and the House of Lords, by the Parliament Act, 1949, can delay only non-financial legislation for a period of twelve months. The absolute legal authority of the Commons is exercised through the Cabinet, and the first duty of the Commons is to provide and maintain a Cabinet that will give direction to the business of government.

In a two-party system with strong party discipline the backbencher is not often called upon to play a part in the making or unmaking of governments. At a general election the party that succeeds in winning a majority of seats in the Commons can expect, in normal circumstances, to continue in office until the next election. The leader of the majority party becomes Prime Minister and appoints other Ministers to their offices; backbenchers can take some part in the original nomination of their party leader, but this may be years before the moment of electoral victory.[2] Revolts or murmurs of rebellion against a party leader, in or out of office, are not unknown but they are rarely successful. In 1930–31, Stanley Baldwin weathered a strong assault by Lords Beaverbrook and Rothermere; and soon after the 1955 Election there were indications that some Conservative

[1] A. V. Dicey, *Introduction to the Law of the Constitution* (9th ed.), pp. 39–40.
[2] Political Promotion is discussed in Ch. 11 *infra*.

90

Members wished to remove Sir Anthony Eden from the Premiership. When Governments fall, however, the issues involved are greater than personalities, and the motivation of attacks on individuals is always questionable.

Changes of government, other than after an election, may be the work of party leaders alone. A Cabinet crisis, resulting from disagreements among its members, can well be settled by negotiations in which the rank-and-file of the Commons are not concerned. The replacement of the Asquith coalition by the Lloyd George coalition in 1916 is one such example:[1] in 1931 Labour Members were astonished when the MacDonald Labour ministry was succeeded by a coalition headed by MacDonald in which the majority of the previous Labour Ministers refused to serve.[2] The resignation of the Baldwin ministry in 1924 and the decision of MacDonald in the same year to seek the dissolution that led to his defeat, were both caused by the actions of the Liberal Party in the Commons, and illustrate the instability which may result when there exist three effective political parties. Yet on three occasions in this century Conservative backbench Members can claim to have influenced the fate of Governments. A meeting of Conservative Members at the Carlton Club on 19th October, 1922, passed by 187 votes to 87 a resolution urging that the Conservative Party should fight the next election independently of the Coalition Liberals.[3] The effect of this meeting was to bring the Lloyd George coalition to a speedy end. On 8th May, 1940, the House of Commons approved the conduct of the war by Neville Chamberlain's administration with a majority of 81—281 votes to 200. As the normal Conservative majority was roughly 200 it was clear that a grave erosion of confidence in the Government had taken place. Chamberlain therefore resigned and was replaced by Winston Churchill. L. S. Amery has described[4] how in April, 1940, a Watching Committee had been formed of Conservative Members and Peers who were disquieted by the half-hearted conduct of the war: this Committee played an important part in the events before the historic vote on 8th May. The third occasion was in 1951 when

[1] D. Lloyd George, *War Memoirs*, Vol. 2, Ch. XXV.

[2] A large number of biographies and autobiographies contain accounts of this event: cf. *inter alia* L. MacNeill Weir, *The Tragedy of Ramsay MacDonald*, ch. 45 *et seq.*, and Snowden, *Autobiography*, Vol. II, pp. 947–54.

[3] Cf. R. T. MacKenzie, *British Political Parties*, pp. 98–109.

[4] *My Political Life*, Vol. III, p. 355 *et seq.*

Conservative Members, by keeping the House sitting for long hours and forcing divisions late at night, caused much trouble to the Labour Government which had but a slim majority. Conservative Members were younger, healthier and more had accommodation in central London that could be reached easily after a late sitting. Earl Attlee in his autobiography commented that the strain placed on Labour Members at this period was very great, and that it was 'not pleasant to have Members coming from hospital at the risk of their lives to prevent a defeat in the House'.[1] There can be little doubt that the Conservative tactics were a factor in his decision to ask for the dissolution of Parliament that led to the defeat of the Labour Government. These examples show how backbench pressure can be decisive only when the Government is already weak. In 1922 the war-time Coalition had long outlived its *raison d'être*: in 1940 the personal foreign policy of the Prime Minister had proved a failure and the outbreak of war had created feeling in favour of an all-party coalition: in 1951 the Government was carrying on with an exiguous majority. It is, then, in rare circumstances that Members can destroy Governments, but they may endeavour to influence them at all times.

When the policy of an individual Department is subjected to heavy public criticism the personal future of the Minister at its head is necessarily involved. Ministers are responsible to Parliament for actions carried out in their name, and must reply to questions and debates about the work of their Departments. But does this mean that the Commons can force the resignation of a Minister whose policy has been a failure? Should a vote of censure on a Minister ever be carried in the Commons, the Minister would immediately resign, and probably the whole Cabinet as well: in practice, party discipline among Government supporters prevents dismissals of Ministers through action in the lobbies. The tradition of collective responsibility in the Cabinet enjoins Ministers to come to the aid of a colleague under attack for applying a Cabinet decision. Normally the spirit of comradeship or political tactics induce such support when the cause of trouble is departmental maladministration, for which the Cabinet cannot fairly be blamed. Has party discipline, therefore, removed all sting from the principle of ministerial responsibility? Opposition criticism, however violent and well-founded, is by itself quite unable to depose a Minister. If dissatisfaction spreads

[1] *As It Happened*, pp. 206–7.

to the Government benches the position is uncertain; the Minister may stay, he may be moved to another office, or he may resign. Three factors influence the outcome, the temper of the backbenchers, the views of the Prime Minister and possibly his most senior colleagues, and the attitude of the Minister under fire. The latter may defend himself and cling tenaciously to his post, or be willing to surrender his responsibilities. It is probably impossible for private Members to oust a resolute Minister who is firmly backed by his colleagues but, if there is wavering in Whitehall, opinion in Westminster can be decisive. Professor Finer has listed ten cases in this century in which a resignation has been influenced by a 'backbench revolt',[1] the most recent being that of Sir Thomas Dugdale in 1954 over Crichel Down.

The political activities of Members are multiplex. They may be public or discreet; they may be individual or collective; they may stem from personal enthusiasms or be prompted by persuasions from extra-parliamentary sources. The more important an issue, the greater the probability that the reactions of Members will be public, collective and dictated by party opinion. The channels for their activities are also divers. Members may write letters to *The Times* or to their own political leaders: when the prospect of a British withdrawal from Port Said was first mooted nearly eighty Conservative Members were reported to have written letters urging the Cabinet to 'stand firm'.[2] It is also open to Members to put down a motion on the Order Paper, not in the expectation of securing a debate, but for propaganda purposes and in order to test the feeling of the House. Other Members who agree with the resolution may add their names; in 1956 a motion urging that the stage be relieved of its burden of taxation obtained the signatures of an absolute majority of the House. Groups of Members urging a particular policy may assume a semi-permanent form, as did the 'Keep Left' group of Labour Members in 1947 and the 'Suez Group' of Conservatives in 1954. Should a group stray too far from official party policy it will attract the displeasure of the Whips and, especially in the Labour Party, issues of party discipline will emerge. Members may also take a leading role in public associations with avowedly political objects—witness the attempt of H. Price (Con. Lewisham, West) to mobilize

---

[1] In 'The Individual Responsibility of Ministers', *Public Administration,* Winter 1956, Vol. XXXIV, pp. 377-96.

[2] *The Economist,* dated 1st Dec. 1956.

the middle classes and the advocacy by Sir Victor Raikes[1] of a 'Third Force', consisting of Britain, Western Europe, Africa and Australasia, which could pursue policies independent of those of the United States.

Meetings between Members and Ministers are frequent and may be held in an atmosphere of intimacy and cordiality, for the Ministers of today are the backbenchers of yesterday and are on good personal terms with most Members, other than newcomers. Apart from more formal meetings with deputations to Ministers or by personal appointment, perhaps arranged through a parliamentary private secretary, many chances for casual conversation occur within the precincts of the House, although with the growing pressure of Departmental business Ministers tend to spend more time in their offices. In the debating chamber itself many hours are devoted to the examination of Government policy and the ventilation of grievances; in the committee rooms further attention is given to matters of detail. Later sections of this chapter will describe how the work of the Commons is designed to facilitate the examination of executive action, and the advocacy of causes great and small. Private meetings of Members are also of much importance, especially among Members who support the Government of the day. Both the main parties have a series of subject committees described below[2] which have watching briefs over the doings of corresponding Ministries. Discussion in these gatherings can be highly influential: a speech by Austen Chamberlain to the Foreign Affairs Committee of Conservative Members is said to have played a large part in forcing the resignation of the Foreign Secretary, Lord Templewood (then Sir Samuel Hoare), over his policy towards Abyssinia.[3] There are quite special difficulties in the way of democratic control of foreign affairs and defence policy, because of the element of secrecy in diplomacy and strategic considerations. Yet Members are by no means powerless: it is more than probable that the withdrawal from Port Said in December, 1956, and the subsequent decision in 1957 that British ships should again use the Suez Canal would both have taken place at an earlier date had there not been such great resistance amongst Government supporters to these actions.

[1] Conservative Member for S.E. Essex 1931–45, Liverpool, Wavertree, 1945–50 and Liverpool, Garston, 1950–57.

[2] pp. 95–105.

[3] L. S. Amery, *My Political Life*, Vol. III, p. 184 *et seq.*

There are, of course, many questions on which the division of views cuts across party lines. Matters of conscience are not subjected to the normal rules of party discipline, and may be decided by a free vote in the House.[1] But the normal pattern of parliamentary business is for the 'whips to be on' and Members are expected to support their leaders and to make personal convictions submit to the demands of party orthodoxy. But rebellions do take place, and the seriousness of a rebellion depends upon the circumstances. If the Opposition is hopelessly uncertain in their attitude to Government policy, as the Conservatives were about accepting the American Loan of 1945, it will lose caste but the fate of the Government is not at stake. Equally, if Government and Opposition leaders agree, a backbench rebellion will not have major political consequences. Should Government supporters agree with the Opposition the implications of a revolt are grave, for it would invite the defeat of Ministers, a reduction in the authority of the Government and an election in which the rebels could not hope for party support. Revolts in this last category are rare. The following sections of this chapter describe the variety of means available for Members to influence policy and administration, but the opportunities, although frequently under-estimated, must be considered in the light of the realities of party discipline.

One further general observation must be made. From time to time Ministers give way and bow to a storm or accept suggestions made by Members: the sum total of such occasions does not represent the extent of the influence of Members. In framing policy Ministers consult interested parties, inside and outside the precincts of Westminster. Unless political principles or expenditure are involved Ministers will usually try to accommodate the representations they receive, and it may be possible to conciliate potential opponents before a word is said in the House. And Members, if they are wise, will try the tactic of private negotiation; it is much easier for a Minister to change his mind before he has publicly committed himself to a particular course of action.

PARTY MEETINGS AND COMMITTEES

Unofficial gatherings of Members in party groups or committees now occupy a considerable amount of time. These private meetings are more popular than the average debate in the Chamber; thus when

[1] Free votes are examined in Ch. 6 *infra*.

the House is thinly attended it is probable that some committee rooms are full. The reason for this preference is not hard to appreciate. Discussion in private is more frank and rewarding, and opinions critical of the policy of a Member's own party can be voiced with less embarrassment. Plans may be laid to exert pressure on a Minister, or information may be gathered for use in subsequent parliamentary speeches. At meetings of Government backbenchers a Minister may be there in person to hear criticism or answer questions; failing a Minister, the appropriate private parliamentary secretary will be present to take notes and report back to his master. At Opposition meetings tactics will be determined for assaults on ministerial policy. It is certain that proceedings at these informal groups have an important effect on the pattern of parliamentary debate and form a major channel through which, by collective action, Members can exert influence. The normal rule is that a Member is permitted to attend meetings of any committee formed by his own party, and notice of these committee and sub-committee gatherings is given on the weekly party whip. In choosing which meetings to attend Members are guided by their interests and experience, and by the nature of the constituencies they represent. Thus, company directors tend to go along to a Trade and Industry Committee; ex-officers gravitate to meetings about the Services; Members from rural areas feel it important to be present at the Agriculture Committee to keep abreast of developments that may be of concern in their localities.

The extent of these party committees has grown steadily in recent years, and a point has been reached at which a number of meetings by Members of one party may be in progress at the same time. According to *The Times*, on 30th January, 1957, the Foreign Secretary addressed a meeting of the Conservative Foreign Affairs Committee, the Minister of Power attended a meeting of the Conservative Fuel and Power Committee and the Minister of Housing and Local Government heard backbenchers' proposals for amending the Rent Bill at a meeting of the Conservative Housing and Local Government Committee. With this volume of activity in the committee rooms it is not surprising the Chamber is often very empty. The difficulty now is that Members often wish to attend two committees which meet simultaneously, and to limit this over-lapping the Conservatives have recently decided that their committees shall meet normally each fortnight instead of weekly. Although party committees have reached a new scale of importance since the war they are not entirely a modern development; the Unionist Agricultural Committee was in existence before 1914. The general meeting of Conservative Members, the 1922 Committee, dates itself, and after its formation a number of specialized groups concerned with each of the Armed Services, Finance, Foreign Affairs and Trade and Industry came into existence.[1] As shown below the energies of Conservative Members have now created 22 committees and a further 17 sub-committees. In the Labour Party the present system of Subject committees commenced in 1944 when Labour Members set to work to consider the many problems of post-war reconstruction. Before this time a number of advisory committees of Labour Members had existed, especially in the late nineteen-thirties, but these became more or less dormant for much of the war. In addition to Subject Groups, Labour Members also have Area Groups and Working Parties whose functions are considered later. In all, it is clear that these party gatherings are an important and fairly new feature of parliamentary life, and one which makes a major demand on the time of Members.

Both parties also have general meetings of Members at least once a week when the House is in session. The 1922 Committee is the Conservative forum and may be attended by all Conservatives, Liberal Nationals and Ulster Unionists. It owes its name to the group of Conservatives, newly-elected in 1922, who started to hold private meetings for the discussion of policy in the belief that there was insufficient consultation between backbenchers and the party leadership. Both Austen Chamberlain's fall in 1922 and Baldwin's unexpected and disastrous dissolution in 1923 helped to strengthen this view. The 1922 Committee, originally frowned on by Conservative leaders, now occupies a position of major importance in the Party organization. When the Conservatives are in opposition, members of the 'Shadow Cabinet' may attend (but not the leader of the Party—the potential Prime Minister) although they have no special *locus standi* and are considered ineligible for election as officers of the Committee. When the Party is in office Ministers attend to discuss policies for which they are responsible, and the Prime Minister may come to talk about the general political situation, especially just before the House goes into recess. The 1922 Committee—the Conservative Private Members' Committee is the formal title—meets normally each Thursday at 6 p.m. and its executive committee of 16 meets for half an hour before the full assembly. A

[1] Sir W. I. Jennings, *Parliament*, pp. 358-9.

Conservative Whip is present at the full meeting to outline parliamentary business for the coming week, and any of the items which are matters of contention within the Party may be discussed. Problems brought forward by one of the functional committees may also be considered.

The 1922 Committee is essentially a political discussion group. Resolutions are not proposed and votes are not taken. The 'feeling of the meeting' is, however, of much importance and is reported back through the Whips' Office to the appropriate Ministers. If the dissatisfaction of a meeting with official policy is great, a deputation may wait upon a Minister, or the Chairman of the Committee might see the Prime Minister; usually the informal channels of communication are found to be adequate. These matters are conducted in confidence and, as the Conservatives are adept at keeping party secrets, it is difficult to estimate how much influence the Committee wields. No doubt, it varies from time to time and between subject and subject. Opponents of the Conservatives frequently allege that the 1922 Committee is the 'core of Tory reaction'; the impression is created of a body dominated by the most militaristic and extreme sentiments. It is often true that privacy is not an aid to moderation. Yet as all backbench Conservatives can attend the 1922 Committee it can claim to be fully representative of opinion in the Party. Should it urge a Conservative Government to follow a more extreme—or liberal—policy, it is arguable that Ministers are out of tune with the prevailing view among their supporters. The guiding principle in Conservative organization is that the Leader of the Party has the right to determine party policy; the 1922 Committee does not question this principle, but the replacement of Austen Chamberlain by Bonar Law in 1922 shows that it is unwise for a Leader to become too far divorced from his followers. Herbert Morrison has suggested that Conservatives have a theory that Ministers, although responsible to the Commons as a whole, should not 'live too closely' with their backbenchers, who, in turn, retain the right to pass critical judgments in private on the policies of their leaders.[1] That is certainly the way that Conservative Members act in practice. It is the task of the Conservative Whips to prevent the growth of rifts among their Members; to persuade the doubtful of the merits of official policy;

---

[1] *Government and Parliament*, p. 131. Morrison has been Labour Member for Hackney, S., 1923–24, 1929–31 and 1935–45, Lewisham, E., 1945–50 and Lewisham, S., since 1950.

to inform Ministers of the extent and intensity of dissatisfaction. This liaison function is carried on with much skill and enables apparently difficult situations to be resolved. When the 1922 Committee discussed the proposed sale of the Trinidad Oil Company to American interests they were reported to be against it 'almost to a man',[1] but at the division in the Commons during the following week on the Government decision to permit the sale a single Conservative, Captain Kerby (Arundel and Shoreham), deliberately abstained.

The full range of Conservative committees existing in the session 1956–57 is set out below. Their structure is flexible; committees, especially sub-committees, die if their subject-matter loses interest, and new committees are formed to study fresh problems as they emerge.

CONSERVATIVE AND UNIONIST PARTY COMMITTEES

Conservative and Unionist Private Members Committee (the 1922 Committee).
Defence
      Sub-Committees: Navy
                            Army
                            Air
Trade and Industry
      Sub-Committee: Films
Foreign Affairs
Finance
Commonwealth Affairs
      Sub-Committees: East and Central Africa
                            West Africa
                            Far East
                            Mediterranean and Pacific
                            Commonwealth Relations
                            West Indies
                            Commonwealth Development
Agriculture, Fisheries and Food
      Sub-Committees: Horticulture
                            Fisheries
Labour
Home Office Affairs
Health and Social Security

[1] *The Economist*, 7th July, 1956.

Housing, Local Government and Works
    Sub-Committee: New Towns
Education
Transport
    Sub-Committees: Shipping
                  Canals
Power
    Sub-Committee: Oil
Atomic Energy
Civil Aviation
Arts and Amenities
Broadcasting and Communications
Scottish Unionist Members
Ulster Unionist Party
Liberal Unionist Group
Lancashire Members
Merseyside Members

These functional committees are in a sense subordinate bodies to the 1922 Committee, and can bring an issue before the general body in order to secure publicity and endorsement of its own views. The 1922 Committee may act as mediator between a functional committee and a Minister; in 1953 the Conservative Fuel and Power Committee advocated a Policy which the Minister (G. Lloyd)[1] was unwilling to accept, whereupon the 1922 Committee heard statements from both sides and decided to support the Minister.[2] This practice seems fraught with difficulty. If the general meeting backed its committee and not the Minister, would the Minister feel forced to resign? There can be little doubt that a Conservative Minister feels happier if he can get along easily and successfully with the group of government supporters who have awarded themselves a watching-brief over his department. A backbencher holding committee office can also feel embarrassed if he strongly disapproves of official party policy and may resign in protest. There are two recent examples of this kind: in 1954 Captain Waterhouse[3] resigned from the Chairmanship of the Conservative Defence Committee owing to disagreement with ministerial policy over Suez, and in 1955 G. Nabarro (Kidderminster)

[1] Member for Birmingham, Ladywood, 1931–45; Birmingham, King's Norton, 1950–55 and Sutton Coldfield since 1955.

[2] R. T. MacKenzie, *British Political Parties*, pp. 60–61.

[3] Member for Leicester, South, 1924–45 and Leicester, South-East, 1950–57.

resigned from the Secretaryship of the Conservative Fuel and Power Committee because of dissatisfaction with the Government's fuel policy.

The corresponding organization on the Labour side of the House is more rigid. The Parliamentary Labour Party has a formal constitution based on democratic principles: resolutions on policy are proposed and decisions are made by vote. In spite of the difference of atmosphere it is difficult to find satisfactory evidence that the individual Labour Member is more influential in the Party than is his Conservative counterpart. During the session the Parliamentary Labour Party meets each Thursday evening to consider parliamentary business for the coming week, and additional meetings are held as required on Wednesday mornings to discuss policy issues. When the Party is in opposition an executive committee—the Parliamentary Committee—of eighteen, including three peers, is elected annually. Contrary to Conservative practice, this is a committee of party leaders and the Leader of the Party is the Chairman.[1] Labour Members form Subject Groups in the same fashion as the Conservatives, and questions of policy are given initial consideration by the appropriate Group which submits a resolution thereon to the Parliamentary Committee. This latter body then approves or amends the resolution and submits it to the full Party meeting. Here the members of the Parliamentary Committee sit together at one end of the room facing the main body of those present: Labour peers may attend and have the right to vote. Frank and sometimes acrimonious discussions take place and, as Labour Members take little trouble to conceal their differences, unofficial reports of these events often appear in the press. There is a fairly continuous struggle in the Party between the leaders and (some of) the led, with the leaders usually advocating more moderate policies. It will be noted that business is so arranged that the Parliamentary Committee can review the enthusiasms of the specialized functional committees.

When Labour is in office strained relationships between Ministers and rank-and-file Members tend to develop. During both the minority administrations of Ramsay MacDonald these difficulties were acute. To prevent their recurrence, in 1945 a small Liaison Committee of Ministers and backbenchers was established to facilitate the exchange of ideas and information. The Liaison Committee had a non-ministerial majority and its Chairman was the Chairman of the full

[1] For further discussion of the significance of these arrangements see pp. 211–12.

101

Parliamentary Party. The Parliamentary Committee did not exist and the officers of the Parliamentary Party were backbenchers. In the period 1945–51, the successive chairmen of the Parliamentary Party and the Liaison Committee were Neil MacLean,[1] Maurice Webb[2] and Glenvil Hall.[3] As Leader of the House of Commons Herbert Morrison was a member of the Liaison Committee throughout the six years Labour held office, and he has testified that meetings of this Committee were uniformly happy. It did not prevent, however, differences of view emerging between Ministers and their supporters. The 'Keep-Left' group of Members maintained determined opposition to the foreign policy of Ernest Bevin, and in 1947 the Government bowed to backbench pressure and reduced the period of national service from 18 months to 12 after 72 Labour Members had voted against the Conscription Bill in the Commons.[4] This is the leading case of the effective influence by Labour Members during these six years: subsequently the period of service was increased to 24 months by the Labour Government owing to the gravity of the international situation, so this example shows the weakness as well as the strength of Labour backbenchers. Meetings of the full Parliamentary Party were held regularly, but there was no question of Ministers seeking Party approval of their actions. On rare occasions votes were taken on critical resolutions, but appeals to party loyalty, the tact of the ambitious and the block vote of up to 70 Ministers were sufficient to sustain Ministerial policy. A Labour cabinet would not be prepared to accept instructions from the Parliamentary Party, but the moral force of a vote in the Labour movement is strong and Ministers of any party are keen to avoid embarrassing expressions of opinion.[5]

When Labour is in Opposition the pattern of organization is necessarily changed. The officers of each Subject Group are elected annually by those Members who opt to join the group at the begin-

[1] Member for Glasgow, Govan, 1918–50.

[2] Member for Bradford, Central, 1945–55. Appointed Minister of Food 1950.

[3] Member for Portsmouth, Central, 1929–31 and Colne Valley since 1939. Financial Secretary to the Treasury 1945–50.

[4] For a full discussion of this event see the article by J. M. Burns in the *American Political Science Review*, December, 1950, p. 865.

[5] In the same way the Parliamentary Labour Party will not accept instructions from the Annual Conference of the Labour Party, although the latter is supposed to be the ultimate source of authority in the Party. This point is argued and illustrated, almost *ad nauseam*, by R. T. MacKenzie, *British Political Parties*.

ning of the session. The Chairman selected is normally the Shadow Cabinet spokesman for the particular subject; at the time of writing only the Education group has a backbench chairman. These bodies meet with varying frequency, depending on pressure of business. That on Foreign Affairs tends to meet weekly, while the Arts and Amenities group is summoned once a month. As with the Conservatives, the organization of groups is kept flexible and can be speedily adjusted to meet changed circumstances. A Trade Union group of Labour Members has also been in existence since the early days of the Parliamentary Labour Party; its task is to safeguard the interests of the unions and it is not a 'Subject Group' in the ordinary sense.[1]

LABOUR SUBJECT GROUPS: SESSION 1956–57

Agriculture, Fisheries and Food
Arts and Amenities
Atomic Energy
Commonwealth and Colonies
Defence and Services
Economic
Education
Foreign Affairs
Fuel and Power
Health Services
Home Office
Housing and Local Government
Legal and Judicial
Social Insurance
Statutory Instruments
Transport and Civil Aviation
Public Information
Films.

There are two further sections of the work of the Parliamentary Labour Party, the Working Parties and the Area Groups. The Labour Opposition now forms a Working Party to give detailed attention to each major item of legislation; these bodies are *ad hoc* but may make

[1] In July, 1957, this group achieved publicity when it complained to the National Executive of the Labour Party about derogatory statements by R. H. S. Crossman (Lab. Coventry, East) concerning the general quality of Labour Members sponsored by trade unions.

a major demand on the energies of the Members concerned. Labour Members also meet in Area Groups according to the geographical location of their constituencies. The present areas are:

Scotland
Wales
Northern
Lancashire and Cheshire
Yorkshire
West Midlands
East Midlands
Eastern
London and Middlesex
South and South Western

A Whip is attached to each group, and it seems that these bodies exist largely for whipping purposes. It is not easy to see how these regions form a sufficient core of common interest to bring Members together; in particular the South and South-Western Group comprises Members from constituencies widely separated by distance and general character. Regional organization among the Conservatives is limited to Scotland, Lancashire and Merseyside and here in each case the *raison d'être* is reasonably apparent. In the past the status of the Labour Area Groups has owed something to the internal stresses within the Party, for in 1947 their function was extended from the consideration of local and regional matters to the examination of national issues. The theory was apparently that each Area formed a microcosm of Labour Members as a whole and that the Whip attached to each group could make its views known to the party leadership. This move was introduced as a counterweight to the activities of the Subject Groups, which tended to be dominated by extremist or specialized opinion, and which had also caused irritation to some Labour Ministers.[1] Area Groups now seem to have fallen back into a minor role, although they may still be important on particular issues. And the study of mental hospitals recently made by the West Midland Group is worthy of note.[2]

The nature of the proceedings at backbench committees, Conservative and Labour, depends very largely on whether or not it is a meeting of Members belonging to the party in power. At gatherings

[1] R. T. MacKenzie, *British Political Parties*, pp. 448–9.
[2] *Observer*, 15th January, 1956.

of government supporters a Minister may come to expound and defend his policy. It is, of course, improper for a Minister to make statements about policy developments which have not been publicly announced, but a Minister may think aloud about the problems which confront him, indicate alternative courses of action and possibly leave behind an impression, not necessarily correct, of the approach he favours. A little judicious kite-flying by a Minister is useful since it can give him an opportunity to judge the reactions of Members to alternative policies. While Ministers must be sufficiently discreet at these meetings, it is also important to them that Members should treat whatever is said as confidential. On occasions the press seems unduly well-informed about these discussions and the displeasure of party leaders has been made known to their followers through the Whips. The attitude of Ministers to their party groups has varied. In the post-1945 period some Labour Ministers treated these bodies with scant respect, possibly because they suspected, with justification, that the Subject Groups were not representative of opinion in the Parliamentary Labour Party as a whole. Conservative Ministers now seem to devote more attention to party committees than was usual for Labour Ministers. Whether this is simply a matter of courtesy, or whether Conservative backbenchers command more influence is very difficult to judge.

Meetings of the majority party are necessarily the more exciting for they are nearer the seats of power. Ministers can be subjected to pressure on specific points, sometimes with obvious success as when the Conservative Government withdrew the clauses of the 1957 Electricity Bill which would have given the Central Electricity Authority power to manufacture electrical equipment. Ministers who resist pressure may be threatened with rebellion and, while most rebellions fade away before the crucial hour, the threat is always stimulating. At Opposition meetings indignation with Ministerial policy is less effective: a group can try to formulate their own policy, urge it upon their party colleagues and perhaps try to convince them of the need to arrange a debate by using a Supply Day. When a debate within its sphere is to take place, an Opposition group may meet to make ready for it. Although party committees have a serious effect on attendance in the Chamber, it is also true that the preparatory work they engender does improve the standard of parliamentary discussion.

The range of all-party committees must also be mentioned. These are concerned with matters that do not directly raise issues of party controversy, such as the need to prevent accidents in the home, the need to provide better and safer roads, or a desire to promote closer relations with a particular country. These bodies wax and wane with the changing zeal of Members, but some, including the first three on the list below, are firmly established. The all-party committees recognized by the whips in the session 1956–57 were:

> Commonwealth Parliamentary Association (U.K. Branch)
> Inter-Parliamentary Union, British Group
> Parliamentary and Scientific Committee[1]
> Parliamentary Home Safety Group
> Parliamentary Group for World Government
> Parliamentary Tourist and Resorts Committee
> Mental Health Group
> Roads Study Group
> Channel Tunnel Parliamentary Committee
> Houses of Parliament Christian Fellowship
> Indo-British Group
> Anglo-Iranian Group
> Anglo-Pakistan Group
> Anglo-Belgian Group
> Empire Industries Association Parliamentary Committee.

Parliamentary life offers unusual opportunities for overseas travel. One illustration is the trip sponsored by the Roads Campaign Council in May, 1957, which enabled 25 Members to study road modernization in France and Belgium. There are also many semi-official deputations to all parts of the world. Each year an all-party delegation attends the Assembly of the Council of Europe, and other groups of Members journey abroad under the auspices of the Commonwealth Parliamentary Association or the British Group of the Inter-Parliamentary Union. Roughly 75% of Members belong to the C.P.A. and the I.P.U. The former was founded in 1911 to facilitate the exchange of information, closer understanding and more frequent intercourse between parliamentarians throughout the Empire: in recent years this organization has done particularly valuable work in arranging courses in London on parliamentary pro-

[1] For an excellent article on the work of this Committee see *Parliamentary Affairs*, Autumn 1956, Vol. IX, pp. 465–9, by Sir H. Linstead (Con. Putney).

cedure for members of the younger legislatures of the Common-wealth. The I.P.U. was founded in 1889 to promote the cause of peace through the development of international co-operation and understanding. Apart from their professed aims, these bodies are of much value in helping Members to study political and economic conditions abroad in a period when hindrances to private travel are still considerable.

THE PASSAGE OF LEGISLATION

Each Bill before it becomes an Act must pass through five stages in the Commons; first reading, second reading, committee, report of committee to the House and third reading. In addition, if the Lords alter the text of a Bill, consideration will have to be given to the Lords' amendments. The first reading is formal and no debate takes place except when the Ten-Minute Rule is used;[1] the Bill is intro-duced by its sponsors and is ordered to be printed. A general dis-cussion of the principles of the Bill follows on the second reading. The only amendment moved to the proposal that 'the Bill be now read a second time' is the official Opposition amendment, if any; it is open to Members to put down other amendments on the Order Paper, but these are merely for propaganda. The Opposition amend-ment may be reasoned, setting out their objections to the measure, or it may advocate delay—'that the Bill be read six[2] months hence'—which is treated as a demand for a complete rejection of the Bill. The financial resolution in committee of the whole House follows immediately; it is moved by a Minister and authorizes expenditure on the purposes of the Bill. Frequently the financial resolution is agreed to with little or no debate.[3] The committee stage of urgent Bills, financial Bills and measures of some constitutional importance is taken in the whole House; minor Bills on which there may be negligible discussion are similarly treated. Other Bills are sent to one

[1] For details see pp. 194–5.

[2] After Whitsun the period of delay proposed is three months.

[3] But in the 1930s there was much controversy over the drafting of financial resolutions which was said to restrict unreasonably subsequent debate. Cf. Pro-cedure relating to Money Resolutions, Select Committee Report; 1936–37 (149) viii, and Sir W. I. Jennings, *Parliament*, pp. 249–64. This problem was again discussed by the Select Committee on Procedure, in 1957: First Report; 1956–57 (110).

of the Standing Committees.[1] These meet on Tuesday and Thursday mornings and consist of the Minister in charge of the Bill with about 45 Members chosen in proportion to the party balance in the Commons. In the 1955 Parliament the Government majority on Standing Committees was three. When the Government has a slim majority, their supporters on the Standing Committees must be assiduous in attendance if the Opposition is to be prevented from winning minor victories. Submission of Bills to Standing Committees does restrict opportunity to join in their detailed examination, and there may be dispute as to whether a Bill ought to go before the whole House. The Conservatives argued that the nationalization measures of the Attlee Government should not have been sent to Standing Committees. Decisions made in committee may be reviewed by the whole House on the Report stage when further amendments can be moved by Ministers and other Members. The third reading follows immediately upon the Report stage and will be brief unless a Bill has aroused such controversy that its opponents wish to restate their objections. After that, unless there is disagreement in the Lords, the Royal Assent will be signified.

The time taken in completing this legislative process is very variable. In moments of crisis, such as the outbreak of war, wide emergency powers are conferred on the executive in Bills which may pass through all their stages in a single day. In normal times the discussion of an important and controversial Bill will be spread over many months. It is the duty of the Opposition to attempt to delay measures which conflict with their principles; not to do so would be regarded as a mark of weakness. Equally it is the business of the Government to ensure the completion of its legislative programme, and this may entail using its majority to restrict the time available for debate. The opportunities for obstruction arise at the committee stage and the Report stage when detailed amendments are proposed and considered: the normal closure motion 'that the question be now put' may be inadequate to prevent interminable discussion. Accordingly two further devices are used, the 'kangaroo' and the 'guillotine'.

---

[1] Procedure. Select Committee, First Report, para. 6; 1945–46 (9–1) ix. Very rarely a Bill is committed to a Select Committee, with powers to send for persons, papers and records, which examines witnesses and memoranda before determining its conclusions. Select Committees consist of backbenchers only: no Minister in charge of the Bill is present. This procedure was used in 1956 for the House of Commons Disqualification Bill.

The 'kangaroo' gives the Chairman of a committee the power to select the most important amendments for discussion, and to ignore, or hop over, the others. The 'guillotine' is a timetable motion which allocates a maximum of so many sittings to a committee or Report stage, and divides the time available between the clauses of the Bill.[1] For example, seven days were allocated for the Committee stage of the Conservative Transport Bill, 1952–53: examination of the first two Clauses had to be completed on the first day, Clause 5 had to be reached at the end of the second day, and so on. At the close of a sitting the 'guillotine' falls, and any amendments not reached on the clauses due to be considered are not discussed. Since 1946 it has been possible to apply the 'guillotine' to Standing Committees[2] as well as to the whole House. The House must itself approve the terms of any guillotine motion, which may be passed either before a committee stage is commenced or during its course if the opposition to a Bill becomes unexpectedly troublesome—e.g., the Landlord and Tenant Bill, 1954. A guillotine both anticipates and invites trouble so a Government will not resort to it lightly; to impose a timetable after a committee stage has started is a moral victory for your opponents.

Any restriction on debate can be portrayed as an infringement on the proper rights of Members. The Opposition, be it Labour or Conservative, will protest that a guillotine is dictatorial, and that the Government is determined to ignore parliamentary opinion and to use the House as a mere rubber-stamp for its proposals. It is a common tactic to waste time in committee on unimportant amendments so that the most vital clauses are not discussed because of the operation of the guillotine. This gives colour to the protests that the Government have allowed inadequate time for the committee stage. It is most regrettable that any part of new legislation should pass without examination but, equally, the time allowed might be adequate if the Opposition used it sensibly and constructively. The application of the guillotine to Standing Committees in particular has been a sore point, yet the allocation of thirty-six sittings for the

---

[1] In 1953 the Conservative Government created a most unfortunate precedent by introducing a timetable motion to restrict discussion on the Lords' amendments to the Transport Bill. These involved matters of substance which had not been considered by the Commons.

[2] Labour Members argued that the timetable for the Town and Country Planning (Scotland) Bill, 1954, left no time for adequate discussion. They walked out of the Scottish Grand Committee and allowed the Bill an uninterrupted passage.

Iron and Steel Bill, 1948–49, was not ungenerous.[1] When a guillotine motion is in operation the position of Government supporters can be unenviable: the Opposition feel entitled to the use of whatever time is available and may make unofficial agreements with Ministers about the progress of the committee stage. These fail to account for the possibility that Members on the Government side of the House may wish to intervene.[2] A spirit of give-and-take between Government and Opposition can obviate the need for timetable motions and they are used less frequently than might be expected: there were but three during the 1945–50 Parliament in spite of the heavy programme of legislation. The Churchill Government 1951–55 made more use of the guillotine, but it also used Standing Committees rather less.

FATE OF PUBLIC BILLS 1945–57[3]

Session	Government Bills		Private Members' Bills	
	Total	Passed	Total	Passed
1945–46	85	83	—	—
1946–47	55	55	—	—
1947–48	70[4]	68	—	—
1948	1[4]	—	—	—
1948–49	102[4]	101[4]	18	5
1950	39	39	—	—
1950–51	60	58	30	8
1951–52	61	56	31	12
1952–53	42	41	26	11
1953–54	64	61	27	13
1954–55	32	25	33	4
1955–56	68	65	32	11
1956–57	53	51	28	12

[1] Some of the sittings on the Gas Bill, 1948, lasted all night and illustrated what can happen if no time limits are applied.

[2] Cf. the Committee stage of the Transport Bill, 1952–53, H.C. Deb., Vol. 508, col. 1592 et seq. On this occasion the motion 'That the question be now put', was moved from the front Opposition Bench!

[3] Excluding Provisional Order Confirmation Bills, Bills under Private Legislation Procedure (Scotland) Act, 1936, and, since 1950, Bills introduced by the Charity Commissioner. Before 1950 'Charity Bills' were designated as Government Bills and one is included in the figure for 1947–48 and one in 1948–49.

[4] Including the Parliament Bill to reduce the delaying power of the Lords which was introduced in three sessions, 1947–48, 1948 and 1948–49. In the third session it was passed over the Lords' veto.

Taking major Bills in committee of the whole House provides greater publicity and incentive for obstruction, and as the time of the House is so valuable it follows that guillotine motions are more likely to be severe.[1]

Not all Bills become law but, as shown in the table on page 110, the chances for Government measures are much brighter than those of private Members' Bills. (For a discussion of private Members' legislation see Chapter 10.) The carnage in 1954–55 was due to the early termination of the session by the dissolution of Parliament.

The number of Acts in the session is not a reliable guide to the volume or the importance of the legislation passed. The average length in pages of the Acts passed in 1946–47 was more than double that of the previous session. It can be argued that 1946–47 made the greatest contribution of any session to the achievement of the aims of the 1945 Labour Government although it produced the lowest total of statutes. Since a Government with a majority does not suffer defeats in the lobbies on its proposed legislation, the failure of a Government Bill to receive the Royal Assent may be attributed either to lack of Parliamentary time or to a Ministerial retreat in face of opposition. Occasionally a Bill will be introduced towards the end of a session for purposes of information, e.g. the Transport Bill, 1952; the intention is to reintroduce it and proceed in the following session. A study of the table above, however, shows that Labour has been more successful than the Conservatives in completing their programmes. Apart from the delay to the Parliament Bill, Labour suffered no major setback, but since 1952 a number of Conservative Bills have foundered. The Judges Remuneration Bill, 1953, to increase judicial salaries and introduce a 'tax free' element into them, was opposed on both sides of the House and dropped. The Teachers Superannuation Bill, 1954, was abandoned in face of hostility from the profession. The Industrial Organization and Development Bill, 1954, and the Shops Bill, 1957, were buried because of the attitude of Conservative backbenchers. If a Conservative Minister produces a Bill that causes contention in his party, the influence of the appropriate 'Subject Group' of Conservative Members may be considerable. The duty of the Government Whips to advise Ministers 'what the Party will not stand' is an important means of forestalling damaging criticism from behind the Treasury Bench.

[1] For further discussion of guillotine motions cf. K. C. Wheare, *Government by Committee*, p. 145 *et seq.*

While few Government Bills are withdrawn, it is common for them to be altered either by suggestions from Members or through second thoughts by Ministers. On the committee stage, amendments hostile to the principle of a Bill are invariably rejected. But if an amendment appears to be helpful to the purposes of a Bill, the Minister in charge may ask that it be withdrawn so that he may look at the matter again. Then he will consult with his Departmental advisers and, if no objection of sufficient weight is forthcoming, the Minister will himself introduce an amendment to cover the point at the Report stage. Even if the Minister is ready at the committee stage to accept the substance of an amendment immediately, he may doubt whether the precise form of words suggested is satisfactory. Drafting of legislation is a highly specialized task and private Members suffer from the disadvantage that they do not enjoy the legal assistance that is available to Ministers: Lieut.-Colonel Lipton (Lab. Brixton) was able, however, to claim that his draft of two additional clauses to the Finance Bill, 1956, had been accepted in their entirety.[1] Such success in committee work demands careful preparation.

As noticed above, many Bills are sent to Standing Committees for detailed examination. Their composition is changed very considerably for each Bill; calls on the time of Members are so heavy that it is not easy to man Committees, and no Member experiences difficulty in securing nomination to the one considering a Bill that excites his interest. In theory, Standing Committees are non-functional as implied by their designation through letters—A, B, C, D. In practice, a Bill comes before a selection of Members, including the chief critics of the measure, who are unusually knowledgeable about its contents. The result may be that a Standing Committee, although politically proportionate, does not truly reflect opinion in the House as a whole. Scottish Bills go to the Scottish Standing Committee which has the normal standing committee membership of 45. It was separated from the Scottish Grand Committee in 1957. The latter body includes all 71 Scottish Members and about a dozen Sassenachs; it considers the principles of Scottish Bills, the Scottish estimates and may debate generally on Scottish problems.[2]

---

[1] H.C. Deb., Vol. 556, col. 788.

[2] Under Standing Order No. 58 any Bill referring exclusively to Wales and Monmouthshire must be referred to a Welsh Standing Committee which has to include all Members representing the area. So far there has been no cause for this Committee to meet.

CONTROL OF POLICY AND ADMINISTRATION

Although the volume of Standing Committee work fluctuates, it is frequently heavy, and the incidence between Members is uneven. In 1953–54, 122 Members each attended more than 25 meetings of Standing Committees while a similar number were quite unconnected with this work. Sir Thomas Moore (Con. Ayr) was the Member most heavily engaged, being present at 53 out of the 74 meetings to which he had been summoned.

STANDING COMMITTEES 1947–57

Session	Number of Committees (including Scottish Committee)	Number of Bills Examined	Members Summoned	Number of Chairmen	Total of Sitting Days[1]
1947–48	5	21	433	13	125
1948–49	6	42	505	12	194
1950	3	4	181	4	4[2]
1950–51	4	23	366	14	57
1951–52	4	26	430	13	66
1952–53	4	28	433	13	62
1953–54	5	28	502	15	155
1954–55	3	9	277	9	27
1955–56	6	31	474	16	170
1956–57	5	27	436	14	134

Source: British Parliamentary Papers, Return of Standing Committees.

Scottish Members are the most involved because they all sit on the Scottish Grand Committee besides sharing in the work of the other Committees. In 1953–54 the palm for regularity of attendance went to Sir I. Horobin (Con. Oldham, East) who was present at all 48 meetings to which he was called: attendance records are poorest among English Members called to the Scottish Committee and in 1952–53 J. Baird (Lab. Wolverhampton, North-East) summoned to 26 Scottish meetings failed to appear once. In general, when

---

[1] Meetings last normally from 10.30 a.m. to 1 p.m. but may be continued in the late afternoon if pressure of business is extreme. The figures in this column exclude meetings of the Scottish Committee to consider Scottish estimates.

[2] This low number indicates the extreme nervousness of the Labour Government about using Standing Committees after the 1950 Election. A strict application of proportional representation left the Government without a majority, but in March, 1951, the Speaker ruled that these Committees should be reconstructed to give Labour a bare majority. Cf. H.C. Deb., Vol. 485, cols. 668–75.

important and controversial Bills are under discussion the Whips are busiest and absenteeism is low; absenteeism is high on the Committee dealing with private Members' Bills, although it is unusual even for this Committee to be adjourned for lack of the quorum of fifteen.

Attendance at the official Committee meetings, however, does not exhaust the task of a Member especially concerned with a Bill. The Labour Opposition forms a 'working party' to examine each Government Bill of any importance; membership of the working party will overlap, but not coincide, with membership of the relevant Subject Group. If a Bill goes to a Standing Committee, Labour Members on the Committee will be included in the working party. This *ad hoc* organization drafts amendments and nominates spokesmen to move them in committee; it also considers Government and any other amendments that may be down for discussion. As a counterpart to the Minister in charge of the Bill, the Opposition nominates a Leader who may propose the major Opposition amendments and will make any quick tactical decisions that may be required as the Committee stage proceeds.

A review of the major Bills of a single session, 1955–56, will illustrate the importance of the committee stage. Many changes were made in the Road Traffic Bill on the initiative of the Minister of Transport. G. Nabarro (Con. Kidderminster) scored victories in Standing Committee on the Government's Clean Air Bill after he had sponsored an unsuccessful private Member's Bill on the same subject. On the Teachers Superannuation Bill a group of backbench Conservatives forced a postponement of six months in the date at which teachers would pay higher contributions, so that it would coincide with their salary increases. Finally, on the Restrictive Trade Practices Bill, taken in committee of the whole House, Labour Members helped the President of the Board of Trade to strengthen the Bill and resist damaging amendments proposed by Government supporters. Backbench victories in committee are achieved by pressure rather than by voting: the pressure is supported by the threat of an adverse vote, but Government defeats are rare.[1] Party

[1] When the committee stage is taken in the whole House the Government is even safer. But in March, 1944, the Government was defeated, 117–116, on an amendment to the Education Bill which aimed to secure equal pay for women teachers. The Government treated the issue as a question of confidence and obtained a reversal of the Committee decision without difficulty.

discipline at the committee stage is now stricter. Ministerial supporters are reluctant to put down important amendments likely to
be unacceptable to their leaders. If such an amendment is moved
from the Government side and the Opposition refuse to permit its
withdrawal, the unhappy proposer is forced either to deny support
to his motion in the division or to act contrary to the 'party line'.
Thus pressure groups find it difficult to get their ideas ventilated
effectively: Opposition Members are more willing to co-operate with
them—but their help is the kiss of death. Public proceedings in
Westminster often have something of a rubber-stamp quality; in
private, the Government are willing to compromise, especially with
their own supporters.

Apart from parliamentary consideration, the content of proposed
legislation is the cause of much consultation for Ministers and their
advisers with interested bodies of many kinds: discussions on a Bill
may continue in the committee rooms of Whitehall after the measure
has been introduced into Parliament. The relative importance of
these negotiations and the activities of backbenchers depends upon
subject-matter. On a topic such as rent restriction, which is of great
political moment but on which the aggrieved are not highly organized,
the influence exerted by Members is considerable. Where voluntary
bodies and professional associations are strongly entrenched, the
role of Members in the evolution of policy tends to decline, except in
the individual case of a Member who becomes the spokesman of a
particular organization. The danger of Ministers making prior agreements with interested parties is that the outcome of parliamentary
debate is prejudged if Ministers cannot modify their position without
defaulting on these commitments.

Private Bills form a quite separate category of legislation. They are
introduced by petition from persons, companies, local authorities or
other public bodies to acquire powers not available under public law.
The second and third readings of these Bills frequently go through
'on the nod', without opposition and without discussion. If when the
second reading is moved any Member says 'object', the consideration
of the Bill is postponed for several days. This interval may allow the
promoters to conciliate the Member who obstructed its passage.
Should further attempts to obtain an unopposed second reading fail,
the Chairman of Ways and Means will put the Bill down for discussion one day at 7 p.m., when the main business is interrupted.

Private Bills run into trouble for political reasons, or because they offend local interests able to persuade Members to represent their views in the House. Conservative Members regularly intervene to prevent local authorities from getting additional trading powers, which they regard as 'socialistic' or as providing unfair competition for other traders. On a number of occasions in 1956 Labour Members tried to ensure that no persons engaged on construction authorized by a Bill should receive any additional payment in return for a promise not to join a trade union. The Liverpool Overhead Railway Bill, 1956, to close this railway, is a good illustration of a measure that arouses local opposition and engages the attention of Members for the area. An alternative to moving the rejection of a Private Bill is to propose an instruction to the Committee that is to consider it. One example is the Labour attitude to influences on union membership noted above; another is the instruction given to the Committee dealing with the British Transport Commission No. 2 Bill, 1956, that the Bill should ensure that no further deterioration be allowed in the condition of the Kennet and Avon Canal.[1] Once a second reading is secured, with or without debate, a Private Bill goes forward to the committee stage. If a petition of objection has been lodged against a Bill, it is sent to a small committee of four Members who must have no interest in the Bill, either personally or as representing their constituencies. What constitutes an 'interest' in these circumstances may sometimes raise delicate questions of conscience. The committees are so small that the attendance of all their Members is essential, and if a Member fails to be present at a sitting he is reported to the House. Proceedings in an Opposed Bill Committee are quasi-judicial in character; the objectors put forward their case through parliamentary counsel—lawyers with experience of this work—and the arguments for the promoters are similarly presented. After the evidence has been heard, the witnesses withdraw and the Committee decides its view on the disputed clauses; the report of the Committee is normally accepted by the House without discussion. A Private Bill that stimulates no objection goes to the Unopposed Bills Committee, consisting of five Members, including the Chairman of Ways and Means and the Deputy Chairman, whose task is to see that the Bill conforms to the relevant precedents, or to be satisfied with the justification for failure to do so.

[1] H.C. Deb., Vol. 550, cols. 318–54.

CONTROL OF POLICY AND ADMINISTRATION

QUESTIONS

Question-time is a major opportunity for backbench Members to claim the attention of the House and, for those who so desire, to obtain publicity. It is also a vital means of enabling the Commons to comment upon and influence the actions of the executive. Parliamentary reputations, including those of Ministers, are much affected by events at question-time, and Departments of state carry on their work in the knowledge that any action may be the subject of challenge in the House.[1]

From Monday to Thursday the first hour of the Parliamentary day is devoted to questions, less a few minutes for prayers and any unopposed items of private business. The three types of questions are those demanding an oral answer, which are starred on the Order Paper, those which ask merely for a written reply that appears in the Official Report, and private notice questions. All questions must be put down at least 48 hours before the time of reply, except those by private notice which are dealt with at the end of question-time and are of relative urgency, thus enabling a Minister to make a statement on some matter of immediate public concern. The advantage of an oral answer is that the Ministerial reply can be followed by further supplementary questions; the Member who initiates a question has the prior right to put a supplementary, but other Members may join in subsequently if the Minister's reply is felt to be unsatisfactory, and if the topic is sufficiently exciting. Ministers read prepared answers to the items on the Order Paper, but only intelligent anticipation can protect them against the supplementaries. It is impossible to forecast when a 'row' will develop at question-time; often one is aggravated should a Minister use an incautious or infelicitous phrase which brings an occupant of the Opposition front bench to his feet with further interrogation. If a Member is not satisfied with a reply he can give notice to raise the subject again on the motion for the adjournment, and it is in the interests of Ministers to be conciliatory wherever they feel such a course to be possible. There is a true element of drama in the question-hour: a full House

[1] In view of the importance of the parliamentary questions in our system of government, it is surprising that there is, as yet, no full-length study of this subject. Patrick Howarth, *Questions in the House*, has described the early stages in the evolution of this parliamentary custom, but the account stops short at 1881 and is largely of historical interest.

and packed galleries provide a large audience for the occasion. Business is carried on at some speed in order to cover as much ground as possible in the time available; the Speaker has constantly to use his discretion in restricting supplementaries. Even so, frequently as few as half of the questions down for oral reply are reached before 3.30 p.m.; the remainder obtain answers in the Official Report in the same way as unstarred questions, unless a Member asks for a postponement to a later date. To save time, a Member who has a starred question on the Order Paper merely rises in his place when his turn comes; if he is not present no oral reply is given and the answer appears along with those to unstarred questions. If an answer is necessarily long and involves many figures it is usual for a Minister to say that 'I will, with permission, circulate it in the Official Report', and the suggestion is normally well received for Members are anxious to save precious minutes. Alternatively, if the reply is long and highly important, the Minister may, with the permission of the Speaker, give it at 3.30 p.m.; like private notice questions this, in effect, lengthens question-time and is a privilege sought infrequently to prevent its abuse. Yet, as noted above, these devices fail to provide for the consideration of all items down for oral reply, and shortage of time for every class of business is a permanent and intractable problem of the House. Since 1920, Members have been limited to three starred questions a day. In spite of the pressure a Member can obtain an oral answer if he is patient; Ministries are placed in a varying order at question-time and a notice of the priority on future days is posted in the division lobby. If, therefore, a Member waits until his quarry is first, second or third on the list of Ministers due to rise after 2.30 p.m., his opportunity will come to produce a carefully prepared supplementary.

The total of questions seeking written answers is much lower than those for oral response; they are less popular as being unlikely to capture public attention or stimulate executive action. However, items of local interest, personal cases and requests for statistical information are often unstarred. If a Member has exhausted his daily ration of three oral questions, he may use this second-best method of raising further matters. Alternatively, should a Member be prompted solely by a desire to elicit facts, uncomplicated by any other motive, an unstarred question may well give him satisfaction.

Rules governing the admissibility and framing of questions are somewhat complex and no attempt will be made to describe them

118

fully: Campion has produced 38 such rules[1] which cover the main principles. Briefly it may be said that the aim of the question must be to press for information or for action; it must not be hypothetical and it must be addressed to someone who has a clear responsibility for the subject. Normally questions are addressed to Ministers, but they may also be directed to other Members holding honorary positions with special responsibilities—the Chairman of the Kitchen Committee, the Parliamentary Charity Commissioner and the Church Estates Commissioner.[2] This limitation often prevents Members from raising matters of contemporary interest and, in particular, no action of a local authority may be challenged unless it can be associated with a government department; police forces outside the Metropolitan Police area are controlled by Watch Committees in each county and county borough, so it is usually impossible to raise questions about the conduct of local police. Special difficulties have arisen over the admissibility of questions on the work of public corporations.[3] Other topics are barred in the interests of constitutional propriety, including any reference to the Royal Family, the grant of honours, the use of the prerogative of mercy, the ecclesiastical patronage of the Crown, or the actions of a court official—including the duties of the Lord Chamberlain in licensing plays. Reference may not be made to any decision of a Court of Law, nor to anything which is *sub judice*. Suggestions may not be made for amending Bills before the House or relating to any topic that has been referred to a Parliamentary Committee or a Royal Commission. There is also a rule against repetition, and allusion may not be made to previous debates or questions in the current session. The actual wording is also carefully vetted by the Clerks at the Table who will excise any superfluous matter, epithets, innuendoes and ironical statements. Members are responsible for the accuracy of facts on which a question is based and a short outline of such facts may be included in the form of a question, but extracts from speeches and newspapers are not permitted.

In contrast to the extent of regulations covering the asking of

[1] Cf. *Introduction to the Procedure of the House of Commons*, pp. 149–52.

[2] Few questions are directed to the Charity Commissioner and the Church Estates Commissioner. J. G. Morrison (Con. Salisbury) Charity Commissioner 1951–56, had three questions addressed to him during this period: one was a written question and the other two were not reached before 3.30 p.m., so in five years he was not called upon to answer orally in the House.

[3] See p. 135.

questions, there are none to govern the nature of replies. Courtesy demands that some reply be made, but if it be brief, evasive or otherwise unsatisfactory to the questioner, he can do nothing except to try and elicit further information by skilful supplementaries. On rare occasions answers may be refused on a plea of national interest; one instance of this kind was the attitude of the Prime Minister (Sir Anthony Eden) to questions about the disappearance of the diver, Commander Crabbe, in Portsmouth Harbour on the occasion of the visit of the Russian warships carrying Mr. Khrushchev and Marshal Bulganin.[1]

Questions differ greatly in subject matter and scale of importance. They are also prompted by a variety of motives. A Minister may be asked to comment on some recent development affecting his department in order to allow the questioner to put a supplementary which expresses a particular point of view. On issues of party controversy a question may be used to express a direct challenge to the policy of the government. Other questions are of a local or 'constituency' character; others are technical, or of limited public appeal, but reflect the special interests of the questioners; others are about personal cases including the affairs of servicemen, pensioners and hospital patients. The above categories are not mutually exclusive and two or three may apply to many questions. In addition, should a Minister wish to obtain publicity for some new aspect of the policy of his department, he may arrange for a government backbencher to ask an appropriate question which thus gives an opportunity for a statement to be made to the House. Members who are active in the question-hour do attract attention and may endear themselves to their constituents or Opposition leaders. The assessment of motive is less easy in some cases than in others: for example, why did Captain Pilkington (Con. Poole) ask the President of the Board of Trade about the addition of hydrozinocarbonylmethyltrimethylammonium chloride to the list of chemicals liable to key industry duty?[2] It should not be thought that the honourable and gallant Member was merely trying to be humorous, for his constituency is the sole place of manufacture of this chemical.

Parliamentary questions are an accurate indicator of the changing political and economic situation. Many are highly topical and the volume of questions directed to any one Minister will reflect the

[1] H.C. Deb., Vol. 552, cols. 1226–9.
[2] H.C. Deb., Vol. 545, cols. 1187–8.

varying degree to which his responsibilities excite public interest. Unemployment or industrial unrest will increase the prominence of the Minister of Labour at question-time; the Secretary of State for the Colonies will be similarly affected by unsettled conditions in Cyprus or other Colonial territories. The total of questions is also associated with the general level of political excitement: in periods of calm it is much lower than at moments of acute controversy. It is dangerous to quote a figure for the daily average as conditions change, but the number for oral answer is often just under one hundred while those unstarred may be less than twenty. Naturally, Opposition Members tend to be the more active interrogators and, unless the Government has a large majority, most questions come from the Opposition side of the House. A Government supporter who intervenes consistently in the question-hour to embarrass his leaders will become unpopular with his party, but displays of independence occur daily on the Government benches, especially when the Labour Party is in office. Parties tend to concentrate on different subjects; the Ministers of Labour and Education receive much attention from Labour Members while Conservatives more frequently engage the Minister of Agriculture. In the period after 1945, when many commodities were rationed, the Conservative Opposition were persistent in their challenge to the policies of the Minister of Food.

The drafting of replies is undertaken by senior civil servants and this task is given regular precedence over other administrative duties. Much care is given to their form which, although strictly truthful, will present departmental actions in the most favourable light possible and attempt to minimize the scope for successful supplementaries. Ministerial time is also consumed for a Minister, if he is wise, will study the implications of each question—with the aid of his advisers —to prepare himself for supplementaries. It follows that here is one sure method of bringing obscure, local or personal matters to Ministerial attention. As a Minister is normally better informed than his critics, he usually defeats them in verbal battle; still, if a Minister has a weak case, pressure at question-time may lead to a subsequent modification of policy. By common consent, parliamentary questions are a most valuable safeguard against bureaucratic excesses, for they ensure that, at quite short notice, any official action may have to be publicly defended by the responsible Minister.

Motion for the Adjournment

The motion for the adjournment is used for several types of debate. It is highly convenient because it allows speeches to range widely, unrestricted by the terms of a reasoned motion. The Government may arrange that the main business of the day shall take the form of a discussion on the question 'that the House do now adjourn' —e.g., the famous two-day debate on the conduct of the war that led to the fall of the Chamberlain administration in May, 1940. Under Standing Order No. 9, the motion for the adjournment may also be used in an emergency to raise a matter of public importance, although there are many procedural difficulties in the way of obtaining such a debate. At the end of questions a Member can move the adjournment of the House to discuss some recent development; the Speaker will not accept the motion unless the subject is specific, urgent, of sufficient gravity and there is no other opportunity in the near future to consider it. If the Speaker accepts the motion, and forty Members support it, the main business of the day is interrupted at 7 p.m. for the emergency debate. The delay until 7 p.m. gives all concerned time to prepare for the discussion, which normally causes much excitement. Requests for an emergency adjournment come usually from the Opposition, but a majority of them fail to meet the severe requirements: in twelve years after the end of war in 1945 only eight of seventy-three such requests were successful.[1]

An attempt to secure an emergency adjournment does place a heavy responsibility on the Speaker in deciding whether it satisfies all the requirements. Rulings from the Chair about Standing Order 9 have been increasingly restrictive, and this has seriously damaged the ability of backbenchers to force Ministers to discuss immediately serious incidents in home, foreign or colonial affairs. Whether an issue is of sufficient gravity, and whether there is a reasonable alternative opportunity for raising it in the near future, may well be matters of opinion. Admittedly if rules about urgency were lax the system might be abused; as it is Standing Order 9 is allowed to operate about twice in each three years, so disuse is a stronger possibility than abuse. In July, 1957, the Speaker refused an emergency debate on the decision to take military action in Muscat and Oman. Wedgwood Benn (Lab. Bristol, S.E.), who was denied the adjourn-

[1] H.C. Deb., Vol. 574, col. 899. These figures were given by D. Chapman (Lab. Birmingham, Northfield).

ment on this occasion, subsequently put down a motion regretting the Speaker's decision. This motion was debated on 29th July, 1957.[1] It was withdrawn after a short but useful debate about emergency procedure, and an eloquent plea by Wedgwood Benn that the rights of backbenchers should be safeguarded.

The daily adjournment debates are of more common concern to Honourable Members as they provide regular opportunities for initiative. Half an hour at the end of business is given to a discussion introduced by a backbencher, and should all other items be disposed of before 10 p.m. on Mondays to Thursdays or before 4 p.m. on Fridays, the adjournment debate may still continue until 10.30 p.m. and 4.30 p.m. respectively. This procedure may not be used to raise issues that would involve legislation, or for which the government has no responsibility. The increased popularity of the adjournment led to the institution in 1945 of a fortnightly ballot to determine its allocation, but subsequently this method was felt not to make the best use of the time available. Under a new scheme, introduced after Easter, 1955,[2] a Member wishing to use the adjournment notifies the Speaker in writing of the matter he wishes to raise. Each Thursday the Speaker chooses the subjects for Tuesday and Thursday of the following week, and in so doing endeavours to give priority to constituency grievances and items of immediate topical interest. Subjects not selected are put into a ballot and luck decides for Mondays, Wednesdays and Fridays; those not successful may be included in succeeding ballots. Anyone who wins a place in the draw is excluded from it for a fortnight, but may still submit subjects for Tuesdays and Thursdays. A Member may not propose more than one topic at any one time; the submission of a subject for the ballot automatically cancels any previous entry by the same Member. The last day of the session and the days immediately before the adjournment at Christmas, Easter, Whitsun and for the summer recess are also devoted to discussions initiated by backbenchers. Members wishing to speak on these days notify the Speaker, who again has the task of allocating the time available and does not necessarily limit each item to half an hour.

Many adjournment debates arise out of matters originally raised at question-time, when an interrogator is not satisfied with the reply

---

[1] Ibid., cols. 880–911. The Speaker may not be criticized inferentially, but only on a specific motion regretting some aspect of his conduct.

[2] Cf. Mr. Speaker's statement. H.C. Deb., Vol. 538, cols. 2076–8.

received, but sometimes broad issues of policy are raised. The usual form of these short discussions is for the time to be shared fairly equally between the Member introducing his case and the Ministerial reply, usually given by the Junior Minister of the appropriate department. Brief interventions may also be made by other Members. The allocation of the adjournment is always given prior publicity to enable the preparation of Ministerial replies. The table below shows the use made of this facility on every sitting day in May, 1956, including the holiday adjournment on the 18th for the Whitsun recess. It will be seen that on some days there was no discussion on the adjournment motion and for this there are three main reasons. The

ADJOURNMENT MOTIONS: MAY, 1956

Day of month	Subject	Number of speakers including Ministers[1]
1	None	–
2	Rural Electrification	2
3	Roger Casement Papers	4
4[2]	None—(House counted out)	–
7	Materials (Flammability)	3
8	None	–
9	Catterick Camp	2
10	War Disabled Pensioners	3
11[2]	None—(House counted out)	–
14	Colonial Sterling Balances	2
15	Suez Canal	3
16	Trawlers (Arctic Ice Conditions)	3
17	None	–
18	Nile Waters	7
	Mill Fire, Keighley	2
	Air Trooping	2
	National Service (Grade III Men)	3
	Mental Nurses (Recruitment)	2
	Whitsun Adjournment	
29	National Health Service	2
30	Great North Road	2
31	Government Surplus Stocks (Disposal)	2

[1] Excluding minor interjections.
[2] A private members' Friday.

House may have been counted out during preceding business; the problem to be raised may have been settled; the Member due to speak may not be in the House when the adjournment was moved. The last possibility is strengthened by the erratic times of adjournment debates for, while normally they commence at 10 p.m., the parliamentary timetable is very variable. Other business frequently continues until later, and occasionally ends earlier, than the usual hour.

Opposition Members tend to be rather more active on these occasions, and 11 of the 16 subjects listed above were introduced by Labour Members. Much fuller ventilation of a grievance is possible on the adjournment than can be secured at question-time, and this device also permits consideration of matters that could not otherwise find a place in the crowded parliamentary timetable. It is a most valuable part of the proceedings of the Commons.

STATUTORY INSTRUMENTS

Many Acts of Parliament now delegate power to Ministers to issue rules and regulations which help to fulfil the purposes of the parent Act. This subordinate legislation—officially designated as Statutory Instruments—is very substantial in bulk, and the number of instruments often exceeds 2,000 a year. Delegated legislation is essential to save parliamentary time and to give an element of flexibility to legislation. It also permits Ministers to consult with interested organizations on points of detail after an Act is passed, but before regulations are issued. In spite of its dangers and some degree of public criticism, delegated legislation is firmly established in the machinery of public administration.[1] The rights of Members to review the regulations vary between different categories of Instruments. Some are 'laid' before the House without any provision for parliamentary control: some are 'laid' and become law immediately, or after forty days, unless a Member successfully moves a 'prayer' to annul it: some need

[1] The classic statement of the need for delegated legislation is to be found in the Report of the Committee on Ministers' Powers; 1931–32 Cmd. 4060, xii. The critics include Lord Hewart, *The New Despotism*, and Sir C. K. Allen, *Law and Orders* 2nd ed., especially Ch. 5. For a full statement of its constitutional forms see *Public Administration*, Autumn 1952, Vol. XXX, pp. 227–61 or the Report of the Select Committee on Delegated Legislation; 1952–53 (310–1) iv. John Eaves, Jun., *Emergency Powers and the Parliamentary Watchdog* contains an excellent survey of the attempt by backbenchers to keep some check on the extraordinary powers granted to the Government in war-time.

an affirmative resolution before they come into effect. Discussions on delegated legislation are often brief, especially when an affirmative resolution is required on some uncontroversial matter.

It is not possible to amend regulations; they must be either accepted or rejected by the House. If a Member challenges an instrument by moving a 'prayer' to annul it, the debate may end in a division; with rare exceptions 'prayers' are defeated, for Government policy is at stake and the Whips are on. In 1951, however, the Conservative Opposition rallied their forces more successfully than the Government Whips and carried a motion to defeat the proposed reduction of the cheese ration from three ounces to two. From the point of view of the housewife this action was ineffectual as supplies of cheese were inadequate to provide a three ounce ration; subsequently a further regulation was issued to enforce the reduction.[1] 'Prayer' debates are exempt from the ten o'clock closure and tend to begin after this hour at the end of the main business of the day. In 1951 Conservative Members took advantage of the absence of a time limit and opposed many Statutory Instruments to keep the House sitting late and so harass Ministers with their small majority. Such tactics may not be repeated for there is now a Sessional Order that terminates 'prayer' debates at 11.30 p.m.[2] In the session 1951–52 time spent on delegated legislation returned to normal proportions; a total of 53 affirmative resolutions were approved and 36 'prayers' against Instruments were moved of which 18 were negatived, 16 were withdrawn and twice the House was counted out.[3] Objections to regulations are made not solely as resistance to Government policy, but may result from allegations that the regulations are in some way constitutionally improper: Sir John Mellor[4] was noted for such forensic battles against Ministers.

A regular review of delegated legislation is undertaken by the Select Committee on Statutory Instruments, or the 'Scrutiny' Committee as it is commonly called. This Committee was established in 1944 in accordance with a motion moved by H. Molson (Con. High Peak).[5] Eleven Members serve on the Committee, most of whom

---

[1] H.C. Deb., Vol. 486, cols. 760–81 and Vol. 487, cols. 515–34.

[2] This followed the recommendation of the Select Committee on Delegated Legislation, Report, para. 107 (1); 1952–53 (310–1) iv.

[3] Ibid., pp. 40–43.

[4] Conservative Member for Tamworth 1935–45, Sutton Coldfield 1945–55.

[5] H.C. Deb., Vol. 400, cols. 202 *et seq.* A Committee on these lines had been proposed in 1932 by the Committee on Ministers' Powers. Report, pp. 67–70, Recommendation XIV B; 1931–32 Cmd 4060, xii.

have legal experience, and they have the assistance of the Counsel to the Speaker; Government supporters are in a majority but the Chairman is drawn from the Opposition. It is not concerned with the policy of Statutory Instruments but with their constitutional propriety and can, therefore, proceed in a non-political atmosphere. The terms of reference instruct the Committee to inspect every Statutory Instrument, or draft of a Statutory Instrument, laid before the House and to consider whether the special attention of the House should be drawn to it on any of the following grounds:

(i) that it imposes a charge on the public revenues or contains provisions requiring payments to be made to the Exchequer or any Government Department or to any local or public authority in consideration of any licence or consent, or of any services to be rendered, or prescribes the amount of any such charge or payments;

(ii) that it is made in pursuance of an enactment containing specific provisions excluding it from challenge in the courts, either at all times or after the expiration of a specified period;

(iii) that it appears to make some unusual or unexpected use of the powers conferred by the Statute under which it is made;

(iv) that it purports to have retrospective effect where the parent Statute confers no express authority so to provide;

(v) that there appears to have been unjustified delay in the publication or in the laying of it before Parliament;

(vi) that there appears to have been unjustifiable delay in sending a notification to Mr. Speaker under the proviso to subsection (1) of section four of the Statutory Instruments Act, 1946, where an Instrument has come into operation before it has been laid before Parliament;

(vii) that for any special reason its form or purport calls for elucidation.

Reports of the Committee are not debated by the House, although material from them is sometimes used in 'prayer' debates. Instruments are now most frequently reported under paragraph (vii) of the terms of reference, and it is common for explanatory memoranda to be supplied by the Ministry responsible for publishing the regulations held to be obscure. Only paragraph (iii) permits straying into the high realm of policy and the Committee is cautious when reporting an Order under this heading. The Committee serves a limited 'watch-

dog' function which ensures that the civil service observe correct procedure and attains a fair standard of clarity in drafting delegated
legislation.

Should the duties of the 'Scrutiny' Committee be widened? Sir
Gilbert Campion, then Clerk to the House, suggested to the Select
Committee on Procedure in 1946 that the Scrutiny Committee might
inquire into grievances arising from Instruments already in operation.[1] But it is difficult to see how the Committee could be involved
in policy questions without becoming an arena for party conflict: the
Government majority would then dominate the Committee which
might rapidly become useless. The 1953 Select Committee considered a number of proposals for strengthening parliamentary
supervision of delegated legislation but did not recommend any
major innovations in procedure.[2]

FINANCIAL CONTROL

The annual expenditure of the British Government is now of the
order of £5,000 million. It is clear that a body of 630 Members
cannot hope to exercise, in a full meeting, any kind of detailed control
over the use of a sum of such magnitude. This is recognized in the
form taken by financial business in the House of Commons. Twenty-
six days each session are allocated to the Committee of Supply—the
Committee of the whole House which considers the supply of money
to the Crown. For the most part these days are spent debating the
work of particular Government Departments; the Opposition have
the right to select the topic to be discussed and to 'put down' for
examination the relevant estimate. Details of expenditure are not
considered and the Opposition uses Supply Days for general criticism
of Ministerial policy. The subjects chosen are those on which the
Opposition disagrees most strongly with the Government of the day,
which are of current public interest or are matters on which the

[1] Third Report, p. xlv; 1945–46 (189–1) ix. A. H. Hansen has also advocated
some extension of the Committee's functions in *Public Administration*, Winter
1949, Vol. 27, p. 284 *et seq.* For a contrary view cf. F. A. Stacey, *Public Administration*, Winter 1950, Vol. XXVIII, pp. 333–5.

[2] It rejected the idea that all Statutory Instruments be submitted to a Standing
Committee in draft form, but in 1957 the Select Committee on Procedure thought
that this might be tried in the case of Statutory Instruments requiring affirmative
resolutions which applied exclusively to Scotland and for which no comparable
Orders had been, or were likely to be, tabled for England and Wales. Second
Report, para. 13; 1956–57 (211).

Government may be most vulnerable to attack. Expenditure can be incurred solely on the recommendation of a Minister, so on Supply Days Members may propose cuts in the estimates but not increases to them. This is why the Opposition may be forced technically to divide the House on a motion to reduce an estimate when the gravamen of their case is the need for increased expenditure. The Opposition may decide that it would be more convenient to take Supply formally and then to propose a motion: thus in July, 1956, a Supply Day was devoted to a motion by the Leader of the Opposition, H. Gaitskell (Lab. Leeds, S.) concerning the salaries of Members. Allocation of time in the Committee of Supply between Government Departments is uneven; Ministries whose work attracts little publicity or controversy will have their estimates passed year after year without a word said, while other Departments more in the public eye will have their work debated regularly. On the last two Supply Days motions to approve the estimates that have not been previously considered are put without discussion. The Opposition may choose to insist on a series of divisions, or their silence may signify assent; in 1956, although the Opposition leadership decided to let the estimates pass without challenge, a small group of Labour backbenchers forced two journeys to the division lobbies.

The annual estimates, which occupy many hundreds of pages, are published in February. They are in four sections, the Navy, Army, Air Force and Civil Estimates; most Supply Days are fitted into the period before the end of July when the Appropriation Act is passed which gives authority for the expenditure of money as set out in the Estimates.[1] Some days may be spent on Supply before February in considering supplementary estimates and excess votes; these debates are more financial in content as some attention is given to their *raison d'être*. Supplementary estimates become necessary when a Department finds that its original estimate was inadequate, and an excess vote is needed when a Department has actually overspent the sum voted to it on some particular item. Excess votes are usually for quite small amounts, but supplementary estimates are an inevitable consequence of any change in policy that implies greater spending. Once the Committee of Supply have approved this additional expenditure a Consolidated Fund Bill must be passed to give statutory

[1] No attempt is made here to set out fully the intricacies of financial procedure in the British Parliament. For a clear, brief account see E. Taylor, *The House of Commons at Work* (Penguin Books).

authority for the issue of the money out of the Consolidated Fund. Consolidated Fund Bills, including the Appropriation Act aforesaid, give further means for general discussions of policy and there is no pretence of examining the details of the expenditure they permit.

Financial procedure, then, enables further criticism of Government policy and administration by backbenchers. Ministerial supporters are in the hands of the Opposition: if a Member of the majority party, for example, wishes to comment on what he feels to be certain shortcomings of the Home Office, he will not have a chance on a Supply Day unless the Opposition decide to 'put down' the appropriate estimate. To this statement one minor qualification must be made. One Supply Day each year, when the Civil Estimates are due for consideration, is devoted to private Members' motions on topics relating to the Estimates.[1] The right to introduce motions is decided by ballot; three motions are chosen, but there is not usually time to discuss more than one or two. This procedure is associated with the historic principle that 'grievances precede supply' and may be counted, in effect, as a small addition to private Members' time.

Detailed examination of expenditure is entrusted by the House to two committees. The Estimates Committee is appointed to consider the estimates and the Public Accounts Committee reviews the accounts of money spent—or comments on the stable door after the horse has bolted. The Estimates Committee, first set up in 1912, has had a tangled and not wholly successful history.[2] Its terms of reference instruct the Committee to suggest the form in which the estimates shall be presented and economies consistent with the policy implied

[1] Technically these are amendments to the motion 'That the Speaker do now leave the Chair'. Until 1957 this system was also used in relation to each of the three Service Estimates. When a Service Estimate was first considered the debate was interrupted about seven o'clock for a backbench motion. This arrangement was terminated in accordance with the recommendation of the Select Committee on Procedure (First Report, para. 9; 1956–57 (110)). The introduction of the amendment tended to divert attention from the main theme of a Service debate on to some matter of detail: on one occasion the debate on the Navy Estimates became a discussion on the merits of phonetic spelling. There is a tendency for Members to enter ballots irrespective of whether they have a topic to raise, and Members who won a place in the draw were not necessarily particularly interested in Service questions.

[2] For a full analysis of the work of the Estimates Committee and the Public Accounts Committee from their inauguration up to 1950, see B. Chubb, *The Control of Public Expenditure*.

in the estimates. Policy is a matter for Ministers who are responsible to the Commons as a whole, and not to any committee of the House. This constitutional doctrine creates difficulties for the Estimates Committee as the bearing of policy on the estimates may be a matter of doubt. Where does policy end, and the administration of policy begin? The Estimates Committee are constantly faced with this intractable problem: if it suggests reductions in expenditure, the charge of interference with policy, the province of Ministers, may always be made.

Since 1945 the Estimates Committee have carried on their task with much enthusiasm. The full body consists of 36 Members and has a quorum of seven. Most of the work is carried out by a series of investigating sub-committees lettered B, C, D, E, F, each of which has seven Members and the Chairman of the full committee, the quorum being three. Sub-committee A has nine Members, including the Chairmen of the full committee and the other sub-committees, and is responsible for the selection of the estimates to be examined. Investigating sub-committees are given one or more topics to review each session and they proceed by summoning witnesses from Government Departments, local authority associations and other bodies. Written evidence is also submitted. The committees hold a large number of meetings and may sit while the House is in recess. The table below gives some idea of the range of their inquiries in the session 1951–52.

ESTIMATES COMMITTEE 1951–52

Sub-Committee	Subject	Number of meetings at which witnesses were present
C	National Servicemen	5
F	Export Credits	4
D	Roads	7
F	Monopolies Commission	4
B	Rearmament	14
E	Schools	11
D	Post Office	3
E	Technical Education	9
F	Assistance to Exporters	7
F	Ministry of Materials	1

In addition, the full Estimates Committee met on 14 occasions and approved reports from the sub-committees. Disagreements in the Committee on the form of their reports are not uncommon, but the division often cuts across party lines. The spirit of the work is non-political and it is usual for chairmen of two sub-committees to be supporters of the Opposition. The Members have the assistance of the Clerk of Financial Committees and his staff who, as parliamentary officials, are independent of the executive. They are, however, 'non-expert' in contrast to the staff of the Scrutiny Committee and the Public Accounts Committee; they are not accountants and have no personal knowledge of Treasury affairs, but their accumulated experience is of great worth.

It is not possible to make an evaluation of the work of the Estimates Committee in precise terms. Concentration is not on the details of the estimates but on general reviews of a sector of departmental activity. Some of their reports are undistinguished and seem not to justify the effort taken in collecting the evidence. The 1954 Report[1] on the Regional Organization of Government Departments amounted to modified approval of existing arrangements: the Report was less than three pages in length but the evidence submitted on the subject occupied 219 pages of (smaller) print. Other reports are more constructive, but may be accused of invading the Ministerial province of policy. One in 1953 challenged the basis of many aspects of the civil defence preparations of the Home Office,[2] and brought forth a spirited departmental reply.[3] It is the practice for Departments to defend themselves in published statements and this ensures that the work of the Committee obtains serious official consideration. The length of replies may be some guide to the quality of work in the investigating sub-committees. If their strictures are rebutted, the Estimates Committee can take little further action. Their reports are rarely discussed in the whole House: yet civil servants are sensitive to parliamentary criticism, and pressure exerted on them is frequently reflected in subsequent departmental activities. The industry of the Committee is considerable. Members seem to enjoy sharing in this work, for it adds to their knowledge of the business of government and may lead to visits of observation at interesting places.[4] Certainly the results are of great assistance to students of public administration

[1] Estimates. Select Committee. Sixth Report; 1953–54 (233) vi.
[2] Estimates. Select Committee. First Report; 1953–54 (19) v.
[3] Estimates. Select Committee. Second Special Report; 1953–54 (74) v.
[4] E. Taylor, *The House of Commons at Work*, p. 223.

as much information is produced that would not otherwise be published.

The Public Accounts Committee is a more powerful guardian of financial probity, and was first established in 1861. It receives reports from the Comptroller and Auditor-General on the appropriation accounts which show how money has been spent. The Comptroller's salary, like that of the Speaker and the Judges, is a direct charge on the Consolidated Fund and so does not have to be approved each year by Parliament. This ensures his independence from Ministerial influence. The Comptroller is assisted by a specially trained staff of some four hundred auditors who have continuous access to departmental accounts. Any expenditure which is not clearly covered by the authority of estimates approved by Parliament, which is wasteful and uneconomic, or which has unusual features will be reported to the Public Accounts Committee. The Committee has fifteen members, a quorum of five, and a Chairman drawn from the Opposition who has had appropriate Ministerial experience.[1] The Chairman plays an important role in guiding the work of the Committee; he does much of the questioning of witnesses that appear before it and, before each meeting, he will discuss with the Comptroller the subjects to be examined. The witnesses are the accounting officers[2] of the Departments whose spending has elicited criticism from the Comptroller, and representatives of the Treasury are also present. Investigations of witnesses may be prolonged and highly technical; they are clearly the result of much careful preparation on all sides. In contrast to the Estimates Committee, the work of the P.A.C. is essentially expert in character, and has also something of a judicial quality since it is concerned with the legality of expenditure. Witnesses are not summoned for pure explanation, but may be called on to defend departmental actions; their presence implies a hint of culpability. Adverse reports from the P.A.C. are treated with the greatest seriousness in Whitehall and are followed by corrective action. Reports are made technically to the Commons, but the House never considers them; in fact, they are directed at the Treasury which writes Minutes on the recommendations to the Departments concerned. These Minutes

---

[1] Attendance at meetings since 1945 appears to have been less good than formerly: cf. Chubb, *The Control of Public Expenditure*, Appendices 8 and 9. It is not possible to quote exact figures: in order to be recorded as present at a meeting it is not necessary to attend for more than a few minutes.

[2] i.e., Permanent Secretaries, the chief officials of Departments.

have much persuasive weight. Herbert Morrison, drawing on his Ministerial experience, testified to this effect before the Select Committee on Procedure.[1] The P.A.C. and the Comptroller are normally treated by the Treasury as valuable allies in restraining unorthodox expenditure. The P.A.C. is, indeed, a major cautionary force because it is able to base its work on the findings of the Comptroller and his staff.

NATIONALIZED INDUSTRIES

The institution of many socialized industries in the period after 1945 created a new problem of parliamentary control. Earlier public corporations—the British Broadcasting Corporation, the Central Electricity Board and the London Passenger Transport Board—had functioned with a minimum of public supervision; their activities were largely uncontroversial and, except for the B.B.C., they made no claim on state revenues. But the second generation of public corporations governed large-scale industries and services whose efficient operation is vital to the national economic well-being. The theory of nationalization followed by the Labour Government contained two central principles; that these undertakings should be monopolies removed from the privately-owned sector of the economy, and that they should retain the freedom for enterprise enjoyed by other commercial bodies. This desire to combine the advantages of public ownership and private enterprise led to difficulties in deciding the relationship that should exist between the new corporations and Parliament. If Parliament could not supervise these bodies, what guarantee was there that they would be conducted in the national interest? Alternatively, if the corporations were subjected to daily parliamentary criticism, much of it activated by political motives, it was feared that their boards and officials would be dominated by a spirit of caution. Initiative and imagination might be frowned upon lest their results incurred displeasure. No private company would take normal commercial risks if shareholders' meetings were held above a hundred times each year.

The result has been an attempt to distinguish between policy and administration, and to preclude Members from raising administrative matters while retaining their right to challenge Ministers on policy. Yet this distinction is not easy to define in theory, nor to follow in practice. Ministers have powers under the nationalization statutes to

[1] Third Report, Minutes of Evidence. Q. 3227; 1945–46 (189–1) ix.

exercise various types of control over public boards and may issue general directions to them, and for any such action a Minister is accountable to parliament. At the other extreme, routine functions do not concern Ministers. But is the closing of a railway line a matter of day-to-day administration? Is the closing of a coal mine a matter of policy or administration? Answers to issues of this kind must be arbitrary and the degree to which Members may examine the work of public corporations has been, inevitably, the source of much controversy.

The problem first became acute in relation to parliamentary questions in December, 1947. Herbert Morrison, then Lord President of the Council, announced[1] that Ministers would not give information on matters of day-to-day administration, for which they had no responsibility. There followed in 1948 a series of discussions in the House of Commons about the admissibility of questions on nationalized industries.[2] Finally on 7th June, 1948, the Speaker made a statement on the subject which had the effect of allowing rather greater freedom of inquiry to Members, and which allayed the considerable disquiet that had developed on both sides of the House. In his statement the Speaker said:

'It is the rule against the repetition of Questions already answered, or to which an answer has been refused that has had the largest share in excluding Questions. The Government, in their desire not to interfere in the day to day activities of the Boards of nationalized industries, have by what might be termed a "self-denying ordinance" refused to answer many Questions on subjects which, by a strict interpretation of the statutes, might be held to fall within their responsibility. They are fully entitled to do so—that is a matter for their discretion. But such a refusal brings into action Rule (26) to which I have referred, and prevents the admission to the Question Paper of all future Questions dealing with the class of matters dealt with by the Question to which an answer was refused. . . . I propose to leave the Rule which excludes Questions on matters outside Ministerial responsibility unchanged. But I am prepared, if it is generally approved, to exercise my discretion to direct the acceptance of Questions asking for a statement to be made on matters about which information has been previously refused, provided that in my

[1] H.C. Deb., Vol. 444, cols. 569–75.
[2] H.C. Deb., Vol. 448, col. 391 *et seq.*, Vol. 451, cols. 208–16, 650–3 and 1649–57.

opinion the matters are of sufficient public importance to justify the concession.'

Since 1948 the new corporations have become more firmly established and are a less strong source of political passion. The desire to ask questions on points of detail appears to have abated. As the range of matters engaging ministerial responsibility is wide, the scope for parliamentary questions is equally wide; it includes the appointment of personnel of the Boards, their tenure, salary and conditions of service, the appointment of auditors, the form of accounts and annual reports, borrowing and capital investment, programmes of research and development and the work of consumer councils. Herbert Morrison has suggested that Members have yet to show their customary ingenuity in framing questions that would be in order.[1] There are other means available to Members of obtaining information about the Boards: Lord Hurcomb, then Chairman of British Transport Commission, told the Select Committee on Nationalized Industries in 1952 that his average correspondence with Members was about 1,700 letters a year.[2] But with minor exceptions the corporations make no charge on public funds and, therefore, the Estimates Committee and the Comptroller and Auditor-General are precluded from inquiring into their activities. The Public Accounts Committee is not so barred as the corporations present their accounts to Parliament, but without the expert aid of the Comptroller the work of the P.A.C. in this field has been ineffective.

There has been a strong body of opinion, especially among Conservatives, that fuller efforts should be made to inform Members on the work of the corporations. After the Conservative victory at the 1951 Election a series of Select Committees were appointed to examine the problem. So far these Committees have been notable for the paucity of their achievements. The first Report issued in 1952 concerned the admissibility of parliamentary questions and indicated unenthusiastic acceptance of the *status quo*.[3] A more significant Report in the following year proposed[4] the establishment of a

---

[1] *Government and Parliament*, p. 261.

[2] Report, minutes of evidence. Q. 549; 1951–52 (332–1) vii.

[3] Cf. 1951–52 (332–1) vii. The Report also proposed that the daily ration of oral questions for each Member be reduced from three to two. No action has been taken on this suggestion which appears to exceed the Committee's frame of reference.

[4] 1952–53 (235) vi.

permanent committee to examine nationalized industries which would keep Parliament informed about their 'aims, activities and problems'. The committee should be assisted by a staff headed by an officer of great administrative experience with a status equal to that of the Comptroller and Auditor-General. H. Molson (Con. High Peak), possibly influenced by his success in the initiation of the Scrutiny Committee, was a leading advocate of the proposal. These recommendations had a mixed reception, however, for it was feared in official circles that a permanent committee of inquiry would limit the administrative freedom of the corporations.

After some delay a further Select Committee was appointed in March, 1955. Being unable to produce any conclusions before the dissolution for the 1955 Election it was renominated with the same membership by the new House. The Committee was not given the services of an officer of high qualifications as proposed in 1953, and its terms of reference were highly restrictive because they embodied what may be called the Morrison theory of public corporations. As a result the Committee were precluded from inquiring into:

(*a*) Matters which have been decided by, or involve the responsibility of, Ministers.
(*b*) Wages, conditions of employment, and other questions normally decided by collective bargaining.
(*c*) Matters which fall to be considered through formal machinery established by statute, e.g., consumers councils.
(*d*) Matters of day-to-day administration.

In November, 1955, the Committee issued a short Report[1] which stated that their present terms of reference left 'insufficient scope to make inquiries or to obtain further information regarding the Nationalized Industries which would be of any real use to the House'. It is clear from the Report that the Committee felt frustrated by the force of paragraph (*a*) above. The Committee received in evidence long lists of Ministerial powers in relation to the various Boards, which were also said to be subject to a general supervision by Ministers through the power of the latter to issue general directions. A witness from the Ministry of Transport stated:[2] 'The Minister has a general oversight in addition to specific powers. He is in constant

[1] 1955–56 (120) ix.
[2] Ibid., Q. 29.

touch with the Chairman of the British Transport Commission. Very many matters are discussed between them . . . but the responsibility for the decisions taken rests with the Commission. The Minister might conceivably feel bound to intervene if he thought that things were going wrong . . . he might feel he had to issue some kind of direction.' Faced with this situation the Committee felt that it was impossible to define the limits of Ministerial responsibility and, therefore, that their own jurisdiction appeared to vanish. In a letter to the Committee the then Minister of Transport, J. Boyd-Carpenter (Con. Kingston-upon-Thames), in stressing the wide range of his responsibilities, even referred to himself as the 'spokesman' for the B.T.C. and the Civil Airways Corporations in Parliament. Such emphasis on Ministerial direction seems to leave no reason for any refusal to answer parliamentary questions about these undertakings. It should be noted, however, that the attitude of the Ministry of Fuel and Power towards the corporations appears to differ from that of the Ministry of Transport.

The Conservatives were unwilling to surrender the attempt to establish an effective Committee and in November, 1956, a further Select Committee was established in spite of objections from the Opposition. The revised terms of reference were 'to examine the Reports and Accounts of the Nationalized Industries', but the Government hoped that the Committee would not intervene in matters of detailed administration or in issues of broad policy that were the concern of Ministers.[1] Much tactical skill will be required for this further experiment to become a success.

There are a large number of opportunities in the parliamentary timetable for Members to consider nationalized industries. Regular debates occur on the Annual Reports which Ministers are required to present to Parliament; the quality and value of these discussions vary, but they are less political in tone than in the 1940s. Any Bill or Statutory Instrument concerning a public corporation is open to discussion, and the affairs of nationalized industries may also be raised in Committee of Supply. Various forms of motion provide other opportunities: they include the half-hour adjournment debates, motions in private members' time, the debate on the Address and any occasion when a Minister moves a motion in Government time to discuss a particular subject relating to a corporation. But it can be argued that these opportunities are of little value unless appropriate

[1] H.C. Deb., Vol. 561, col. 599.

information is available, and the ability to debate does not satisfy the desire of some Members to invoke some measure of parliamentary control.

The hostility of Conservatives to the concept of nationalization has led to deep suspicion of the activities of publicly-owned industries. This suspicion has centred on the National Coal Board and has been aggravated by steady increases in the price of fuel and the high cost of the Board's capital development programme. On 10th May, 1956, there was a Conservative backbench revolt against the second reading of the Coal Industry Bill which sought to increase the borrowing powers of the N.C.B.; 25 Members went into the lobby against the Government while the Opposition abstained from voting. Labour reaction to this kind of pressure is to argue that fuller parliamentary supervision of the public boards will lead to an increase in political sniping and general interference with their smooth operation: Labour is too ready to defend the nationalized industries while some Conservatives are too ready to attack. Preconceived attitudes of this kind are inimical to any constructive review of the corporations. If they again become a major source of party friction, the problem of how Parliament can best safeguard the public interest will not be solved satisfactorily.

MEMBERS AND CIVIL SERVANTS

A common criticism of the Civil Service is that it stifles initiative and insists on excessive adherence to prescribed administrative routines. This, it is said, leads to a lack of inventiveness, the desire for a quiet life and failure to see the problems of tomorrow. In order that no indiscretions shall be committed each grade of civil servant has a limited power of decision; matters exceeding the competence of an official must be passed up to the next step in the hierarchy. A civil servant is responsible to his superiors and ultimately his Minister; the supreme crime for him is to cause his Minister embarrassment. The result of the activities of Members may well be to strengthen the inherent tendencies to official caution beyond desirable limits—the problem of how far parliamentary commentary would damage the efficiency of nationalized industries is one that applies to all Departments of State. It also increases the cost of administration, for much care is given to the preparation of evidence for Select Committees and to the content of Ministerial replies and speeches. Senior officials give top priority to parliamentary business; other matters are perforce delayed. The price of parliamentary inquiry is high, but it must be paid to secure some protection from bureaucratic actions. The financial aspect is of less significance than the cost of fear and frustration. Left-wing critics who favour large-scale and imaginative state action are distressed by the effect of the restraining voice of Parliament, even although its value is admitted. H. R. G. Greaves[1] has urged that the force of the parliamentary question on officials would be lessened if Ministers were more willing to admit mistakes and imperfections in the work of their Departments. But the legend of the infallibility of the Civil Service will not be surrendered easily, and in a period of narrow majorities in the Commons this is an idealistic solution.

The attitudes of civil servants and Members towards each other are too ingrained for much change to come quickly. Naturally these vary, and may result from a lack of personal contact. Yet many Members gradually come to know those officials at the principal or assistant secretary level whose work is of greatest interest to them. The relationship is a little strange; it is overshadowed by the absent figure of the Minister who may be called upon by the Member to defend publicly the decision taken by the official in his (the Minister's) name. Civil servants may well think of legislators as interfering busy-bodies, or as lobbyists seeking special favours. The Member, for his part, is convinced of his duty to make representations in response to complaints that come his way: much experience of such complaints may make him feel that the Civil Service is unsympathetic, parsimonious, inflexible and adept at procrastination, however much he may respect the officials he happens to encounter. The anonymity of the civil service is also irritating. Most of the decisions that Members challenge are made by officials and are, of necessity, unknown to Ministers. The cloak of Ministerial responsibility shields the individual administrator from criticism and also safeguards his independence, for no Civil Servant feels that his personal future depends on willingness to act in a way that is pleasing to influential Members. After the Crichel Down inquiry, in which details of public administration received unparalleled publicity, there was some demand among Members[2] for wider retributive action against officials

---

[1] Cf. *The Civil Service in the Changing State*, pp. 62–64.

[2] Cf. the debate on Crichel Down. H.C. Deb., Vol. 530, col. 1218 (A. Hurd, Con. Newbury), col. 1238 (R. Crouch, Con. N. Dorset, 1950–57), col. 1247 (C. Davies, Lib. Montgomery), col. 1277 (Viscount Lambton, Con. Berwick) and

who were criticized in Sir Andrew Clark's Report.[1] Crichel Down also led to an official restatement of the limits of the doctrine of Ministerial responsibility,[2] which may be summarized as follows. If a civil servant carries out a direct order from a Minister or acts properly in accordance with the policy laid down by the Minister, the responsibility of the Minister is absolute. If a civil servant makes a mistake, but not on an important question of policy, the Minister should acknowledge the mistake and accept responsibility, although not personally involved, and subsequently take corrective action within the Department. If a civil servant acts reprehensibly there is no obligation on the Minister to defend actions of which he has no knowledge and which he believes to be wrong, although he must still account for his stewardship to Parliament. But these principles may not provide a clear prescription covering any particular case, for the extent to which a policy has been laid down by a Minister (or by his predecessors, and not countermanded) can be a matter for argument. The restatement of these rules is unlikely to have satisfied Members who felt that civil servants enjoy too great a degree of security of tenure; that while exhaustively conditioned to avoid mistakes, the public official is over-protected if he errs. The case of MacLean and Burgess, the two Foreign Office employees who decamped to the Soviet Union, helped to strengthen this view. When the full record of the previous behaviour of these men became available, many Members were shocked that they should have been permitted to retain positions of trust.[3]

To discover means which will secure democratic control of the mass of government action is an intractable problem in the modern state. The effective political difficulties in the way of making the doctrine of ministerial responsibility imply penalties for Ministers who incur widespread parliamentary displeasure were discussed in the opening section of this chapter. The main devices fashioned by Parliament to bring the work of the executive under review have also been outlined; their operation was shown to be partial, uneven and somewhat spasmodic. It has been suggested that they are not without effect, but that any extension of intervention by Members would

col. 1271 (A. S. Irving, Lab. Liverpool, Edgehill). Other Members expressed contrary views during the debate.

[1] 1953–54 Cmd. 9176, xi.
[2] H.C. Deb., Vol. 530, cols. 1290–1.
[3] Cf. H.C. Deb., Vol. 545, col. 1487 *et seq.*

violate the authority of Ministers and the structure of cabinet govern-ment. And any closer connection between Members and Government Departments would impose demands on the time of the former which could not fail to have other repercussions on the character of the House of Commons. Institutional change within Parliament is not the answer to seek: whether such changes are needed outside Parlia-ment is a wide question beyond the scope of this study.

6

Party Discipline

Unity is an essential condition for the success of a political party. Fissions and internal feuds are exploited by political opponents and do grave damage to the degree of public confidence that a party can command. In the Commons the Government must organize its supporters to secure a constant majority, and the Opposition must keep together if its ability to provide an alternative government is to be beyond question. The repeated inability of Liberal Members since 1916 to vote together in the same division lobby has done much to accelerate the decline of their party: the strife within the Parliamentary Labour Party before the 1955 general election cannot fail to have had some effect on the election results. But while politicians understand the need to restrict controversy in the interests of their party, the internal strains within parties are severe; when these become too powerful to be restrained by pleas for unity, some form of eruption must follow. 'Damn your principles and stick to your party' may be sound tactical advice but it not infrequently fails to appease rebellious spirits. In a Parliament dominated by two parties, the range of opinion within each must be wide. Members of the same party have a variety of interests, experience, social background and temperament which can but lead to conflict. They represent constituencies that are quite dissimilar in composition. From the nature of their calling it is inevitable that most Members possess unusual qualities of vigour and determination and are not easily amenable to the discipline demanded by team-work. It is in this setting that the Whips of each party must try to promote harmony by smoothing tempers or, more rarely, by indicating pained displeasure at the waywardness of an erring soul in their flock.

The two major parties each have about twelve Whips.[1] In the

---

[1] The original term, 'whipper-in', was drawn from the language of the hunting field where a whipper-in has the duty of preventing hounds from straying from the pack. Cf. I. Bulmer-Thomas, *The Party System in Great Britain*, p. 109.

143

Conservative Party they are appointed by the Leader of the Party: the Parliamentary Labour Party elects its Chief Whip and he nominates his assistants. Most of the Whips of the party in office hold Government appointments: the Chief Whip—usually known as the Patronage Secretary—is the Parliamentary Secretary to the Treasury, five of his assistants are Lords Commissioners of the Treasury and three more hold positions in the Royal Household, as Treasurer, Controller and Vice-Chamberlain. A further three or four additional assistant Government Whips hold no office and receive no payment for their added responsibilities.[1] All the Opposition Whips are unpaid. Whips of each party have an office and these are the nerve-centres of party organization in the House. From here are issued on Fridays the weekly 'documentary whips' which inform Members of forthcoming business and request their attendance. Additional whips may be sent out during the week if it is thought to be necessary. The extent of the underlining of the request to attend a debate indicates its degree of significance. A single underlining intimates that no division is anticipated: double underlining means that the business is of importance and that a division is expected: three-line whips are issued when a vital vote is due to take place, and on these occasions no excuse for absence is acceptable, barring serious illness. Each Whip has special responsibility in relation to roughly thirty supporters and Members are divided into geographical groups for this purpose: regional Labour groups have a Whip who represents a constituency within the area, but this practice is not followed by the Conservatives. The first task of a Whip is to interpret the somewhat formal contents of the documentary whip to his group by explaining party tactics and—in the case of the Opposition—when a major assault on Government policy is planned. Attempts may be made to keep such information confidential and it is not thought suitable to commit to paper. A Whip must also see that his group are in the appropriate lobby for every division and, therefore, have a shrewd idea of where missing Members may be found. As Members hurry from all parts of the House when the division bells are rung they need guidance on which lobby to enter. Even those in the Chamber may be confused, for the form of some motions is a little complex—e.g., 'that the words proposed to be left out stand part of the question'. The Whips act as tellers in divisions. Other Members are tellers only

[1] But the unpaid Whips are not barred, as are members of the Government, from other activities that attract remuneration.

when there is a free vote and the Whips are off, or if they are leading a rebel group that has forced a vote in defiance of party policy.

Whips of both main parties have a roster to ensure that some are always present in the House, and they spend longer hours in the Palace of Westminster than most Members. One is always on duty on the Treasury bench. Government Whips must not only keep Ministers in office, they must also organize the work of the House so that government business proceeds successfully, and without unexpected delay. It is, therefore, a part of their function to 'keep a House' by maintaining the presence of a quorum of 40 Members. On 26th November, 1952, the first day of a two-day debate on the Second Reading of the Iron and Steel Bill, Colonel Wigg (Lab. Dudley) called attention to the fact that forty Members were not present. Labour Members had been advised to keep out of the Chamber and, as enough Conservatives could not be rounded up, the sitting was adjourned. Such incidents disturb the smooth flow of parliamentary work and represent a failing on the part of the Government Whips. If a division is to be challenged it is necessary to keep more supporters in the House than the Opposition can muster; even if the Opposition appear disinterested, and most of them go home, the Government still require an attendance of a hundred to move successfully the motion 'that the question be now put'. Failure to have this motion accepted might mean that the business would be 'talked out' and no decision reached. Government Whips tend to lose their identity as individual Members. They never speak in the House, except to move procedural motions. As Junior Ministers they are not called on to serve on Select Committees. Constituency business they deal with by correspondence with Ministers: their public speeches are careful, restrained and devoid of announcements of policy developments which may attract publicity to the words of other Ministers. Opposition Whips are not so constrained in their parliamentary activities, and their whipping duties are more limited. It is not for them to command the order of business and prevent procedural hindrances, and they can but try to maximize the opportunities for initiative available to their own Members.

A Whip should possess a good understanding of the opinions of Members, above all of those who are in his special charge: this enables the Whips Office to forecast reactions in any political situation. When the Conservatives are in office their Whips are allocated a sphere of governmental activity, covering one or more Ministries, in which they are required to take a particular interest. They attend all relevant backbench committees and have to report to the Chief Whip on the trend of the discussions, and on the views of Members as a whole, on topics within their range. In some measure the work of Government Whips may overlap with that of Ministers' private parliamentary secretaries,[1] and they must be well informed on policy developments so, if necessary, Members can be persuaded of the merits of the official attitude. One has the impression that the Conservative Whips' Office is now run on the lines of a military staff headquarters in which liasion duties are carefully distributed to each individual in the organization.

New Whips, especially in the Conservative Party, are often chosen from Members who have served in the House for a short time, and many Whips, therefore, have devoted by far the greater part of their parliamentary life to this function. Not all Members are suitable for the task. Great reserves of passion and an overpowering sense of political mission are natural disqualifications. A Whip must be utterly loyal to his party;[2] he must be discreet, tactful and approachable; he must also be a 'political animal', able to sense the climate of opinion. It does not matter if he is devoid of strong convictions if he can still guide backbenchers as the party wishes. Yet the popular conception of a Whip as a man who dragoons his flock is far too simple: he is, in turn, advocate, lightning conductor and interpreter. The success of the Whips may be measured by the degree of party harmony, and they accomplish far more by quiet persuasion than by threats.

In the Labour Party the policy that Whips have to urge on the recalcitrant has usually been decided at a meeting of the Parliamentary Labour Party, and the issue tends to be one of obedience to party decisions. Conservatives do not decide policy in such a formal manner and for them discipline is a matter of loyalty rather than obedience. This helps to explain why expulsions—the withdrawal of the whip—are far more common in the Labour Party, but Labour rebels who repent are treated with magnanimity. Three Members,

---

[1] For a discussion of the work of a P.P.S. see p. 207.

[2] In April, 1954, three Labour Whips, K. Robinson (St. Pancras, N.), C. Royle (Salford, W.) and J. Taylor (W. Lothian) supported an amendment to the Atomic Energy Bill against the advice of their leaders. They were immediately asked to resign their positions.

PARTY DISCIPLINE

A. Bevan (Ebbw Vale), Sir Stafford Cripps[1] and G. R. Strauss (Lambeth, Vauxhall),[2] who were expelled from the Labour Party in 1939 for advocating a 'Popular Front' with Communists and other Left-wing groups, subsequently attained Ministerial office in Labour Cabinets. K. Zilliacus who lost the whip in 1949 and his seat in 1950, was subsequently readmitted to the Labour Party and returned to the Commons in 1955. Before the 1955 Election the whip was hastily restored to eight rebels: A. Bevan (Ebbw Vale), G. Craddock (Bradford, S.), S. O. Davies (Merthyr Tydfil), E. Fernyhough (Jarrow), E. Hughes (S. Ayrshire), J. McGovern (Glasgow, Shettleston), S. Silverman (Nelson and Colne) and V. Yates (Birmingham, Ladywood). In November, 1954, the Parliamentary Labour Party decided to abstain on the vote ratifying the London and Paris agreements. Six of the above had voted against the agreements while McGovern had voted for the Government. The eighth case, that of Bevan, is described below. Withdrawal of the whip is an extreme measure and does not normally follow isolated acts of rebellion; more frequently rebels are reprimanded by the Chief Whip and warned to be of better behaviour in future. And ambitious young men are well aware that undue independence of spirit will not ingratiate them with their leaders.

The Parliamentary Labour Party is acutely aware of disciplinary problems and has a set of Standing Orders which embody the duty of Members to support party decisions. The existence of these Standing Orders, however, has not prevented overt disagreements in the Parliamentary Party. In 1946 the Standing Orders were suspended as an experiment, it being hoped that this action would help to foster good-fellowship and co-operation between Ministers and their back-bench supporters. The right to withdraw the whip was retained as an ultimate sanction. In spite of a number of large-scale rebellions these Standing Orders remained in abeyance until March, 1952, when 57 Labour Members defied a three-line whip in a division on defence. This action was the cause of wide disquiet in the Party and Standing Orders were thereupon revised and reinstated. Paragraph One is of the greatest importance and reads as follows:

'The privilege of membership of the Parliamentary Labour Party involves the acceptance of the decisions of the Party Meeting. The Party recognizes the right of individual Members to abstain from

---

[1] Member for Bristol, East, 1931–50.

[2] Member for North Lambeth, 1929–31, 1934–50 and Vauxhall since 1950.

voting on matters of deeply held personal conscientious conviction.' The 'conscience clause' in the previous Standing Orders had been more narrowly drawn with an implication that it referred particularly to religious and temperance questions. No such limitation is now suggested and it would appear that a Labour Member can summon conscientious scruples to his aid whenever he disagrees profoundly with a party decision. Earl Attlee, when still leader of the Labour Opposition, was constrained to observe that 'conscience is a still, small voice, not a loudspeaker'. Other Standing Orders authorize the withdrawal of the whip by the Parliamentary Party and lay down procedure to deal with breaches of discipline. But the restoration of Standing Orders has not been efficacious, for during the following three years Labour Members were often reft with serious feuds.

Between the Elections of 1945 and 1955 there were thirteen major Labour rebellions; the average number of participants was nearly fifty and over 200 Members were concerned in one or more incidents.[1] Nine of these occasions took place in the period 1946–49 when the Labour Government with a large majority could afford a little latitude: the remaining four occurred between 1952 and 1955 and reflected a major struggle for power within the Party. Eight of the rebellions were staged in the division lobbies, four involved the tabling of motions critical of official Labour policy and the other incident was the Nenni telegram.[2] The dominant causes of dissent were foreign policy and defence, including conscription and the use of atomic weapons. Trouble also developed over the Government of Ireland Bill, 1949, and the clause in the Civil Aviation Bill, 1946, authorizing the appointment of part-time directors of the Airways Corporations. The failure of Aneurin Bevan to agree with his more moderate colleagues led to his resignation, together with H. Wilson (Huyton) from the Labour Government in March, 1951; after the 1951 Election, and the relegation of Labour to the Opposition benches, Bevan's challenge to the party leadership led to infringements of discipline by his supporters. The restoration of Standing Orders in March, 1952, failed to inhibit the activities of Labour

[1] Cf. the admirable analysis by W. L. Guttsman in the *Manchester Guardian* dated 14th April, 1955.

[2] A number of Labour Members signed a telegram of support for Signor Nenni just before the Italian general election in April, 1948. Nenni was the leader of the left-wing group of Socialists in alliance with the Italian Communists. The Labour whip was subsequently withdrawn from the instigator of the telegram, J. Platts-Mills, Member for Finsbury 1945–50.

Members supporting 'Bevanite' policies, and they continued to hold separate meetings with the object of attracting wider support. Their critics alleged that they were creating a party within the Party, and in November, 1952, the Parliamentary Labour Party passed a resolution calling for the 'immediate abandonment of all group organizations within the Party other than those officially recognized'. Shortly after this decision it was made known that the Bevan group would cease to hold meetings, but a cleavage of opinion remained which needed merely the emergence of an appropriate issue to bring it once more to the front. In April, 1954, F. Beswick (Lab. Uxbridge) moved a new clause to the Atomic Energy Bill designed to prevent the new Atomic Energy Authority from producing nuclear weapons unless authorized to do so by a resolution passed by both Houses of Parliament: contrary to the advice of their leaders, 65 Labour Members supported the proposed clause. In the same month Bevan resigned from the Shadow Cabinet as a protest against the failure of the Labour Party to oppose the formation of the South East Asia Treaty Organization, the Pacific N.A.T.O. But the Bevan dispute did not come to a head until the beginning of 1955. In February Bevan and 113 other Labour Members tabled a motion condemning the Government's refusal to open talks with Soviet leaders before the London and Paris agreements on the future of Western Germany had been ratified. On 24th February, the Parliamentary Labour Party, by a vote of 132 to 72, passed a resolution regretting the tabling of this motion in defiance of Party decisions. On 2nd March, 1955, at the end of a two-day Commons debate on defence, Bevan questioned Attlee on the attitude of the Labour Party towards the use of thermo-nuclear weapons.[1] This was an extraordinary challenge to the authority of the party leader and an overt demonstration of the rift within the party, which was further emphasized by the failure of 62 Labour Members to vote for the official Opposition amendment to the Government motion on defence. Such an incident could not pass unheeded and the Parliamentary Labour Party subsequently agreed by 141 votes to 112 to withdraw the whip from Bevan. Withdrawal of the whip, however, does not automatically imply expulsion from the Labour Party. The latter penalty is reserved to the National Executive of the Labour Party and is subject to an appeal to the Party Conference. On this occasion much support rallied to Bevan in the constituencies after his loss of the whip, and the National

[1] H.C. Deb., Vol. 537, col. 2176.

Executive decided against his expulsion from the Party. The incident closed when the whip was hurriedly restored just before the General Election.

The Bevan case is most instructive for its shows that if a minority group is sufficiently large and determined, sanctions for indiscipline become ineffective. To expel a leading politician from a parliamentary group by a majority of 29 in a total vote exceeding 250 serves mainly to emphasize the extent of party disintegration. Politicians in such a situation have the choice of allowing a relaxation in discipline or of surrendering hope of an early acquisition of power. When imposed by a narrow margin the penalty of expulsion loses much of its sting. It is true that if a Member loses the whip he can expect normally to lose his seat at the next election, but the position is changed if the rebel is a man of importance who can attract sympathy in the party at large as well as overwhelming support in his own constituency. Bevan's strength in the Labour Party was sufficient to obtain his election as Party Treasurer in 1956, and there can be little doubt that he would have been returned for Ebbw Vale in 1955 even had he been forced to stand as an unofficial Labour candidate. Party discipline can exterminate from the Commons those Members who are eccentric or who move towards kinship with their nominal adversaries, but it is helpless when a party divides almost evenly against itself.

The storm-centre within the Conservative Party in recent years has been the Suez Canal. In July, 1954, the 'Suez Group' mustered 28 Members to oppose the Government motion to approve the agreement with Egypt over the future of the British base in the Canal zone. Military action against Egypt in 1956 caused rebellion on both wings of the Party: initially a few Conservatives opposed the use of force in Egypt, and after the decision to withdraw from Port Said was announced fifteen Members of the Suez Group abstained on a vote of confidence. No disciplinary action followed these manifestations of independence, but in moments of great tension the Conservative Whips exercise their art of persuasion to the limit. P. Maitland (Con. Lanark), one of the fifteen Suez rebels mentioned above, subsequently spoke of the 'Westminster machine' using 'extraordinary and unexampled pressures, some of them altogether underhand, to force the Tories into line'.[1] The last major

[1] Reported in *The Times*, December 8th, 1956. Colonel Wigg (Lab. Dudley) tried to use this statement as the basis of a complaint of breach of privilege. The

150

challenge to the Party's leaders was in May, 1940, and led to the resignation of the Chamberlain government. Five years earlier roughly 70 Conservatives led by Sir Winston Churchill[1] had voted against the second and third readings of the Government of India Bill. None of the incidents recorded in this paragraph led to the withdrawal of the whip.

Minor and individual overt acts of protest by Conservative Members are not uncommon as can be seen from the following examples in the session 1955–56. In May, 1956, 25 Conservatives voted against the second reading of the Coal Industry Bill. On the motion to approve the White Fish Subsidy Scheme in December, 1955, none of the Ulster Unionist Members voted for the Government. In February, 1956, a few Conservatives voted against the second reading of the Licensing (Airports) Bill. Lord Hinchingbrooke (Dorset, South) and Major Legge-Bourke (Isle of Ely) voted against the Government motion to increase purchase tax in October, 1955. The following month Lord Hinchingbrooke tabled a motion for the rejection of the Government's Housing Subsidies Bill, and in December, 1955, J. C. Jennings (Burton) voted against the second reading of the Teachers' (Superannuation) Bill. The policies of a Conservative Government are a constant source of backbench criticism: there can be no smoke without fire, and the resolution of many rebels weakens as the division bells are rung.

Conservative practice is to take away the whip in cases where a Member becomes seriously at odds with the Party machine. Sir W. Wayland[2] lost the whip for a period after he had supported the Independent candidate in the famous 1931 by-election at St. George's, Westminster. The whip was withdrawn from Captain Cunningham-Reid[3] in 1942 because of his independent approach, but two years previously he had refused a request from the St. Marylebone Conservative Association to resign. J. H. McKie, Member for Galloway

attempt failed because only Maitland could initiate a complaint about the nature of the pressures to which he had been subjected. That the activities of Whips might constitute a breach of privilege is a novel and stimulating doctrine; if ever it were accepted, the effects on the character of the House of Commons could not fail to be profound! (Cf. H.C. Deb., Vol. 561, cols. 32–34 and 227–30).

[1] Conservative Member for Oldham, 1900–6; Liberal Member for Manchester, N.W., 1906–8, Dundee County, 1908–22; Conservative Member for Epping 1924–45 and Woodford since 1945.

[2] Member for Canterbury, 1927–45.

[3] Member for Warrington 1922–23, 1924–29 and Marylebone 1932–45.

since 1931, did not receive the Conservative whip 1945–48 as he had been elected as an Independent Conservative in 1945 following a dispute with his local Association. Other Conservatives have voluntarily relinquished the whip, e.g., E. Gandar Dower[1] in 1948 after differences with his local supporters. In 1954 two Conservatives refused the whip for a few months as a token of protest against some aspect of policy: Major Legge-Bourke objected to the Government's policy on Suez and Sir John Mellor[2] took exception to proposals to increase the payment of Members. In May, 1957, a body of eight Conservatives forsook the whip because, according to a statement issued at the time, they felt that the Government had 'capitulated to Nasser' by allowing British ships to again use the Suez Canal. They were J. Biggs-Davison (Chigwell), A. Fell (Yarmouth), Lord Hinchingbrooke (Dorset, South), P. Maitland (Lanark), A. Maude (Ealing, S.), Sir Victor Raikes,[3] L. Turner (Oxford) and P. Williams (Sunderland, S.).

The two main parties differ appreciably in their treatment of disciplinary problems. For the Conservatives a decision to withdraw the whip is made by the Leader and not by a party meeting: such an event is therefore less likely to cause controversy than in the Labour Party. The Conservatives are also more tolerant. Withdrawal of the whip is a rare penalty and is imposed on those who offend the Party organization, central or local, rather than for heresy in the House. A number of examples have been cited above of Conservatives refusing the whip as a method of protest: this tactic is unknown in the Labour Party, possibly because of its quasi-religious sense of devotion to 'the movement'. Left-wingers do not leave the Labour Party voluntarily, and if forced out tend to reach for a martyr's crown. The spectacle of an Independent Conservative Member, who refused the whip, speaking on trade policy at the 1957 Conservative Conference is unlikely to have a parallel in the Labour Party. But the main distinction is that among Labour Members it is traditional to settle differences by vote. This is normal democratic procedure but it does weaken the position of dissenters. The right to vote in a private meeting is held implicitly to exhaust the moral right to object. Should the minority still continue to argue

[1] Member for Caithness 1945–50.

[2] Member for Tamworth 1935–45 and Sutton Coldfield 1945–55.

[3] Member for S.E. Essex 1931–45, Liverpool, Wavertree, 1945–50 and Liverpool, Garston, 1950–57.

152

and agitate, they can be charged with challenging the authority of the party meeting. If no resolution is put to a meeting, no firm decision is reached and no 'party line' is formulated: when division of opinion has been profound, the atmosphere created is one of doubt and dissatisfaction. Against this background it is much easier to carry the argument to the Commons' Chamber. Thus a confirmed individualist may well be happier on the Conservative benches. There he will be urged to be loyal to his leaders, but he will not be told to obey a caucus pronouncement.

II

For private members' business, questions of privilege and, infrequently, for Government business, the Whips are taken off and Members are free to vote as their own inclination chooses. In addition, no whipping takes place on Select Committees. The latitude in private members' time extends to both Bills and motions on Fridays and also to Bills introduced under the Ten-Minute Rule, but if the Government is strongly opposed to a private member's Bill its influence will normally prevail.[1] When Government policy or legislation is under discussion the Whips are removed only if the subject involves quite special political difficulties, for if Ministers allow a free vote they are inviting their own defeat. This is true *a fortiori* when the Opposition is united in their objections to Government proposals; the Labour demand that a free vote should be allowed on the Bill to initiate commercial television was politically unrealistic. It is easier for a divided Opposition to take off the Whips as the consequence can be merely an increase in the Government's majority. Thus the second reading of the Licensing (Airports) Bill, 1956, was carried by 239 votes to 89, in a division for which the Labour Whips were withdrawn.

A review of free votes on Government business over the last thirty years will illustrate how far they have been permitted on issues where moral considerations are paramount. In 1927 and again in 1928 the Commons refused to approve the revised Prayer Book, and Ministers opposed one another both in debate and in the division lobbies. During the last war the Government proposed that theatres should be permitted to open on Sundays for the benefit of

[1] For a discussion of private members' time see Chap. 10.

troops who were away from home. The Home Secretary (Herbert Morrison) urged the Commons to support the Government, but a free vote was allowed and Sunday opening was defeated by eight votes. Morrison had been connected, more successfully, with a free vote on a previous occasion: in 1930 as Minister of Transport he was responsible for the Road Traffic Bill which *inter alia* proposed to end the speed limit, and the abolition was carried without the intervention of the Whips. The controversy over the death penalty has been a fruitful source of free votes in recent years, although their effect has been limited.

It is instructive to examine the parliamentary struggle over the death penalty in some detail. The story commences with the Criminal Justice Bill, 1948, which was a measure designed to make a wide range of reforms in the administration of the criminal law and the treatment of offenders. On the Report Stage a new clause was tabled by Members from all political parties which sought, for a trial period of five years, to replace the death penalty for murder by life imprisonment. Contrary to the advice of the Home Secretary this clause was added to the Bill on a free vote by a majority of 23—245 votes against 222. The House of Lords deleted the new clause and the Government thereupon suggested a compromise that retained the death penalty for certain categories of murder which implied 'express malice'. This compromise clause was carried in the Commons by 307 votes to 209, but the Government Whips were on. The Lords rejected the new proposal as impractical and confronted the Labour Government with a difficult situation. If the Labour majority in the Commons insisted on retaining the compromise, the whole Bill would be lost. Further, the machinery of the Parliament Act could not be used to overcome the Lords' veto as the disputed clause had not been part of the Bill when it first left the Commons. In order to save the remainder of the Bill the compromise was dropped and a Royal Commission was subsequently appointed to give further study to the whole question, but its terms of reference were deliberately framed in such a way as to preclude a straight recommendation for or against capital punishment. After a pause of four years the issue was again raised in July, 1953, when Sydney Silverman (Lab. Nelson and Colne) unsuccessfully attempted to obtain leave to introduce a Bill under the Ten-Minute Rule to abolish the death penalty, his opponents arguing that the question should be delayed until the report of the Royal Commission was published.

The Report[1] subsequently proposed a number of alterations in the law relating to capital punishment. The more important were that the age below which sentence of death may not be imposed should be raised from 18 to 21; that in all other cases the jury should have discretion to decide whether there are such extenuating circumstances as to justify the substitution of a sentence of life imprisonment; that the McNaghten Rules, which in England and Wales determine the tests of criminal responsibility, should be abrogated. In February, 1955, the Commons considered a Government motion to 'take note' of the Report. It was announced that Ministers had come to provisional views about the Report which would be re-examined in the light of what was said in the debate. An amendment urging the suspension of the death penalty for a trial period of five years was rejected on a free vote by 245 votes to 214. Nine months later the attitude of the Government to the recommendations of the Report was made public and the main suggestions, noted above, were turned down. The following week Sydney Silverman again produced a Bill under the Ten-Minute Rule to end capital punishment; this time, rather surprisingly, leave to introduce was accorded without a division. On 16th February, 1956, the Commons debated a Government motion 'That this House is of opinion that, while the death penalty should be retained, the law relating to the crime of murder should be amended'. An amendment asking for the abolition or suspension of the death penalty was carried on a free vote by 292 votes to 246: 47 Conservatives voted for the amendment, eight Labour Members voted against it, and a number of Ministers deliberately abstained. Faced with this verdict, the Government decided to provide time for the further consideration of Silverman's Bill and in March its second reading was carried on another free vote by 286 votes to 262. The committee stage subsequently occupied the whole House for two and a half days and hostile amendments were proposed. In all, there were eight divisions in committee. The opponents of the Bill scored a single and temporary victory when, by a majority of four, the House agreed that the death penalty should be retained for a murder committed by a person serving a sentence of life imprisonment; this decision was reversed at the Report Stage. Finally, the Bill went to the Lords where it was heavily defeated.

After the vote of February, 1956, all death sentences had been commuted to life imprisonment by the use of the royal prerogative

[1] Cf. 1952–53 Cmd. 8932, vii.

155

in accordance with the 1948 precedent when no executions took place during the period when the Commons were on record in favour of their abolition. It was impossible, therefore, for the Government to allow the matter to rest with the defeat of the Silverman Bill in the Lords. A further measure—now the Homicide Act, 1957—was produced by the Home Secretary which initiated a distinction between capital murder, for which hanging is retained, and non-capital murder, punishable by life imprisonment. These categories are amoral: the forms of capital murder are designed to dissuade professional criminals from violence and to protect their victims, the police and prison staffs. Thus they are concerned with deterrence, not the heinousness of any particular crime. The 1957 Act reached the statute-book with the aid of the Government Whips but, as the Labour Party is now committed to the ending of capital punishment, the end of the controversy is not in sight.

The success of the Death Penalty (Abolition) Bill in the Commons had been entirely due to the determination of its small band of Conservative supporters. Although the Whips were off, the Tory abolitionists were subjected to heavy pressure from their party colleagues in Westminster and the constituencies. The protracted course of the debates allowed plenty of opportunity for second thoughts, and it is sad that such courage and resolution proved to be of no immediate avail.

It is clear that Cabinets allow their supporters the luxury of a free vote on rare occasions, when they are faced with major political difficulties on an issue that cuts across the normal lines of party loyalty and party controversy. There is a marked tendency for Ministers to attempt to evade questions of this kind—for example, gambling, divorce and Sunday observance. The result of a free vote is often embarrassing to the Government, for backbenchers, given a formal right to ignore the advice of their leaders, are not unwilling to take the opportunity. In particular, Ministers can expect trouble should they refuse to accept a verdict reached with licensed liberty— witness their confusion over capital punishment and Members' pay.[1] And the recent history of free voting provides a further illustration of how much easier it is to prevent change than to enforce reform. A single division and a majority of eight prevented the Sunday opening of theatres: a long campaign and many victories in the lobbies have not yet ended the death penalty.

[1] The 1954 free vote on Members' pay is described on p. 233.

7

Members and their Constituents

I

'Gentlemen: I have received your letter about the excise, and I am surprised at your insolence at writing to me at all.

'You know, and I know, that I bought this constituency. You know, and I know, that I am now determined to sell it, and you know what you think I don't know that you are now looking out for another buyer, and I know, what you certainly don't know, that I have now found another constituency to buy.

'About what you said about the excise: may God's curse light upon you all, and may it make your homes as open and as free to the excise officers as your wives and daughters have always been to me while I have represented your rascally constituency.'

Thus Antony Henry is reputed to have replied to those of his constituents who asked him to vote against the budget of 1714. When Honourable Members receive similar requests in our own time, their replies certainly lack the admirable pungency of the style of Henry. From the above it would appear that the problems of a corrupt electoral system, based on a limited and variable franchise, would be those of delicate private negotiations, possibly financial in character; more theoretical issues concerning the nature of the representative function would seem not to emerge. But this was not so. Exactly sixty years after Henry's letter, and nearly another sixty before the first Reform Bill, Burke made his famous speech to the Electors of Bristol in which he argued that an elected Member must use his own judgment at all times and was not a mere delegate appointed to carry out the instructions of those who sent him to Westminster.

'Certainly, gentlemen, it ought to be the happiness and glory of a representative to live in the strictest union, the closest correspondence, and the most unreserved communication with his constituents.

Their wishes ought to have great weight with him; their opinion, high respect; their business, unremitted attention. It is his duty to sacrifice his repose, his pleasures, his satisfactions, to theirs; above all, ever, and in all cases, to prefer their interest to his own. But his unbiassed opinion, his mature judgment, his enlightened conscience, he ought not to sacrifice to you, to any man, or to any set of men living. These he does not derive from your pleasure; no, nor from the law and the constitution. They are a trust from Providence, for the abuse of which he is deeply answerable. Your representative owes you, not his industry only, but his judgment; and he betrays, instead of serving you, if he sacrifices it to your opinion.

'My worthy colleague says, his will ought to be subservient to yours. If that be all, the thing is innocent. If government were a matter of will upon any side, yours, without question, ought to be superior. But government and legislation are matters of reason and judgment, and not of inclination; and what sort of reason is that, in which the determination precedes the discussion; in which one set of men deliberate, and another decide; and where those who form the conclusion are perhaps three hundred miles distant from those who hear the arguments?

'To deliver an opinion, is the right of all men; that of constituents is a weighty and respectable opinion, which a representative ought always to rejoice to hear; and which he ought always most seriously to consider. But *authoritative* instructions; *mandates* issued, which the member is bound blindly and implicitly to obey, to vote, and to argue for, though contrary to the clearest conviction of his judgment and conscience—these are things utterly unknown to the laws of this land, and which arise from a fundamental mistake of the whole order and tenor of our constitution.'[1]

Similar views to those of Burke have been expressed by other eminent writers. In his *Representative Government* (1861), J. S. Mill argued that pledges should not be required of a parliamentary candidate, although the voters were 'entitled to a full knowledge of the political opinions and sentiments of the candidate'.[2] Walter Bagehot in *The English Constitution* (1867) objected to any increase in the influence of constituencies over Members because it would lead to the pursuit of less moderate policies urged by those who lack

[1] Edmund Burke, *Speeches and Letters on American Affairs*, pp. 72–73 of the Everyman edition.
[2] Ch. XII of *Representative Government* is a discussion of pledges.

understanding and responsibility.[1] The case against turning Members into delegates of the constituents was again pressed with great cogency by Lord Bryce in *Modern Democracies* (1921). It would lead to four unhappy results: men of independent outlook would not enter Parliament; the value of parliamentary debate would be diminished; the power of local party committees would be increased; the power of the Cabinet would be increased.[2] But Bryce did not advocate complete freedom for Members. They should not act contrary to any promises made at their election, and a Member who leaves one party and joins another should resign his seat; but on issues on which no pledge has been given, or which have emerged since his election, a Member should be free to follow his conscience.

Sir Ivor Jennings' well-known work *Parliament* (1939) contains a subsection on 'Members and their Constituencies',[3] but in it will be found no echo of Burke. The reason is that Jennings recognized the over-riding character of party considerations in both the selection and the parliamentary activities of Members. Voters support a party and not a candidate, and Honourable Members are those fortunate enough to have been adopted by the dominant party in a constituency. Once elected, the behaviour of a Member is dictated by considerations of party loyalty. He will, of course, advance the interests of his constituency when possible, deal with individual grievances, be concerned with the prospects of local industries and the like, but when the sheep-dogs bark he will be shepherded into the appropriate lobby. On this analysis, the basic truth of which is not denied, constituency opinion becomes unimportant. The strictures of Burke on those who seek to impose their will on Members would fall in our century, not upon voters, but upon Party Whips. Yet constituencies cannot be cancelled from the reckoning altogether. Recent events have shown that Members are as likely to encounter serious trouble from their local supporters as from the Whips. Such friction can develop either after a Member has strayed from the party line or because of his attitude on a topic when the House was allowed the luxury of a 'free vote'.[4] An example of the latter is the local opposition encountered by those Conservative Members who supported

[1] Cf. p. 129 of the World's Classics edition.
[2] Vol. II, p. 387.
[3] pp. 26–30.
[4] Free votes are discussed *supra*, Ch. 6, Section II.

the abolition of capital punishment: the repercussions of the Suez action provide an illustration of the former. Difficulties may also be more personal in character or be caused by local pledges.[1]

The greatest crime a Member can commit in the eyes of his local constituency association is to appear to have some sympathy for the views of his political opponents. A local party organization exists primarily not for political debate, but for political struggle; ardent party members, especially among Conservatives, are not to be deflected by the alleged rights or wrongs of a current controversy. If the wisdom of party policy is questioned publicly in a way that suggests some slight merit for the views of opponents, party enthusiasts are scandalized. This the cautious Member will bear in mind, particularly if he be the representative of a constituency Conservative Association with a large and vigorous membership. The experience of S. Evans (Lab. Wednesbury) and N. Nicolson (Con. Bournemouth, East, and Christchurch) is a warning. Evans refused to denounce military action against Egypt, while Nicolson refused to support it: the Wednesbury Labour Party called on Evans to resign and he did so, while the Bournemouth East and Christchurch Conservatives decided by a majority of 3 to 1 to seek another candidate for the next election. Other Conservative Members who shared Nicolson's view received varying treatment. Relations between Sir Frank Medlicott (Central Norfolk) and his local Association were badly strained and Sir Frank announced that he would not contest the next election. At Birmingham (Handsworth) Sir Edward Boyle[2] fared rather better: a statement issued by the Handsworth Conservative Association recognized the right of a Conservative Member to act in accordance with his sincere convictions. Anthony Nutting (Con. Melton) who resigned as Minister of State for Foreign Affairs over the Suez issue, also gave up his seat in the Commons: the local association sent a message of support to the Prime Minister without giving Nutting an opportunity to defend his opinions. Nutting was, therefore, condemned unheard. Whether Melton Conservatives would have acted in the same way as Nicolson's constituents cannot be known because of Nutting's unsolicited application for the

[1] For examples cf. pp. 16–17 *supra*.

[2] In November, 1956, Sir Edward resigned his post as Economic Secretary to the Treasury on the Suez issue: in January, 1957, he was appointed Parliamentary Secretary to the Ministry of Education in the Macmillan Government but he did not recant from his earlier views.

Chiltern Hundreds, but it should be recorded that both Nicolson and Evans had been a target for criticism by some of their local supporters even before the Suez incident.

It is instructive to compare the troubles of left-wing Conservatives with the position of the right-wingers. When eight of the latter resigned the Conservative whip in 1957—a step much graver than abstention in a single division—there was no report of constituency objection to their conduct. Only Members who are thought to be too near the political centre encounter hostility from local supporters, although in the Labour Party this truth is limited by the case of those suspected of Communist sympathies. Labour Members who lost the whip in 1954 were in no danger from their local associations and in 1949 the Gateshead Labour Party still defended K. Zilliacus[1] when he was no longer acceptable to Transport House. The words of Bagehot on this matter are still valid.

'Constituency government is the precise opposite of parliamentary government. It is the government of persons far from the scene of action, instead of the government of moderate persons close to the scene of action; it is the judgment of persons judging in the last resort and without a penalty, in lieu of persons judging in fear of a dissolution and ever conscious that they are subject to an appeal.'[2]

There is little evidence that constituency pressure affects voting in the Commons. One reason must be that local opinion often becomes articulate only *after* the relevant debate in the House, and criticism of the Member takes the form of an inquest on his behaviour rather than a guide for future action. If public discussion on an issue has many months in which to become effective, its impact is necessarily the more powerful—witness the willingness of Nigel Nicolson to modify his advocacy of ending the death penalty. But when the Whips allow a free vote, the spirit of Burke is resurrected and Members become jealous of their independence. As free votes are limited to questions on which party alignments are inapplicable, no one can be accused of lack of party loyalty. Even so, Members do not care to offend what they know to be a majority view in their constituencies, but if Welsh Members oppose a Bill to liberalize the law relating to Sunday observance are they submitting to local opinion or merely following their own inclinations? On questions which involve party discipline a Member will oppose his party only

[1] Member for Gateshead, East, 1945–50 and Manchester, Gorton, since 1955.
[2] *The English Constitution*, p. 129, World's Classics edition.

if his convictions are strong: a man willing to stand up to the Whip will not be influenced by his constituents.

Electors have no immediate legal remedy when angered by their Member; the recall is unknown to the British Constitution.[1] The problem of how a representative should act in conditions of strain is either tactical or ethical, and if passions are sufficiently aroused tactical considerations lose their force. Members who resign from a party, perhaps join another, and retain their seats, seem morally to be in a weak position, for they are acting contrary to commitments made at the previous election. (They may protest that the party is out of step with them and not vice versa, but this argument is frequently unconvincing.) Yet the custom is to remain at Westminster until the next general election; the conduct of Sir Richard Acland[2] in this matter was exceptional, that of Colonel Banks,[3] R. Blackburn,[4] A. Edwards,[5] T. Horabin,[5] I. Thomas[5] and E. Walkden[6] was typical.

The position of unorthodox Members who still adhere to their party is entirely different, the more so if the cause of dissension has arisen since the previous election. They are guilty of no breach of faith. If reproached for exercising their judgment their reply can be that no other source of judgment is compulsive. It is always open to any individual or association to lobby Members, but there can be no justification for attempting to give instructions. A resolution passed by a meeting of a Member's constituency association is indicative only of the sentiments of those at the meeting; they may not coincide with majority opinion in the constituency as a whole, or among those who voted for the Member at the previous election, or even among all

[1] The 'recall' is a device used in a number of States in the U.S. whereby a petition signed by a given proportion of the voters has the effect of making an elective office become vacant. The incumbent can defend his stewardship by contesting the ensuing by-election.

[2] Sir Richard Acland resigned from the Labour Party owing to his opposition to the manufacture of the hydrogen bomb. He also gave up his seat in the Commons intending to defend his cause at the by-election, but he was overtaken by the dissolution of Parliament and was forced to stand at a general election, under probably less favourable circumstances: Member for Barnstaple as a Liberal and then a Common Wealth supporter 1935–45, Labour Member for Gravesend 1948–55.

[3] Member for Pudsey, Conservative 1950–56, Independent since 1956.

[4] Member for Birmingham (Kings Norton), Labour 1945–51, Independent 1951.

[5] See p. 44.

[6] See p. 224.

those who belong to the local party organization. No single gathering can claim to speak for a whole constituency. And government cannot be conducted by continuous plebiscite. A Member who follows his inclinations is merely doing his duty, provided that he does not contravene earlier *professions de foi*. The successful demand of the Wednesbury Labour Party in 1956 that their Member, S. N. Evans, should resign is contrary to British practice, and it is to be hoped that this precedent will not be followed. Evans had not been deprived of the Labour whip and he continued general support for Labour policy. This is not to argue that constituency associations should refrain from criticizing their Members nor, indeed, select an alternative candidate if dissatisfied with their present representative on personal or policy grounds. Members can have no right to the permanent loyalty of their local party.

Equally, however, enthusiastic party adherents should not be over-hasty in denouncing Members who show independence of mind. A parliament of puppets is in the interests of no one. And the Whips are quite strong enough to maintain an adequate standard of party discipline without further support from the constituencies. This self-denying ordinance must be a difficult prescription for active party workers to swallow, for why should they canvass, subscribe and drive at elections to aid the return of a Member who does not please them? Their voluntary sacrifice is required for the return of every Member to Parliament; the candidate as an individual is a negligible quantity, and he owes all to his adoption by the party. Yet as the more lively of amateur politicians in the same party rarely agree among themselves, a Member cannot satisfy them all if he departs from dreary repetition of party platitudes. It is inevitable that a Member of merit should sometimes cause offence to those who have supported him in the past. One new element in this situation is the growth of party membership, notably in the Conservative Party, for more people now feel that their Member has some obligation to them. In the small political organization with a largely inert membership, sources of friction may be removed in the secrecy of a committee room; local officials may resign quietly if irritated by their Member and others are found to replace them, or the Member may discover urgent personal, health or business reasons which will necessitate a by-election. In a large-scale organization which includes ward branches, women's branches and Young Conservatives, public controversy is more likely. Honourable Members are perhaps not the most sensitive of men and women, but adverse comment from your 'own side' must be unpleasant and disquieting. There is much in favour of the growth of active political life at the constituency level, for it helps to strengthen the reality of democracy: it is an unhappy paradox that increased interest in politics may weaken the independence of a legislature.

The volume of constituency criticism is restricted by the admiration shown for the qualities of courage and independence. The Member, through his position, automatically commands a significant degree of respect. Only a minority of the Members who stray from the flock in Westminster are disowned or replaced by their local association. Two generalizations may be made about the attitude of constituency supporters. They are more likely to challenge a Member if his majority is considerable; in a marginal seat any dissension in the camp offers too great a prospect of victory for opponents. Secondly, as was argued above, Members of very moderate opinions are more suspect than those with extreme views. An extremist is not a good candidate for a marginal seat—for example, J. Amery (Con. Preston, North)—but he is less likely to be thrown over by his party than one near the political centre representing a safe seat. How far Members are influenced by the size of their local majority cannot be determined. Those holding marginal seats have a special incentive to give satisfaction when dealing with constituency business; they may also be sensitive about any unpopular Government policies. It was noticeable in 1957 that Conservative Members with very slim majorities were among those who offered strong resistance to the rent decontrol of middle-class properties.[1]

II

Routine constituency business occupies a significant proportion of the time of Honourable Members. Although many of the tasks must become tedious, they are carried out, in general, with a marked degree of goodwill and enthusiasm. There is political benefit to be gained from building a reputation for being a 'good constituency man', but it is quite wrong to suggest that Members bestir themselves to deal with the problems of electors out of a shrewd calculation of advantage; willingness to give service to others is a traditional feature

[1] For example, R. C. D. Jenkins (Dulwich).

of the public life of this country. It is now an established social custom that those who have a grievance against a public authority may carry the plea to their Member, and parliamentary candidates know that a penalty of success is that they are expected to become a sort of Citizens Advice Bureau-cum-preliminary court of appeal. How far Members can really assist constituents with complaints is considered below, but a Member is thought to have done his duty if he takes a sympathetic interest in the troubles brought to him and communicates with the appropriate authority.

A majority of Members find it convenient to live in or near their constituencies, for their diaries contain many local engagements, especially at week-ends. Before adoption, candidates from distant parts are frequently asked if, once elected, they will come and reside in the area: a negative response diminishes chances of selection. In geographically small, densely populated urban neighbourhoods it is less likely that a Member will have an address within the actual constituency, but he will normally be sufficiently near to keep in close touch with the area. The nature of his commitments is influenced by the type of constituency. A representative of a borough of medium size will receive a greater number of invitations to appear at civic ceremonial than one who represents a scattered rural area. Many of the public appearances requested are for non-political occasions, including charitable and sporting functions, religious services, Speech Days or meetings of bodies such as the United Nations Association. It is common for Members to hold (honorary) office in a variety of local bodies. A small number of Members remain actively engaged in local government administration: T. Lewis[1] combined the leadership of the majority party on the Southampton Borough Council with attendance at Westminster for over four years. All Members are involved in the activities of their local supporters, for they are the standard-bearers of the party in the constituency and must help to keep the organization in fighting trim. Between elections the enthusiasm of party adherents must be maintained to provide the subscriptions to meet running expenses. So attendance at political dances, political bazaars and political meetings is a regular part of the 'week-end in the country'. The general run of constituency speeches by Members is dreary. Addressing the faithful, Members feel their task to be the restatement of current party policy, and excitement is likely only at moments of deep crisis

[1] Labour Member for Southampton 1929–31 and 1945–50.

or if some local controversy stirs feeling. Clearly, the meeting of a ward association is not the place for a Member to ventilate doubts about the wisdom of party leaders or party attitudes which he may express in private. Back in the House, Members are pursued by those, curious about our parliamentary institutions, who make requests for tickets (Admission Orders) to obtain entrance to the Strangers' Gallery and listen to a debate. In the recess Members are often to be seen ushering groups of visitors round the Palace of Westminster.

The more important type of constituency problem is that which is collective in character. Growing unemployment in an area will always engage the attention of the local Member. A recession in the cotton trade will agitate representatives from Lancashire constituencies: recession in the motor industry will lead the Members for Coventry to urge the government to take action to ease the position: the political strength of farming grows from the large number of Members it can summon to its aid. Controversial changes in local government are difficult to bring about because of the extent to which they stimulate constituency pressure on Members. In any local disaster, for example severe flooding, the local Member will be active in doing whatever is possible to secure relief. Each part of the country is keen to secure a good share of services provided by the Government and parliamentary representatives are urged to complain about alleged shortcomings in hospital accommodation, postal organization, broadcasting and television reception, the number of local offices of government departments, etc. Major issues affecting local amenities and the planning of land use—the siting of atomic energy stations—also stimulate local opinion. The examples could be multiplied endlessly, and a glance through a volume of *Hansard* will show how Members raise in the House a great variety of items that are of concern to their electors: it is on matters of this nature that backbenchers supporting the government most easily voice criticism of the policies of Ministers.

Correspondence received by Members tends to fall into four main groups: individual expressions of opinion of topical issues; circulars from national organizations seeking support for a wide range of causes; general constituency problems, as discussed above; requests to give assistance in personal problems. No more than a rough indication of the volume of mail can be given, for backbenchers differ in the estimates they give. A common average would appear to be between twelve and twenty letters a day; doubtless, some constituencies are more demanding than others. The volume of comment on public affairs will vary with circumstances, but personal troubles seem to be more acute in the winter months. Or do the dark evenings provide a greater temptation to write to Members? Further personal cases also arise from the 'surgeries' that most Members hold to deal with individual problems by interview. These surgeries are often held on Friday evenings or on Saturdays at the local party offices, and Members can all produce stories, tragic and comic, of their experiences on these occasions. A gentleman released on licence from an institution for those of unsound mind, who has called to learn his Member's views on capital punishment, may be followed by a father, accompanied by adolescent daughter, the father being in a high state of indignation because of his daughter's adverse school report. More common is the plight of those who come because of housing difficulties.

The growth of this type of social case work is partly a product of the philosophy of the Welfare State: it is now assumed that the processes of public administration should provide for those in need. Expansion of the armed forces and the effects of government-imposed economic controls have also made a contribution. The removal of various restrictions and the alleviation of shortages since the immediate post-war period have done something to ease the burden on Members. But why are they a target for those with a grievance? Presumably, because it is believed that the intercession of a Member will produce more favourable treatment than could otherwise be obtained. If it were true that Members could use their position to secure such privileges, the practice would be an abuse and a denial of the principles on which modern social legislation is based. In fact, Members can often do little to help. When a complaint seems justified—and sometimes when it is less convincing—they pass it on by letter to the government department or other public authority concerned. This type of correspondence has multiplied in post-war years: in 1938 the Financial Secretary to the Treasury wrote 610 letters to Members, and in 1954 this figure had grown to 3,349.[1] The Financial Secretary, being concerned with detailed administration of financial policy, is subjected to greater pressures than many other Ministers. Part of the additional letters received in the post-war period referred

[1] K. E. Couzens, 'A Minister's Correspondence', in *Public Administration*, Vol. XXXIV, pp. 237–44.

to issues that did not exist in 1938—for example, post-war credits, purchase tax, tobacco duty relief, war damage, compulsory acquisition of land or property and planning legislation. The expanding functions of the state confer extra rights and extra burdens on the individual and both are fruitful of representations to those holding public office.

Apart from trying to please a constituent, there are two possible motives that may prompt Members to take up a case. One is to claim that a decision should be altered because the case requires some form of exceptional consideration: the other is merely to bring a matter to the personal attention of the Minister, to ensure that the decision made really was intended by him, and that the civil servant who authorized it correctly interpreted his Minister's wishes. A Member's intervention may expose the fact that a plain mistake has been made. One example is that of the student whose university award from his local education authority was stopped after a single term, although he knew of no strictures about his work or conduct. A complaint to his Member led the latter to initiate inquiries with the local education authority which discovered that a clerk had confused the reports on two scholarship holders with the same name. Two Members were involved in rectifying this error, for the Conservative Member who received the initial protest also communicated with the Labour representative of the constituency where the University was situated; this is also an illustration of how Members may co-operate in handling constituency business. It is highly probable that a mistake of this nature could be rectified, without so much palaver, by a direct approach to the local authority. In such a case the Member clearly helps, even if his aid might have been unnecessary. He can also assist constituents unable to draft their case to the best advantage or who do not know where to address their plaint—indeed Members themselves are sometimes in doubt on the latter. Wisdom, sympathy and consolation can also be offered to those in distress but, apart from the type of circumstances mentioned in this paragraph, Members can be of assistance only if they can produce fruits of influence. How far is this possible?

To examine this problem further it is useful to compare the fate of a letter sent to a Minister by a Member with that of a letter in the same terms sent by an ordinary individual, but as practice varies between Departments only an outline description can be given. Correspondence from the general public is sorted in the registry of a government Department and despatched to the appropriate section of the office. It will proceed to go up the hierarchy of civil service grades until it reaches an official sufficiently senior to have the authority to send an answer. The ultimate destination depends, therefore, on the complexity of the issues raised; letters do not get past the level of Higher Executive Officer (H.E.O.) unless they are of a nonroutine nature, although replies on topics that look awkward or unusual are scrutinized by a Principal or Senior Executive Officer (S.E.O.). Letters will not rise even as far as an H.E.O. if they appear to come within a category that may be dealt with by the lower grades. The danger is that a junior officer will decide that a letter merits a stock answer without appreciating factors in the case which demand more competent consideration. In contrast, the letter from the Member to a Minister has a quite different career. It goes to the Minister's private office and is handled by the private secretary to the Minister, a young official in the administrative class, either a Principal or Assistant Principal, who sends an immediate acknowledgement to the Member. The letter is forwarded to the registry and is encased in a special type of file which indicates that the contents must have prior attention over other business. It tends to miss some lower levels of the hierarchy on the upward journey and the reply is considered carefully by a Principal or S.E.O. who, when satisfied, will pass the file up to an Assistant Secretary: whether the reply is reviewed by even higher officials, an Under Secretary, Deputy Secretary or the Permanent Secretary himself, will depend upon the conventions within the department and the delicacy of the issue at stake. Probably in a majority of cases the file will be sent back to the private secretaries' office by the Assistant Secretary, and the reply will then be placed in front of the Minister personally for signature. How far Ministers read what they sign is a question that defies analysis: it is reasonable to suppose that Junior Ministers have more time in which to be conscientious. There is a possibility that a Minister will be dissatisfied with the answer prepared and give instructions that the case be further examined. Yet if he wishes to amend any decision, the senior civil servants concerned will have an opportunity to advise him as to the possible implications of any alteration; to create a precedent may—according to the circumstances—constitute a new departure in policy affecting all subsequent cases of a similar nature. The strict tradition is that the Members' letter does not call forth a different decision to that which would be given to any other analogous case, unless very rarely it induces a Minister to initiate a change in policy. If a Minister does wish to change a decision the result may affect but a very small aspect of a wider general policy, and it may also be possible to have more than one interpretation of the proper implementation of general policy in a particular instance.

What emerges, then, is that although Members' letters get preferential treatment, they do not win any special favours for those on whose behalf they are written. Since the Minister's correspondence has priority they are dealt with more speedily: there is a Prime Minister's instruction that Members' letters shall receive at least a preliminary reply within a fortnight. In addition, since they are considered by senior officers, the replies will be more carefully scrutinized. Whether the replies are also fuller is less certain. A lengthy explanation which attempts to justify departmental practice may smooth away doubts in a Member's mind, but it may also provide grounds for further argument and correspondence, or even discussion in the House. Alternatively, a complete statement might be so long and technical as to be virtually incomprehensible; or it could involve an improper, and therefore impossible, disclosure of confidential information. The general character of the replies prepared to send to Members varies, in fact, between Departments and within Departments. Possibly the greatest advantage of a Member's letter is that it suffers no danger of receiving a stock answer that is inappropriate to the case.

As an alternative to correspondence, Members may see Ministers personally about a constituent's troubles; they have a conventional right of access to Ministers and no civil servant has the right to refuse a Member such an interview. From the point of view of equitable administration this practice has its dangers. A Minister, buttonholed in the corridor of the House, may be presented with a persuasive but highly one-sided story of a complaint: if he is unwise or inexperienced a Minister may thereupon give an undertaking which subsequently proves to be embarrassing. The path of wisdom is to be friendly but utterly non-committal, and to ask for a statement on paper which can then be subjected to the normal procedure for dealing with Members' letters. What happens when a Minister gives a private, unconsidered oral promise which is contrary to previous policy? Clearly, either the Minister breaks his word or the Member secures exceptional treatment. In the latter case, permanent civil

170

servants will suffer very proper pangs of conscience, and they may also exercise much ingenuity in demonstrating on office records that the case had special features that separated it from similar instances. This can be important for future reference. If standard practice is that an application of type A receives decision Z, and a case occurs which gets decision Y, it is urgent to be able to show that the Y decision was justified because the case does not fall within type A. Otherwise all future type A applications should earn Y treatment.

It is not suggested that Ministers frequently incur obligations in a rash manner, or that it is a bad thing for Ministers and Members to converse. A Member who is unsatisfied about a constituent's problem may be mollified if the Minister arranges to see him by appointment, and before the interview the Minister will have been carefully briefed by his officials. This technique is of value, especially when the Department is not prepared to commit to paper some of the grounds that have guided the decision. It may be felt that Ministers and their permanent advisers are over-cautious in suppressing information, but it would be unwise of them to rely always and entirely on the discretion of Members, many of whom have a habit of passing Ministerial replies back to complainants. In the greater freedom of conversation, however, it may be possible to give satisfaction to the supplicant Member. To relieve a hard-pressed Minister it is sometimes arranged for a Member to discuss a case with a permanent official within the administrative class, but no civil servant will talk business with a Member without the consent of his superiors.

Each personal case raised by a Member consumes much administrative manpower. Because the time occupied is largely that of senior officials, the cost is considerable. The volume of work thus created varies very greatly between Departments and between different sections of the same Department: while some Principals scarcely ever see a Member's letter, others are faced with a succession of them. In a section that suffers a sudden increase of parliamentary attention there is a grave danger that other important work relating to policy formation may be seriously impeded. If the delayed modifications of policy are related to the cause of Members' letters, a vicious circle could be created: even if this be a rare event it is always a logical possibility. When a flood of correspondence is broadly of a single nature it becomes easier to produce a stereotyped reply. To civil servants, Members may seem tiresome or worse. Some Members appear incapable of seeing more than one point of view, that of their constituent. Others can never be placated since they are fundamentally opposed to the policy which it is the task of officials to administer, and may seem to specialize in collecting grievances of a particular kind. Yet while the cost of trying to satisfy Members is heavy, it must be borne, since it forms another means of making the executive reconsider and justify its actions; the 'checks and balances' in our system of government are precious.

A Member who finds that private negotiation with the Minister about a personal case is of no avail can proceed to raise it in the House either by a question or on the motion for the adjournment.[1] Although this is another important constitutional safeguard it is not likely to produce satisfaction: what is not conceded in private is rarely granted in public. Common advice given to new Members is: 'If you want to get something done, try writing to the Minister; if you want to make a row, raise it in the House.' For the Member who does ventilate constituency business in the Commons, there is the satisfaction that the local electorate may feel he is active in working for their interests. Quite apart from any political advantages, it is always pleasurable to command esteem. But the argument of these pages has been that although many channels exist for Members to press matters of individual or local concern, there is but rare opportunity to obtain exceptional treatment for those they represent, even should they wish to do so. This is, indeed, a reflection of the British method of conducting public business.

[1] See pp. 123–5.

8

Members and the Public

Outside their own constituencies most Honourable Members are unknown to the general public. Senior Ministers and ex-Ministers are better remembered, but few are so widely recognized that the political cartoonists can dispense with adding names to their likenesses. The backbencher is allowed but a minor claim to public attention and his news value is lower than that of the personalities from the worlds of show business or sport. His speeches in the House are noticed, if at all, only by the more serious of the national newspapers. Publicity is certain should he be engaged in a lawsuit and, on a lesser scale, if he resigns or dies. Presence at a distinguished social gathering may be recorded in *The Times*. But to achieve fame a Member must act in a way to excite the interest of journalists or, possibly, be a journalist himself. Thus the public will be made aware of Members with outspoken or extreme views, especially if they relate to an issue that is easily understood: the attitude of Dr. Summerskill[1] to boxing is a good example. A Member who is near the scene of events of international importance will also be featured in the headlines: two recent cases are the negotiations undertaken in Cyprus by F. Noel-Baker,[2] and the journeys to see President Nasser by Colonel Banks.[3]

With the decline of the public meeting, the remaining platforms for opinion become the printing press and the microphone. Members produce a steady flow of books and articles, some of which are motivated by a desire to persuade the reader of the validity of a particular viewpoint, while others are quite non-political in content. In the latter category fall the novels of M. Edelman (Lab. Coventry, N.)

[1] Labour Member for Fulham, West, 1938–55 and Warrington since 1955.
[2] Labour Member for Brentford 1945–50 and Swindon since 1955.
[3] Member for Pudsey: Conservative 1950–56, Independent since 1956.

and the authoritative *Life of Addison* by P. Smithers (Con. Winchester). Historical and autobiographical works may contain a message for tomorrow, but it is usually of secondary importance. Other books are quite clearly written as political testaments—Aneurin Bevan's *In Place of Fear*, *Task for Giants* by P. Maitland and *The Future of Socialism* by C. A. R. Crosland.[1] J. Strachey[2] may be regarded as a leading theoretician in the Labour Party. Other Members have written about our system of government: outstanding in this class is Herbert Morrison's *Government and Parliament*. Political pamphleteering is perhaps a dying art but Members contribute regularly to quarterly, monthly and weekly reviews about matters of contemporary interest. The mass-circulation papers conceive their business to be entertainment rather than instruction, and offer limited scope for articles about politics. Members do, however, talk freely with journalists and may, through them, influence the content of political news and gossip that is published.

In this connection the Lobby correspondents have a pre-eminent role. They are a select band of newspapermen who have the right to enter the Members' Lobby: their task is not to report the debates—which is done by a larger corps of journalists in the Gallery—but to gather information which enables them to forecast, explain and generally comment upon parliamentary affairs. About twenty journalists are admitted to the Lobby and they represent the London dailies, the leading provincial dailies and the 'quality' Sunday newspapers. The tradition is for each Lobby correspondent to be on close terms with a very small number of Members: these relationships are regarded as strictly confidential and it would be dishonourable for a Lobby journalist to disclose the name of a Member who communicated information to him.[3] Intimate contacts of this nature are often facilitated because a number of Members are themselves ex-journalists and have old friends in the profession, and much of the political commentary that appears in the Press has its source in the conversation of Members.

Broadcasting and television are now the most pervasive media of mass communication, and both are subject to some degree of public

---

[1] Labour Member for South Gloucestershire 1950–55.

[2] Member for Birmingham, Aston, 1929–31 and Dundee since 1945.

[3] See Minutes of Evidence, Q. 1525 *et seq*; 1946–47 (138) ix, for a formal statement of the activities of Lobby journalists. This document is the Report of the Committee of Privileges on the Allighan case (see p. 224).

control. The use of the microphone confers at least as much influence as the control of an editor's pen, so it is natural that Members should be sensitive about the character of political programmes. Proposals that any part of parliamentary proceedings should be broadcast have been vigorously opposed; for this there are two good reasons. The addition of a vast, unseen and external audience would seriously damage the intimate character of parliamentary debate. And if a part of debates were transmitted, the problem arises—which part? How could a fair share of time be allocated to the opposing parties, and possibly between front benches and back benches, without destroying the spontaneity of argument? Yet, in relation to other programmes, this sensitivity has had unfortunate results. It formed the stimulus for the 'Fourteen-Day Rule' which imposed limitations on political broadcasting and the liberty of discussion that is central to the health of democracy.

The 'Fourteen-Day Rule' had a curious history,[1] for it originated from a most laudable intention of the B.B.C. to prevent Ministers from securing an improper advantage over their political opponents when introducing contentious legislation in Parliament. The series of events can be said to start with a broadcast by the President of the Board of Education (Mr. R. A. Butler) on the eve of the second reading of the 1944 Education Bill: following this broadcast the Governors of the B.B.C. resolved that 'when a debate on a major matter of public policy is imminent or is actually taking place in Parliament, the B.B.C. cannot allow the broadcasting of Ministerial or other *ex parte* statements thereon'. Matters affecting the war effort were excluded from the operation of this rule. At the end of hostilities the B.B.C. decided to depart from the pre-war policy of avoiding political controversy. Discussions were held with representatives of the major political parties and it was agreed that comment on any legislation passing through Parliament should be barred. In December, 1946, the restriction was extended to cover any topic to be discussed in Parliament. The B.B.C. subsequently found this new principle to be unduly restrictive and, in 1948, a further agreement was reached with representatives of the parties. No discussion or *ex parte* statement was to be broadcast on any topic to be debated in Parliament in the following fortnight; no Member should participate in any discussion on a current Bill; the Budget was to be

[1] Cf. Broadcasting (Anticipation of Debates). Select Committee Report, pp. 23–29; 1955–56 (288) vi.

excluded from these arrangements. Thus, for the first time, Members were placed at a distinct disadvantage. The B.B.C. seems to have been constantly unhappy about this scheme and initiated a number of abortive attempts to modify it. In 1953, the B.B.C. sought to terminate the arrangement, but neither the Government nor the Opposition would agree. Finally, in order to formalize the situation, the B.B.C. asked to be given a direction by the Postmaster-General in accordance with the terms of its Licence; this direction was issued in 1955 and embodied the terms of the 1948 agreement, except that no reference was made to special treatment for the Budget.

The B.B.C. wished to define the position in order to free itself from responsibility for the consequences. The advent of commercial television—which received the same edict—made it important to clarify the restrictions, so that the new competitor should suffer equally. And the issue of the formal direction also served to excite public discussion about the desirability of limiting political controversy. Before 1955, the 'Fourteen-Day Rule' had been applied with a degree of elasticity, especially to the somewhat less serious discussion programmes like 'Any Questions?': rigid use of the rule, after the direction had been received, caused regular last-minute reorganization of programmes. This dislocation drew attention to the existence of the 'gag' and created widespread indignation.

A free vote in the Commons in November, 1955, approved the curb on political broadcasting by 271 votes to 126, but also authorized the establishment of a Select Committee to inquire further into the operation of the limitation. Both parties were deeply divided on this issue, and it is clear that those who upheld the 'Fourteen-Day Rule' did so from a mixture of motives. The Leader of the Opposition (Mr. Attlee) urged that the B.B.C. must not become the mouthpiece of the Government and echoed the spirit of the resolution passed by the Governors in 1944.[1] The main formal argument used was the need to preserve the primacy of Parliament as a forum for public debate; that the authority of Parliament would be undermined if its proceedings were anticipated in sound and television broadcasts. Stripped of their pretensions, what do these assertions mean? Can it be thought that Parliament may suffer real damage if backbenchers broadcast comment on topics due to be debated in the Chamber?[2] If so, Parliament would seem to be a fragile institution.

[1] H.C. Deb., Vol. 546, col. 2340.
[2] Parliamentary fear of radio and television is curiously similar to parlia-

The danger would come only if leading spokesmen of both parties regularly appeared on sound or television on the eve of major parliamentary occasions, for this would mean that major speeches in the House would become a sort of second hearing. A sense of anti-climax might be inevitable. But there is no evidence that the B.B.C. or I.T.A. wish to arrange programmes of this kind: nor is it clear that parliamentary leaders would be willing to participate, for it might be highly embarrassing to have to commit themselves prior to a debate. In any case this possibility could be avoided by some regulation much less draconian than the 'Fourteen-Day Rule'.

There were, however, two other powerful factors at work which strengthened the pressures in favour of restriction. The choice of Members to broadcast inevitably stirs an amount of personal feeling, as some Members are used frequently and others not at all.[1] A regular and successful performer may build a national reputation, and this could conceivably assist promotion to a ministerial post. But again there is little evidence to support the view that the broadcasters of today are the Ministers of tomorrow; except for Dr. C. Hill (Con. and Lib. Luton), who was the 'Radio Doctor', it is not possible to find a Minister who first achieved prominence through broadcasting. The B.B.C. exercises great care in this matter. A Member is never used continuously so that no one should have too much publicity, and this applies even when a Member broadcasts on matters other than politics, e.g., sport.[2] The Radio Doctor won fame long before he entered the Commons, and the B.B.C. cannot be held responsible if any of those whom they employ subsequently develop political ambitions.

Party headquarters also keep a wary and suspicious eye on political broadcasting to ensure that their opponents do not gain any unfair advantage. It is relatively easy to secure an even balance of opinion as between the political parties; the trouble is to arrange for a due proportion of speakers to represent the various shades of opinion within a party. The B.B.C. chooses Members to appear on the basis of their ability as broadcasters and, no doubt, those who

mentary fear of the Press in the eighteenth century. Cf. Francis Williams, *Dangerous Estate*, Ch. III.

[1] During the year ending March, 1956, there were 401 broadcasts on B.B.C. sound and television by a total of 159 Members. Annual Report and Accounts, 1955–56; 1955–56 Cmd. 9803, xi.

[2] Cf. House of Commons Disqualification Bill. Select Committee, Special Report, minutes of evidence, Q. 1598 *et seq*; 1955–56 (349) ix.

are careful to follow the 'party line' are less entertaining than those with unorthodox opinions. As a result it has been under pressure to give greater weight to the official viewpoints in the major parties, and the original panel[1] of the television programme 'In the News' was broken up as it was held to be unrepresentative. At one time the B.B.C. also decided to ration the appearance of those Labour Members associated with the views of Aneurin Bevan.[2] A feeling grew that some Members had been unfairly excluded from broadcasting: allegations on this matter were examined by the Select Committee on Broadcasting (Anticipation of Debates). The Committee found that the B.B.C. had not been subjected to improper influences, and that the pressure exerted by the Whips had been solely directed towards securing a reasonable balance of political views.[3] But it is certain that dislike of political free-lances made the party organizations keener to limit controversial broadcasting.

Granted the combined power of those who wished to sustain the 'Fourteen-Day Rule', why did it come to an end? The severe application of the rule by the B.B.C. after the issue of the direction served to stress the difficulties inherent in its operation. It became clear that any Member could prevent other Members from broadcasting on any subject for the whole of a parliamentary session by the simple expedient of introducing a Bill; the fact that there might be little likelihood of finding time to discuss the measure was irrelevant. An even more serious problem was how the B.B.C. and the I.T.A. were to know the contents of the parliamentary agenda a fortnight in advance, when business for the following week is announced after question-time each Thursday. The answer was that the 'usual channels'—the Whips—would be able to give guidance on topics likely to be discussed within the prohibited period. This, however, implied that broadcasting officials would become better informed about future parliamentary business than the average Member—a situation not conducive to the dignity of Parliament, which the Rule was supposed to conserve. Added to these factors were the constant dislocation of programme arrangements and the widespread public

---

[1] Sir R. Boothby (Con. E. Aberdeenshire); W. J. Brown (Lab. Wolverhampton, West, 1929–31 and Ind. Rugby 1942–50); M. Foot (Lab. Plymouth, Devonport, 1945–55); A. J. P. Taylor.

[2] Broadcasting (Anticipation of Debates). Select Committee Report, Minutes of Evidence. Q. 1096 et seq; 1955–56 (288) vi.

[3] Ibid., paras. 14–15, and Minutes of Evidence, Q. 180 et seq.

objection to the bar to freedom of speech. Further, as events showed, it was not easy to see how the Rule could be upheld in an emergency.

The Select Committee on the Anticipation of Debates was precluded from considering the principle of limitation, and had to confine itself to examining its application in practice. After a review of the difficulties described above, the Committee recommended a major reduction of the restrictions. Limitation on broadcasts should apply only from the time of the formal announcement of future parliamentary business, and should not begin to operate until seven days before the scheduled parliamentary discussion.[1] Members should be treated in the same way as all other persons in regard to these regulations.[2] Even the modified 'Seven-Day Rule' should be flexible and be relaxed at the discretion of the Postmaster-General in particular instances; for this purpose the Postmaster might be advised by a small committee of Members.[3] Before this Report was debated the Suez crisis occurred. Both the Prime Minister (Sir Anthony Eden) and the Leader of the Opposition (Mr. Gaitskell) broadcast their views on the issues involved, which were also being debated regularly in Parliament. Lord Chesham, speaking for the Government, subsequently admitted that these broadcasts were probably a violation of the existing Rule, since Ministerial broadcasts were not exempt.[4] Finally, in December, 1956, the complete abandonment of the Rule for a trial period was announced,[5] and on 25th July, 1957, the Prime Minister (Mr. Macmillan) stated that the suspension of the Rule would continue indefinitely.[6]

The reverse side of the problem of communications between Members and the public is how our elected representatives are to be made aware of movements of opinion in society at large. One solution is the Gallup Poll, but Members probably tend to discount the evidence of these figures especially if it happens to be unfavourable. Members for marginal constituencies are, no doubt, prone to persuasion by indications of a swing of political feeling, and government supporters with slim majorities are the more likely to urge

[1] Ibid., para. 7.
[2] Ibid., para. 9.
[3] Ibid., paras. 11–12.
[4] H.L. Deb., Vol. 200, col. 230.
[5] H.C. Deb., Vol. 562, cols. 1099–1101.
[6] H.C. Deb. Written answer.

Ministers to moderate unpopular policies. Yet the Commons are well aware of the representative character of our democracy: there is little danger that Britain will slip into a form of government dominated by Gallup plebiscites.

Individuals and organizations who wish to press their opinions on Members have the choice of writing letters or attempting to see them in person. The latter process is more difficult, but also more satisfying. Enthusiasts for a particular cause often assemble at Westminster and try to gain admission to the Central Lobby where they ask for their local Members. Professional lobbyists of the Washington type are fortunately unknown in this country where lobbying, although organized, is essentially amateur. If a deputation is too large, mass lobbying cannot proceed smoothly, and not all those who wish to reach the Central Lobby may be able to do so: big numbers are more likely to lead to unpleasant incidents than to reasoned argument. But smaller groups of twenty to thirty can be accommodated without difficulty, and are well received by Members, who recognize the value and importance of the right to lobby. A constituent who comes to Westminster without an appointment has no guarantee that his Member will be available to meet him. Further, a Member who is in the Palace, and who is not otherwise engaged, need not appear to talk with anyone who asks for him, whether the caller has arrived alone or as part of a group. One Scottish Member has declared that in thirty years' experience he has never felt disturbed by any incident of lobbying. 'If there is a crowd in the Central Lobby—I just walk through it.'[1]

Mass lobbying seems to be on the increase.[2] When an industry is adversely affected by government action or is threatened by economic recession, it is common for shop stewards to come to the parliament buildings urging remedial measures. The British Peace Committee has organized a steady flow of deputations of considerable size. Questions of equal pay and pensions stimulate much lobbying; representatives of old age pensioners, spinsters, ex-servicemen, teachers and civil servants have congregated to urge their claims on Members. In particular, the London Schoolmasters' Association and the British Limbless Ex-Service Men's Association have made many appearances in the Lobby; in 1954 some 180 bakers and confectioners came to raise the issue of night baking; between 1949

[1] *The Times*, 30th November, 1955.
[2] Ibid.

and 1952 London taximen protested about the number of taxi licences issued. The activities of the National Union of Bank Employees show how successful this kind of pressure can be in arousing interest among Members. In May, 1957, a strong deputation urged Members that the Union should be the recognized negotiating body for bank employees; subsequently T. Leather (Con. N. Somerset) and A. Robens (Lab. Blyth) called a meeting attended by 250 Members at which the case of the N.U.B.E. was put in more detail. Over-efficient lobbying may have a reverse effect to that intended by the organizers. The intense efforts of the National Union of Teachers, through the post and by journeys to Westminster, over the changes in their superannuation scheme were said by *The Economist* to have stiffened Members' resistance to these entreaties, lest any success should provoke other associations into arranging a similar barrage. *The Economist* approved of this development: 'At a time when there is far too much government by pressure group, this first faint sign of some kicking against the pricks is an attitude to be encouraged.'[1] Yet the real brake on the influence of sectional interests is party discipline; it is rare to be able to persuade a Member to vote against a firm policy decision by his own party. In 1949, after much activity by local branches of the British Legion, a total of 272 Members agreed to support the Legion's claim for a Select Committee to consider the problem of pensions; but after the Government opposed the establishment of such a Committee only 149 Members remained to support it in the division lobby.[2] Growing realization of the effect of the Whips has caused some transfer of pressures from Members to Government Departments: trade associations now concentrate their efforts in Whitehall rather than Westminster.[3]

Many of the deputations that come to the Commons arrive with petitions that specify their grievances. These are now presented to the House by a Member after prayers and before questions commence: since 1836 no discussion has taken place on a petition at the time of presentation.[4] The volume of these protests fluctuates greatly. The largest petitions are those sponsored by powerful organizations: the entertainment industry collected over three million signatures to

[1] 10th December, 1955, p. 924.
[2] G. Wootton, *The Official History of the British Legion*, p. 290.
[3] Political and Economic Planning: *Industrial Trade Associations*, pp. 87–88.
[4] For a full discussion of this topic see Colin Leys, 'Petitioning in the Nineteenth and Twentieth Centuries', *Political Studies*, Vol. III, pp. 45–64.

protest against the increase in entertainments tax in 1950–51, the Automobile Association had over two million supporters of its petition on petrol taxation in 1948 and pensioners' societies gathered over a million signatures in 1946. Another notable example was the demand for the prohibition of atomic weapons which amassed above a million and a quarter names in 1950–51. By itself petitioning is not an effective method of bringing pressure to bear on governments; it does, however, promote discussion of a grievance and obtains further publicity. And if petitions form no more than a fragmentary link between Members and the public, they are a concrete and harmless focus for agitation.

9

Members and their Interests

The interests of Honourable Members must, in great measure, depend on the sorts of people who are elected to the House of Commons. This, in turn, rests on the choices of constituency selection committees. But the outlook of Members is also affected by factors that need play no part in the process of local nomination— their sources of income, their previous experience and their personal or non-political enthusiasms. Full information about the private lives of Members is not available, and it follows that no complete analysis of Members' interests can be attempted. Yet a study of the standard works of reference does reveal both a similarity of background among certain groups of Members and the great diversity of their connections. There must be few types of activity in Great Britain that cannot find, when necessary, a friend in the Commons.

Much of Chapter 1 on the selection of candidates is relevant to the present discussion, but need not be repeated here. The opinions of Members are affected by their age, sex, education, social status and the like. And if a Member is nominated by a particular organization, it is also reasonable to suppose that he will reflect the attitude of the sponsoring body on issues which concern the latter. Thus, the interests of trade unions will never be overlooked in a House of which nearly a hundred Members are union nominees; the voice of the miners will always be heard, and so will the views of the other large unions. In 1955, the number of union nominees elected was 96, the lowest since the parliament of 1935–45. Of these the National Union of Mineworkers sponsored thirty-four, the Transport and General Workers Union, fourteen, the Union of Shop, Distributive and Allied Workers, nine, the National Union of Railwaymen, eight, the Amalgamated Engineering Union, six, the Transport Salaried Staffs Association, five, and the National Union of General

183

and Municipal Workers, four. A few associations other than unions affiliated to the T.U.C. also have political funds that may be used to give financial assistance to parliamentary candidates. The British Medical Association has such a fund, but details of its management are not available for publication.[1] The National Farmers' Union has a similar fund which, however, appears to be largely unused: at the end of 1956 it amounted to no less than £87,000, but the N.F.U. have not given any financial assistance at elections since 1945. The National Union of Teachers have a scheme under which they may contribute not more than 50% of the election expenses of up to four candidates from each of the Conservative, Liberal and Labour Parties, subject to a maximum of £400. In 1955, six candidates aided by the N.U.T. were elected—J. C. Ede (Lab. South Shields), W. G. Cove (Lab. Aberavon), J. C. Jennings (Con. Burton), Dr. H. M. King (Lab. Southampton, Itchen), I. J. Pitman (Con. Bath) and T. G. Thomas (Lab. Cardiff, West). The Co-operative Movement also sponsors parliamentary candidates, but in this case the position is somewhat different because the Co-operative Party is a separate political organization. Under an agreement made in 1946 between the Labour Party and the Co-operative Party, it was possible for constituencies to nominate joint Labour and Co-operative candidates; in these constituencies the co-operative movement makes a major contribution to Labour election expenditure. In 1957, when there were twenty Labour and Co-operative Members, the Labour Party terminated the 1946 agreement because *inter alia* other sections of the Labour Movement were jealous of the strength of Co-operative representation within the Parliamentary Labour Party.[2]

In addition to assistance in meeting election costs it is common for trade unions to give their Members other forms of help, which include direct monetary payments, reimbursement of travelling and other expenses incurred as a result of parliamentary duties, the provision of clerical and research facilities. The monetary payments are modest in amount; they varied between £50 per annum and £200 per annum in 1956.[3] It would, of course, be utterly improper

[1] The annual statement of accounts of the B.M.A. contains no reference to the political fund. Cf. the Supplement to the *British Medical Journal*, dated 25th May, 1957.

[2] At the time of writing a new agreement between the Labour Party and the Co-operative Party is under negotiation.

[3] B. C. Roberts, *Trade Union Government and Administration in Great Britain*, p. 387.

and a breach of parliamentary privilege if the unions attempted to influence the conduct of Members by financial means. These payments are, and must be, entirely *ex gratia*,[1] or else be made for services unconnected with parliamentary business. Equally, it would be idle to deny that such aid does strengthen the link between the sponsored candidates and the unions. One illustration of the frank recognition of this link is the practice adopted at the annual conferences of the National Union of Mineworkers and the Amalgamated Society of Woodworkers where a parliamentary report is presented by, or on behalf of, the Members sponsored by these unions.[2] The relationship that exists between the trade unions and the political side of the Labour movement is ambivalent; although the unions are keen to have strong parliamentary representation, they are equally determined not to be dominated by parliamentarians. When serious labour disputes are discussed in the Commons it is notable that Labour Members seem to have little to say that is definitive or constructive. The reason is simple. It is clearly understood in Labour circles that the conduct of strikes and wage negotiations is the business of the union leaders, not of politicians. When the Labour group of Trade Union Members appointed younger and more energetic officers, G. Brown (Belper) and C. Pannell (Leeds, West), it is reported that the late Arthur Deakin, Secretary of the Transport and General Workers Union, attended a meeting to explain to the group the proper limits of its functions.[3] Another symptom of this combination of love and fear is that most unions do not permit Members to sit on their executive committees,[4] and many unions also restrict the right of their full-time officials to become parliamentary candidates.[5] Yet not all unions share this distrust and the Parliament elected in 1955 contained four Labour Members who were also general secretaries of smaller unions— R. Edwards (Bilston), D. Houghton (Sowerby), Sir T. O'Brien (Nottingham, West) and A. Palmer (Cleveland). Two other Labour Members, E. Gooch (Norfolk, North) and W. Padley (Ogmore), were the Presidents respectively of the National Union

---

[1] See pp. 226–8.

[2] B. C. Roberts, *op. cit.*, p. 187.

[3] S. Jacobsen and W. Connor, 'The Trade Unions and Parliament', reprinted in *Parliamentary Affairs*, Vol. IX, pp. 470–7.

[4] V. L. Allen, *Power in Trade Unions*, p. 152.

[5] Ibid., pp. 244–5.

of Agricultural Workers and the Union of Shop, Distributive and Allied Workers.

On the Conservative side of the House the predominant occupation is that of company direction. An examination of the *Directory of Directors* for 1956 reveals the following information about Members elected at the 1955 general election.

MEMBERS ENGAGED IN COMPANY DIRECTION

Party	Number of Members	Number of Companies
Conservative	92	402
Labour	6	16
Liberal	1	1
Totals	99	419[1]

But the figures in the table under-estimate quite considerably the extent to which Members are concerned with the control of business because the *Directory* does not cover all private firms. In consequence, it does not include the names of many Conservative Members who are described as company directors in other works of reference such as *Who's Who* and *The Times House of Commons*.[2] When considering the proportion of Conservative Members engaged in this form of activity, two other factors must be remembered. In 1955 some seventy Conservatives were ineligible to be directors because they held ministerial office: unwillingness to sacrifice directors' fees has led some Conservatives to refuse offers to join the Government. Secondly, directorships tend to be gathered with advancing years, together with accretions of wealth, contacts and experience. After an election there is an influx of new and relatively young Conservative Members, many of whom have not yet been introduced into board rooms, but who will certainly be in them as time passes.

The range of business concerns with which Members are associated is extremely wide. It covers all the major sections of industry and commerce including, for example, banking, insurance, aircraft, motors, brewing, publishing and various forms of engineering. Less

[1] This figure includes a small element of double counting because a few concerns have more than one Member on their boards of directors.

[2] According to J. F. S. Ross, *Elections and Electors*, p. 442, in the 1951 Parliament 142 Conservative and 25 Labour Members were company directors. These figures include companies too small to be noticed by the *Directory*.

obvious items on the list are cremation and greyhound racing. A spokesman in the House is usually available for most large-scale forms of trading activity. The world of business—in the same way as the trade unions—keeps a watchful eye on all projected developments in public policy, and, when appropriate, sympathetic Members are carefully briefed. The Federation of British Industries regularly approaches Members in this way.[1]

It is clear that both employers and employed are abundantly represented in the Commons. So also are other social groupings. A wide variety of voluntary organizations, actively concerned to influence state policy on particular issues, have their headquarters in London and are in regular touch with one or more Members. What is more natural than for an association for the Prevention of X or the Encouragement of Y to ask a Member, interested in these objects, to become a Vice-President or to serve on an Executive Committee? This is a sensible and desirable extension of the representative nature of the House of Commons, for it enables Members to put the viewpoint, not merely of constituencies, but also of specific ideals and causes. Frequently these are matters that do not arise in party political controversy. A sectional pressure group must not be regarded as something evil or even sinister; it is merely a body of persons which endeavours to make its opinions effective. Whether pressure is improper or undesirable depends on the methods used to achieve influence, and the process of lobbying those elected to a legislature scarcely deserves condemnation. The wider the range of Members' interests and the fuller their information, the better can Parliament perform its function as the Grand Inquest of the Nation. There is a danger that unorganized opinion will go by default, but this is unlikely to happen in the House of Commons where normally some Member is always ready with an opposing argument.

No detailed analysis can be made of the extent to which Members are connected with the myriad of voluntary associations, but it is possible to sketch the broad categories into which these associations fall. The simplest classification is between the selfish groups and the 'do-gooders'. The National Federation of Property Owners seeks to achieve economic advantage for a limited section of the community, while the R.S.P.C.A. may fairly be termed altruistic. But this distinction is open to challenge. Such bodies as the Association of

[1] Cf. S. E. Finer, 'The Federation of British Industries', in *Political Studies*, Vol. IV, p. 61 *et seq.*

British Chambers of Commerce and the National Union of Manufacturers may urge that the prosperity of traders and industrialists is vital to the well-being of our society as a whole. Further, there could well be disagreement on whether professional, religious and other organizations were selfish in their objects—for example, the Association of University Teachers, the Lord's Day Observance Society and the Automobile Association. A fuller classification of pressure groups would recognize the distinction between purely economic interests, professional aims, women's organizations, regional and ethnic groups, governmental organizations (for example, the Association of Municipal Corporations and the County Councils Association), religious bodies and humanitarian associations.[1] All these types of groups attempt to claim the attention of Members, frequently by the dispatch of circulars that go quickly to the waste-paper basket. But a Member who is active in support of a pressure group can be used in many ways; apart from speaking in the House or in Standing Committee, he can put down questions designed to attract public attention, if not a favourable response, and facilitate the making of direct representations to a Minister. In the case of the female campaign for equal pay 'M.P.s sometimes led deputations to Ministers. . . . Usually, however, M.P.s played little part in the deputation; their chief service was to help to gain access to Ministers who often refused to see the (Equal Pay Campaign) Committee.'[2] Many of the Bills introduced by backbenchers through the ballot or under the Ten-Minute Rule are also inspired by organizations with an axe to grind.

What induces Members to busy themselves at the behest of interest groups? No clear assessment of the motives of six hundred odd individuals can be made, but an argument is not advanced insincerely merely because it happens to coincide with the economic connections of the advocate. It is natural that a teacher should urge the need for more spending on schools; that a motor manufacturer should press the claim for better roads; that an ex-miner should demand improvement in welfare facilities for miners. So long as Members believe in the justice of the proposals they put forward, these activities are a healthy development of the democratic process.

[1] Cf. Allen Potter, 'British Pressure Groups', *Parliamentary Affairs*, Vol. IX, p. 421.

[2] Allen Potter, 'The Equal Pay Campaign Committee', *Political Studies*, Vol. V, p. 57.

Venality can exist in any powerful assembly. The danger is recognized by the Standing Order of the Commons that no motion to impose a charge on public revenues be proceeded with without the consent of the Crown: this prevents Members from introducing measures which would be of direct financial benefit to their constituents or some other limited group of persons. Another provision is that no Member may take part in a division if he has a direct pecuniary interest in the result. But owing to a ruling by Speaker Abbot in 1812, this restriction is applied very narrowly: it does not extend to any issue of public policy, and to be barred from voting a Member's interest must be immediate and personal. Thus it is very difficult to challenge the validity of a vote on grounds of financial interest; Labour Members discovered this in 1953 when they queried whether certain Conservatives should be permitted to vote on the Bill to institute commercial television.[1] Nor is it improper for a Member to ask a question because he has a financial interest in the answer. There has been a somewhat nebulous tradition that a Member who intervenes in debate should declare a personal interest if he has one. Sir Winston Churchill has put it thus: 'It is always the understood thing in the House that everybody makes himself perfectly safe by declaring any special interest he has in any matter about which he speaks.'[2] In practice this rule of conduct is not followed by Members for the reason given by Speaker Morrison: 'If on every separate Question an Hon. Member declared his interest it would be very difficult to carry on.'[3] Declarations of interest are made not to obviate allegations of impropriety, but to establish a claim to special experience of the subject of discussion. The following statement by Dr. Broughton (Lab. Batley and Morley) is an excellent example: 'In my constituency there is a café which is run by a small company of which I am one of the directors. In saying that, I declare a personal interest and at the same time lay claim to a little knowledge in this field.'[4]

The rules of the Commons, by themselves, play but a small part in establishing a standard of conduct for Members. Far more im-

[1] H.C. Deb., Vol. 522, col. 206 *et seq.*

[2] Cf. *Parliamentary Affairs*, Vol. X, p. 324.

[3] H.C. Deb., Vol. 522, col. 994.

[4] H.C. Deb., Vol. 530, col. 1793. This and other useful quotations are cited by Frank C. Newman, 'Reflections on Money and Party Politics in Great Britain'; *Parliamentary Affairs*, Vol. X, pp. 308–32.

portant are four other factors; the traditions of British public life, the prevalence of the non-conformist conscience, the over-riding demands of party loyalty and the resistance of the Civil Service to claims for special treatment. Of these, it is arguable that the impartiality of the Civil Service is the most effective safeguard. Members have influence, but they do not command the power of the executive: if they wish to seek favours, they must negotiate with those who can make decisions. It is significant that Mr. Stanley directed his activities towards Ministers and not to backbenchers.[1] Men who enjoy economic security are less likely to abuse a position of authority for personal gain, and if Members do not suffer pressing financial needs an element of strain is removed. To quote W. Elliot in a debate on Members' pay: 'There is also a tendency towards the "kept men" in this House, and a House composed entirely of "kept men" would be dangerous, especially if men are kept by bodies able to pay more than the State is willing to pay for their services. . . . We pay a cashier very much more than other people . . . because we put a heavy strain on his honesty which it would be dangerous for us to make too heavy.'[2] The Commons is no longer a largely patrician assembly and it is important to recognize that possibilities of temptation exist; in addition, the scope for temptation widens as the machinery of state plays an increasing role in the direction of the nation's economy.

The case of W. J. Brown[3] in 1947 attracted public attention to the question of the connections between Members and outside organizations. But this incident arose from the strained relationships between Brown and the C.S.C.A., and the peculiar nature of the contract that existed between them. It was, therefore, rather separated from the core of the problem. If Members manage their private affairs discreetly and keep on good terms with their sources of income, embarrassing publicity will be avoided. The influence of money in politics will not be eliminated by regulation, and it is well that the House has not acted on Brown's own suggestion that it should be 'obligatory upon Members to disclose the nature of any such rela-

---

[1] Cf. Report of the Lynskey Tribunal; 1948–49 Cmd. 7616, xviii.

[2] H.C. Deb., Vol. 530, col. 75. Walter Elliot was Conservative Member for Lanark 1918–23, Scottish Universities 1946–50, and Glasgow, Kelvingrove, 1924–45 and 1950–57. The problem of the remuneration of Members is discussed in Ch. 13.

[3] See p. 227.

tionships to their constituents and to this House'.[1] It would be difficult to define precisely the type of agreement that involved publicity; the edict might also be avoided by a sufficient combination of ingenuity and informality. Positions of authority are always a possible gateway to financial advantage, but there is no evidence either that Honourable Members are corrupt, in the crude sense of that term, or that they are deflected from what they conceive to be their duty by considerations of self-interest.

[1] H.C. Deb., Vol. 440, col. 303.

191

10

Private Members' Time

The growth of the activities of the State, the authority of the Cabinet and of party discipline have together steadily increased Government dominance of the parliamentary timetable. Backbenchers now determine the character of business on but twenty Fridays during the session: these Fridays are known as 'private members' time'. At the commencement of the nineteenth century one day a week was reserved for the Government, in 1837 the Government took a second day, and in 1852 a third day. Further restrictions on the initiative of backbenchers came in 1902 when it was agreed that Government business should have precedence at all sittings, except on some Fridays and on half of certain Tuesdays and Wednesdays. A further rearrangement in 1927 gave private Members precedence on about eight Wednesdays and thirteen Fridays.[1] Even this slim ration could be abolished in any session if the Cabinet, backed by the Whips, demanded the whole time of the House, as in 1928–29, 1931–32 and 1934–35. In the 1914–18 war virtually no time was found for private Members and in 1939–45 there was none at all. Pressure of reconstruction legislation in each of the first three postwar sessions 1945–48 again involved the sacrifice of the opportunities of Members, but they did not surrender their rights without protest.[2] In 1945 A. P. Herbert[3] threw a bundle of thirteen Bills, fully drafted and ready for presentation, on to the floor of the House to add colour to his objections to the motion which gave absolute priority to the Government. On the Labour benches there was also much regret at

---

[1] Sir W. I. Jennings, *Parliament*, p. 110.

[2] Cf. H.C. Deb., Vol. 413, col. 133 *et seq.*, Vol. 430, col. 93 *et seq.*, and Vol. 443, col. 88 *et seq.*

[3] Independent Member for Oxford University 1935–50; see his *Independent Member*, pp. 374–6.

the continued loss of private members' time, and each year R. Stokes[1] hoped for better things next session. Finally in the session 1948–49 the Government relented slightly and allowed ten Fridays for private members' Bills, but no time was made available for unofficial motions. In the brief session of 1950 five Fridays were allowed for private members' motions and in each session since backbenchers have had the use of twenty Fridays, ten for Bills and ten for motions.[2] It is peculiar that the Standing Orders governing private members' business introduced in 1927 still remain, but in each session since 1939 their operation has been suspended by a sessional order.

Members ballot for the use of their twenty Fridays: a single ballot is held soon after the commencement of the session for the right to introduce Bills, but a separate ballot is held sixteen days before each Friday allocated to motions. The Fridays are devoted to Bills and motions alternately so a ballot to introduce motions is held fortnightly during the greater part of the session. The first six Fridays for Bills are occupied by second reading debates, and the remaining four are given to those Bills that have already advanced furthest along the road to the statute book; the highest priority goes to any Bill for which Lords' amendments are awaiting consideration, and the lowest priority is any Bill the second reading of which is not completed. This is to ensure that Bills which have most nearly finished the parliamentary journey shall not be lost through shortage of time.[3]

There exist two methods of introducing Bills other than by obtaining a place in the ballot, but they offer little prospect of time for discussion and, therefore, of ultimate enactment, unless they are exceptionally uncontroversial. Under Standing Order No. 35 a Member may present a Bill without obtaining leave from the House and the Bill shall be read a first time without any questions being put and shall be printed. Bills introduced in this way are termed Unballoted Bills. They receive no further consideration unless one of three things takes place: it is allowed an unopposed second reading

---

[1] Labour Member for Ipswich 1938–57.

[2] Except in 1954–55 when part of this time was lost because of the dissolution of Parliament in April, 1955.

[3] In accordance with the recommendations of the Select Committee on Procedure in their Third Report, para. 51; 1945–46 (189–1) ix. The Report also proposed a single combined ballot for Bills and motions in which Members would have the choice of presenting a Bill or a motion and of an appropriate Friday, according to their precedence in the ballot.

—the Government provides time for it to be debated—or all balloted Bills down for discussion on any Friday are disposed of before the end of the sitting. The second and third possibilities are highly unlikely, but five Bills became law under the first possibility in the period 1950–55. A Member who hopes to get an unopposed second reading will bring forward his Bill at the close of the main debate on a Friday, but the attempt will fail if any other Member says the single word 'Object'. It is, therefore, essential to conciliate all interested parties, including the Department(s) concerned, before a Bill is brought forward in this way.

This method of introducing Bills, withdrawn in 1939, was restored on a Government proposal in November, 1950. The other means whereby private Members may initiate legislation, the Ten-Minute Rule, was also restored in November, 1950, through a Government defeat on the issue by 235 votes to 229.[1] Under the Ten-Minute Rule (Standing Order No. 12) a Member may introduce a Bill at the end of question-time on Tuesdays or Wednesdays with a short speech not exceeding ten minutes. A single speech of similar length may also be made in opposition, and then the motion for leave to introduce the Bill is put. The Bill may be unopposed or there may be a division: if the Bill is unopposed, or is successful in a division, it is available for further consideration in the same ways that apply to the unballoted Bills described in the previous paragraph. In the period 1950–55 eight Bills introduced under the Ten-Minute Rule reached the statute book, seven of which obtained an unopposed second reading, while the eighth, the Slaughter of Pigs Bill, 1953, introduced by Brigadier Rayner[2] was sufficiently fortunate to obtain time for discussion on a Friday after business on balloted Bills had been concluded.[3]

Two quite separate purposes may be served by the Ten-Minute Rule. The short speech that it permits a Member to make may succeed in satisfying any opponents to his measure and may smooth the path towards an unopposed second reading. Alternatively, it permits a Member to make a demonstration on some more controversial topic in the hope that the interest and support aroused by the brief introduction may improve the chances of legislative action in a subse-

[1] H.C. Deb., Vol. 480, col. 976.

[2] Conservative Member for Totnes 1935–55.

[3] P. A. Bromhead, *Private Members' Bills in the British Parliament*, Appendix E, describes in detail the passage of these Bills from 1948 to 1954.

quent session. Sydney Silverman (Lab. Nelson and Colne) twice used the Ten-Minute Rule to bring in a Bill to abolish the death penalty. On 1st July, 1953, leave to introduce the Bill was refused by 256 votes to 195; on 15th November, 1955, leave was given without a division[1] and Government time was subsequently made available for further discussion. This Bill has now become the most famous private member's Bill of the post-war period and is discussed fully in Chapter 6.

The Ten-Minute Rule procedure introduces an attractive element of flexibility into the parliamentary time-table. When it results in a division, the Whips are not on and, indeed, party leaders have had little time to consider their attitude to the proposal. On a Bill that cuts across the lines of party controversy, both sides may be hopelessly divided: Sir Edward Keeling[2] obtained leave to introduce the Death of the Speaker Bill by 172 votes to 149, but only half of the votes cast in his support came from his Conservative colleagues.[3] A good attendance is assured because the discussion takes place normally within half an hour of the end of question-time. The Ten-Minute Rule does give the backbencher an admirable opportunity to command the attention of the House: there is no need to win a place in a ballot, and a better audience is available than for an adjournment motion.

To introduce a Bill under the ballot is, of course, the main opportunity for the backbencher to initiate legislation, but the obstacles in his path are formidable. Each session twenty Bills are brought in under the ballot while between 250 and 300 Members compete for the right to be among the twenty.[4] It follows that a Member who enters the ballot with a passionate desire to legislate on some subject will find that his chances of winning a place are rather worse than one in twelve. Not all Members who enter the ballot have a Bill that they wish to introduce; if they have the good fortune to win a place they can obtain a Bill either from the Whips or from a Member imbued with reforming zeal who was unlucky in the draw. A. P. Herbert has given this description of how he secured the intro-

[1] H.C. Deb., Vol. 517, col. 414 and Vol. 546, col. 210.

[2] Conservative Member for Twickenham 1935–55.

[3] H.C. Deb., Vol. 511, col. 2095.

[4] P.A. Bromhead, *Private Members' Bills in the British Parliament*, p. 21.This book contains a full account of the procedural difficulties facing private members' legislation.

duction of his Matrimonial Clauses Bill by Sir Rupert, then Mr., De la Bère.

'Two other Members with Bills in their beaks descended on us and tried to carry him off. But I was able to claim priority and bullied them away. He, too, already had a Bill in his hand, an innocent little thing about municipal elections, which the Whips had given him. My heart sank when I saw that: but I did not know Mr. De la Bère.'[1]

Sir Alan was indeed fortunate for he had been unacquainted with De la Bère before this meeting, and his colleague-to-be had won second place in the ballot, hence any measure he introduced was certain to be discussed. As noted above, six Fridays are devoted to the second readings of Bills and three or four fall to be considered on each of these days: if the debate on the first Bill occupies the whole of the time available, the other Bills due to be discussed on that day go to the end of the queue and will almost certainly die for lack of time. Alternatively, the time left for the second (or third) Bill may be too brief for any reasonable discussion of it to take place, and the Bill will be 'talked out' without any decision having been reached. Only Members who secure one of the first six places in the ballot are guaranteed a full hearing, although probably not more than five out of the twenty Bills fail to obtain any attention at all. It is possible that the debate on the first Bill will be unnecessarily prolonged in order to obstruct the passage of another and highly controversial Bill due for examination on the same day. Another problem is to keep the House in session. On Fridays the call of constituencies and the week-end encourage Members to be absent from Westminster. A Member introducing a Bill must do his own 'whipping' to keep his supporters present; if a count is called and less than forty Members are available, the rest of the day will be lost, even if the Bills on the Order Paper command virtually unanimous support. One example can be used to illustrate both these difficulties. The debate on the Intestates' Estates Bill, a measure that commanded general agreement, was prolonged to block the introduction by T. Steele (Lab. Dunbartonshire, West) of the Housing (Temporary Prohibition of Sale) (Scotland) Bill, designed to prevent the sale of council houses in

---

[1] A. P. Herbert, *The Ayes Have It*, p. 84. R. De la Bère was Conservative Member for Evesham 1935–50 and South Worcestershire 1950–55. Sir Alan's unsuccessful attempt to find a Member to introduce his Bill on Newfoundland in 1948 is described in *Independent Member*, pp. 425–8.

Scotland: in revenge, Labour Members successfully called a count and the Intestates' Estates Bill failed to get a second reading.[1]

Even when a Bill is supported by a majority of Members present, it is sometimes difficult to obtain a decision on the second reading, for its opponents will keep the debate going to try and avoid a vote. If no decision is reached by four o'clock, the Bill is 'talked out' and it is improbable that time will be available for further consideration. The sponsor of the Bill can claim to move that 'the question be now put', but the Speaker may refuse the motion if he is of the opinion that the Bill has not been adequately discussed. Alternatively, if the motion is put and carried by a majority, it still needs one hundred Members in support to be successful. On 17th February, 1956, R. Mason (Lab. Barnsley) moved the closure in an attempt to obtain a second reading for his National Insurance (Industrial Injuries) Bill; the vote in favour of the closure was 87 to 60, but the Bill was lost because its supporters were thirteen short of the necessary hundred.[2]

Apart from these technical difficulties of obtaining a decision on a second reading, there is the further problem of attempting to ensure that the decision will be favourable. At this stage the fate of a Bill depends on two factors—its general character and the quality of the preliminary negotiations undertaken with interested parties. The more important the subject of a Bill and the wider its scope, the more likely it is to arouse objections from sectional interests, other Members and Ministers. If a sponsor is able to announce that he has the support of the appropriate outside bodies and the Government indicates something approaching benevolent neutrality, his Bill may obtain a second reading without a division. Measures to strengthen the law on prevention of cruelty to animals frequently come into this category. The more unexciting a Bill, the better are its chances of survival. Introducing his Small Lotteries and Gaming Bill, Ernest Davies (Lab. Enfield, East) stated the position with clarity.

'When a private Member is fortunate enough to draw a place in the Ballot for Private members' Bills he is faced with the problem of whether to introduce a Bill which may not have much chance of getting through the House but is on a major issue and will give an opportunity for debate. On the other hand, he may prefer to intro-

---

[1] H.C. Deb., Vol. 498, cols. 1077–1147. The Intestates' Estates Bill was subsequently allowed to go forward as an unopposed Bill and ultimately was passed into law.

[2] H.C. Deb., Vol. 548, col. 2766.

duce a Measure which represents some urgently needed reform which is perhaps not sufficiently important for the Government themselves to undertake or which the Government, for some reason, might have refrained from undertaking. If such a Bill can be of a non-party character and largely non-controversial, it has that much better opportunity of reaching the Statute Book.'[1]

In the inter-war period there was a marked tendency for Labour Members to introduce measures of a partisan character that led inevitably to their defeat in a division that took place on party lines. Since 1948 Labour Members have tended to introduce Bills of a non-political character. A Government must be expected to use its influence against Bills which represent a direct challenge to its policy, although the fate of the Cabinet is not brought into question by a defeat in private members' time. If Government hostility fails to kill a Bill at the second reading, it normally prevails at a later stage. The Industrial Rating Bill obtained a second reading in March, 1956, after a division in which the Labour Opposition obtained a majority of 21 (104 to 83), but the Conservatives managed to secure its defeat on the third reading by 179 votes to 134.[2] The Government may also experience difficulties with Bills sponsored by their own supporters, witness the combination of Labour Ministers and Conservatives needed to defeat the Hairdressers (Registration) Bill in 1949.[3]

The second reading is the major hurdle but a Bill that has surmounted it can be either amended or obstructed in committee. In 1957 the Maintenance Orders (Attachment of Income) Bill, introduced by Miss J. Vickers (Con. Plymouth, Devonport) was killed by the refusal of Members to provide a quorum at the committee stage. One Standing Committee is wholly devoted to private members' Bills but the Committees must work with speed if all such Bills are to obtain consideration before the last of the Fridays allocated to them.[4] The Pools Betting Act, 1954, sponsored by F. Mulley (Lab. Sheffield, Park), underwent important changes in

---

[1] H.C. Deb., Vol. 546, cols. 1811–12.

[2] H.C. Deb., Vol. 550, cols. 783 and 2223. The Bill was not initiated entirely as a party measure for the second reading was seconded by F. Harris (Con. Croydon, North-West). Harris voted in favour of the second reading but failed to record a vote on the motion for the third reading.

[3] H.C. Deb., Vol. 466, col. 1733 and Bromhead, Appendix B.

[4] A Select Committee on Procedure has proposed that the quorum at the private members' bills Committee be lowered from 14 to 12 of its 35 Members. Second Report, para. 5; 1956–57 (211).

committee that made it more acceptable to the promoters of football pools. The National Insurance Benefits Act, 1956, which raised the limit of earnings retired persons could attain without loss of benefit, was amended in the committee stage to incorporate the recommendations of the National Insurance Advisory Committee on this subject which the Government had decided to accept.[1] Virtually, a private member's Bill was turned into a vehicle for promoting Cabinet policy. A Standing Committee may kill a Bill altogether by reporting adversely on each of the clauses, as happened in 1951 to the Road Transport Bill of J. R. Bevins (Con. Liverpool, Toxteth). It is also possible that the sponsor of a Bill may think it wise to withdraw the measure at the committee stage: Mrs. White (Lab. East Flintshire) took this course in 1951 with her Matrimonial Causes Bill for, owing to Cabinet hostility, it had no real chance of being passed, and the Government had offered to set up a Royal Commission on the subject.

The chief menace to Bills on the Report stage and third reading is shortage of time on the four Fridays now devoted to the later stages of private members' Bills. Obstruction is less likely at the third reading for the Speaker is more willing to put the question after a short debate. Except in unusual circumstances, as when a Bill obtained a second reading contrary to the wishes of the Government, the third reading is carried without difficulty. Once through the Commons the last hurdle is the Lords, but before the rejection of the Abolition of the Death Penalty Bill in 1956, the Upper House had not refused to pass a private member's Bill for a quarter of a century. The timetable of their Lordships' House is sufficiently flexible to accommodate all Bills sent up to them with a minimum of delay. The Lords frequently amend private members' Bills and often amended Bills are returned to the Commons after the last Friday for them has passed; when this occurs the Government normally provides the time necessary for the consideration of the Lords' amendments.

It is clear that for a backbencher to become the author of an Act of Parliament he must have obtained general support for his proposals. He also needs a little luck and, possibly, some outside aid. The task of drafting a Bill is highly technical, and many Members would not feel competent to undertake it without assistance. The legal profession is heavily represented in the House, and a Member may obtain help in formulating his Bill from a colleague; less often

[1] H.C. Deb., Vol. 552, cols. 845–50 and 1573 *et seq.*

the Government may be willing to make the services of parliamentary draftsmen available. A third source of aid can be a voluntary society that is interested in the contents of the measure, and the source of inspiration for some measures comes entirely from such associations; the volume of legislation concerning the protection of animals is not unconnected with the R.S.P.C.A. Some of the outside influence is clearly economic in character. Sir Ivor Jennings has described the efforts of N.A.L.G.O. before 1937 to promote legislation to obtain superannuation rights for local government officials.[1] If a Member agrees to adopt a Bill prepared by outside experts, or one obtained from the Whips, he will save himself the troubles of drafting his measure.

The activities of pressure groups in this field are limited, however, by the Standing Order which forbids the introduction of any proposal to spend public money other than on the recommendation of the Crown. Only the Government, therefore, can bring in a Bill which seeks to impose a charge on the national revenues. If a private member's Bill implies incidentally an amount of State expenditure, it can proceed only if an appropriate resolution is moved in Committee of the whole House by a Minister. This is a most valuable safeguard against any abuse by Members of their right to introduce Bills, for it eliminates the possibility of their trying to obtain special facilities for their constituents or other sectional interests by this means. In the past this limitation has not applied to any Bill which would increase the rate-borne expenditure of local authorities but, with the growth of central financial assistance to local authorities, increased local expenditure usually has repercussions on the Exchequer. It is accepted, however, that the Government will not normally refuse a money resolution on these grounds.[2]

Hence to succeed a private member's Bill should conform to certain principles. It must not spend public money; it must be generally acceptable to Ministers; it must not be so wide in scope or so controversial as to irritate interested parties into organizing determined parliamentary opposition. Because of these restrictions the legislation initiated by private Members tends to fall into two broad categories: reforms of a legal nature and the regulation of social (or anti-social) activities. Not all private Members feel inhibited by the principles set out above. Sir Alan Herbert's Marriage Bill was

[1] *Parliament*, p. 183 *et seq.*
[2] Bromhead, *op. cit.*, p. 25.

not uncontroversial: Miss Ellen Wilkinson's Hire Purchase Bill, 1938, dealt with a most complicated subject.[1] Sydney Silverman's assault on the death penalty is another reminder that private members' Bills may deal with major questions of policy on which the Government is unwilling to take action. Even if the greater number of these Bills are of minor importance, it is impossible to look down the lists of those that have been enacted in recent years and not feel that they have made a contribution to human and animal well-being. Any selection of titles must be arbitrary, but the following will give some indication of the range of topics covered by private members' Acts—Session 1948–49, Adoption, Married Women (Maintenance); Session 1950–51, Slaughter of Animals, Fireworks; Session 1951–52, Defamation, Heating Appliances (Fireguards), Affiliation Orders, Corneal Grafting; Session 1952–53, Pharmacy, Road Transport (Rear Lighting), Accommodation Agencies; Session 1953–54, Protection of Birds, Law Reform (Limitation of Actions), Pool Betting. During the period 1948–57 a total of 76 private members' Bills became law; of these 57 were introduced under the ballot, thirteen under the Ten-Minute Rule and six were unballoted Bills. It seems that sponsors of Bills are becoming more adept at securing the passage of their measures, for in the first post-war session in which Members had a chance to initiate legislation only five of their Bills were passed, while in 1953–54 eleven balloted Bills were successful and two others. Or it may be that Members are more willing to deny themselves the right to speak on Fridays in order to speed up business.

Although roughly half the balloted Bills still fail to become law, it does not follow that the House wastes half the ten Fridays devoted to Bills, for many of those that fail won a low place in the ballot and, therefore, were not discussed at all. Further, if a Bill is debated and does not pass, the House may well have had a most useful debate. Examples of this kind are the Bills on Spelling Reform, Censorship of Plays, Analgesia in Childbirth, Women's Disabilities, Press Council, Sunday Observance and Safety in Employment. The unsuccessful Bill may stimulate Government action; in 1955 G. Nabarro (Con. Kidderminster) withdrew his Clean Air Bill in response to a

---

[1] Ellen Wilkinson was Labour Member for Middlesbro', East, 1924–31 and Jarrow 1935–47. Her Hire Purchase Bill was drafted by the Haldane Society, a body of lawyers associated with the Labour Party. Cf. Sir W. I. Jennings, *Parliament*, pp. 184–5.

Ministerial promise to introduce legislation on the subject, and the Clean Air Act was duly passed in the following Session.

Those who opposed the restoration of private members' time in the post-war period argued that this facility should be surrendered because of the great pressure of Government business. It remains true that most Departments have measures they desire to introduce, but for which no time can be found. Does this imply that the ten Fridays allocated to private members' Bills could be better used by Ministerial legislation? To make a firm judgment on this matter is impossible, since it is not known what use the Government would make of the additional time. The main case for private members' Bills is that they do provide an alternative source of inspiration for legislative action. This is highly desirable, for there are topics on which the Departments hesitate to move, especially those that arouse the moral indignation of Members. Individual Members suffer no such inhibitions and they produce ideas for legislation which are frequently a nuisance to the Government. These come from a variety of sources, apart from their own personal enthusiasms. It seems that the Conservative backbenchers committee on Social Services was connected with the National Insurance Bill of 1956.[1] A private member's Bill may stem from the recommendations of an official report that has not commanded the energies of the Government: the complex Defamation Bill sponsored by N. H. Lever (Lab. Manchester, Cheetham) followed the publication of the Report of the Porter Committee.[2] Other possible channels, mentioned above, are voluntary associations of all kinds and the Whips. The priority allocated to these measures by the luck of the draw is not rationally defensible, but it is an admirable feature of the British Parliament that the programme of legislation is not dominated entirely by Ministers and their advisers. Writing in 1938 H. J. Laski[3] condemned private members' Bills as being ill-suited to modern conditions. No Bill, he argued, can pass without the approval of the Government, and if Ministers do not feel keenly enough on a problem to legislate about it the matter would be so unimportant as to fail to justify the attention of the House. Such faith in the wisdom of Ministers is touching but unfounded, and an examination of the roll of private members' legislation since 1948 completely fails to substantiate Laski's thesis.

[1] H.C. Deb., Vol. 548, col. 1218.
[2] Law of Defamation. Committee Report; 1948 Cmd. 7536, i.
[3] Cf. *Parliamentary Government in England*, p. 166.

The other use made of private Members' Fridays, the introduction of motions, produces fewer features of interest. The allocation of each of these Fridays is determined by a separate ballot in which the names of three Members are drawn. Accordingly, three notices of motion are given for each Friday, but it is most unusual for the third topic to be reached, and on a majority of these occasions the whole day is occupied by the debate on the first motion. The range of subjects raised by private Members' motions is wider than that raised by their Bills because a motion can encourage the Government to undertake increased expenditure. It is also possible for foreign or Commonwealth affairs to be considered, although this is done infrequently. A general picture of the type of motion brought forward can be obtained from the following table:

PRIVATE MEMBERS' MOTIONS:
SESSION 1955–56

Date	Subject of Motion	Party Allegiance of Sponsor	Result
18.11.55	Export Trade	Conservative	Talked out
2.12.55	Noise	Conservative	Counted out
16.12.55	Ancient Monuments	Labour	Agreed
	Railway Closures	Conservative	Talked out
10.2.56	Film Industry	Labour	Withdrawn
24.2.56	Productivity	Conservative	Agreed
	Employment of the Disabled	Labour	Conservative amendment carried without a division
9.3.56	Betting and Lotteries	Labour	Agreed
23.3.56	Channel Tunnel	Conservative	Withdrawn
	Machinery of Government	Conservative	Withdrawn
20.4.56	Defence Expenditure	Labour	Talked out
4.5.56	No Par Value Shares	Conservative	Counted out
8.6.56	Civil Service	Labour	Conservative amendment carried without a division
	Police	Conservative	Agreed

Some of these debates followed the orthodox lines of party controversy, but other motions commanded support on both sides of the House, e.g., the Channel Tunnel and Railway Closures. Labour Members do not always use their luck in the draw to grind political axes—witness their motions on Betting and Ancient Monuments. Divisions on private members' motions are uncommon; in 1955–56 there were none, and in the previous session there was a single division on an unsuccessful attempt to move 'the motion be now put'. It will be noticed that amendments to motions by Government supporters obtain acceptance without a vote being challenged. Attendance on these Fridays is often poor, even when the house is not counted out.[1] Motions do not stimulate outside interests in the same way as private members' Bills and this, combined with the unlikelihood of a division and of the later motions being reached, helps Members to feel that the demands of their other duties are pressing. On Fridays the House is less compelling as a debating society than as a legislative assembly.

This does not imply that time devoted to motions is ill-spent. Many have a topical character or provide a chance to ventilate a problem that would not otherwise be discussed. They also may allow a Member, unplaced in the ballot for Bills, to bring his pet subject to the attention of the House. On a matter like the closing of branch railways Members are enabled to make 'constituency' speeches. And if Motions on Fridays give a little relaxation to Members, they may do good in countless ways.

Private members' time is of high value in providing parliamentary life with a much needed degree of variety. On twenty Fridays a session the atmosphere is changed and Members have an alternative to the routine of criticizing or supporting official policy. Political opinions remain unchanged but they are not regimented by the Whips. Members on opposite sides of the House may join each other in common cause. A sense of freedom prevails because Members are not limited to commentary on, or registration of, Government decisions. It may be that in a period when political tempers run high private members' time would not be used as constructively as it has been in recent years; but that is no reason to minimize its present worth.

---

[1] For example, cf. H.C. Deb., Vol. 550, col. 1729.

Political Promotion

The aim of a party in opposition is to acquire power; the desire of the party in power is to retain office. Ambitions of the individual are related to those of his group, and politicians, excited by their intense consciousness of the pursuit of power, are activated also by visions of personal advancement. It is more than probable that most new Members aspire to ministerial rank although conventions of modesty limit the publication of their hopes. But most Members spend the whole of their parliamentary career on the backbenches, for the number of posts available is sufficient to accommodate but a fifth of the Government supporters if the Government has a bare plurality in the House, and the ratio diminishes as the size of the majority increases. This is a vital safeguard to the independence of the legislature. A government could use the patronage at its disposal to quell objection to its policies, and the limitation of patronage in this country has been closely linked with the growth in the independence of the Commons. The total of Ministerial posts is closely controlled by legislation, and the Select Committee on Offices of Profit has expressed disquiet[1] about the rise in the number of parliamentary private secretaries—Members who act as unpaid and semi-official assistants to Ministers—lest this should lead to a further growth of official influence on the backbenches.

In spite of the odds against promotion Members remain optimistic, at least for some years. It is easy for one who is a centre of attraction in his own constituency to over-rate himself, and new Members may not appreciate the range of qualities that are required for ministerial office. Also they may not at first be aware of the intensity of the competition for preferment or the pressure of talent on the back-

[1] Report, para. 24; 1940–41 (120) iii.

benches seeking occupation. When the elderly show no disposition to retire, and many senior positions are held by Peers, the frustration among both Junior Ministers and the rank-and-file may be acute; such was the position after the 1951 Election.

There are various means through which Members can advance their claims to recognition. Members tend to concentrate their attention on particular topics so that their contributions to debate may be well informed. They will attend the party committee(s) dealing with their special interests; one who shows much ability and energy at these meetings may subsequently be elected an officer of a committee. This is a small step forward, but it can lead to greater things as shown by two appointments in 1957: C. Orr-Ewing (Con. Hendon N.) who became Under Secretary for Air had previously been Secretary of the Conservative Air Committee and J. Vaughan-Morgan (Con. Reigate) was chosen as Parliamentary Secretary to the Ministry of Health after a period as Chairman of the Conservative Health Committee. Personal qualities are further displayed in the Chamber itself, and an aspirant to office must first prove himself in debate. Opposition Members have a greater freedom of manœuvre in this regard; the Government is always facing them and may be attacked on any suitable opportunity. Government supporters may offer constructive criticism of their leaders, yet they should not afford comfort to the enemies of their party. Alternatively, they may counter-attack those on the Opposition benches, but this technique does not easily build great reputations for so often it leads merely to a restatement of the Government's case, with an addition of some party polemics. Yet there are exceptions to this rule. Iain Macleod's (Con. Enfield, West) victory in a debating duel[1] with an ex-Minister, Aneurin Bevan (Lab. Ebbw Vale), may have influenced his early promotion to become Minister of Health. If a Member on the Government benches hopes for promotion he is ill-advised to challenge a Minister, for political memories are uncomfortably long. A sortie in the wrong division lobby is also damaging to personal prospects, although Enoch Powell (Con. Wolverhampton, S.W.) became Parliamentary Secretary to the Ministry of Housing and Local Government the year after he had voted with the Suez Group against the Government. In 1957 J. Amery (Con. Preston, N.) became Financial Secretary at the War Office a month after he had refused in a division to support the policy of evacuating Port Said, but this

[1] H.C. Deb., Vol. 498, col. 886 *et seq.*

rather exceptional nomination was partly due to a desire to conciliate extremist opinion among Government supporters.

The first step up the ladder for many Members on the Government side of the House is to become parliamentary private secretary to a Minister—the common abbreviation is P.P.S. This is entirely a personal arrangement between a Minister and a backbencher; the position carries no payment and it has no official status. Most Ministers have a P.P.S., and the general function of the latter is to act as an additional pair of ears and eyes for his Minister and so keep him informed of trends of opinion in the Commons. But it is not possible to generalize in detail about the tasks of a P.P.S. because Ministers vary in the extent to which they invite assistance. A Minister may require little more than the arranging of 'pairs' for him when a two-line whip is in operation and a division is expected, thus allowing the Minister to be absent from the House. At the other extreme a Minister may not only wish for full reports on backbenchers' views but will invite comments on projected developments in Departmental policy. It is usual for a P.P.S. to attend all party committees concerned with the functions of his Minister. Notebook and pencil in hand, his presence serves to give these meetings a greater sense of importance; knowing that they will be privately reported, Members may speak with greater care and a heightened sense of responsibility. A P.P.S. should also be well informed on developments in Opposition policy in relation to his Department so that he can forewarn his Minister of probable lines of attack in future debates. Members with a minor matter to raise in relation to a Department may decide to see the P.P.S. as an alternative to putting down a question: they may also go to him to seek help, e.g., over arrangements for a projected visit to Cyprus. It follows that a good P.P.S. can probably save his Minister a lot of trouble in the House. To do so he must be well liked and it is a help if his Minister is also well liked. And if a P.P.S. is known to enjoy his Minister's confidence he may get access to more information: the House is shrewd in its assessment of personal relationships and is aware that his role varies from nominal to influential. In the Department the position of the P.P.S. is delicate. He has no official standing yet he may be frequently closeted with the Minister and be on terms of some intimacy with him. To do his work effectively he must have access to an amount of 'inside' information, and he may be present when important policy matters are under discussion. Often he has modest accommodation in the Department and may see copies of all correspondence between Members and his Minister. The nature of the task makes it an admirable training ground for future office-holders, but it also imposes certain limitations that have become conventional. A P.P.S. must never speak in the Commons upon the work of the Department with which he is associated; outside the House he may so speak if he has an official brief. On other matters the P.P.S. is free to act as he chooses but should show restraint; if he is critical of another Department the Minister concerned may feel a temptation to complain to *his* Minister. In addition, the doctrine of collective responsibility which binds Ministers to support each other on all occasions tends also to engulf the P.P.S.s, and five of them who voted against the Labour Government in 1948 on the Government of Ireland Bill failed to retain their positions.[1]

The other honorary office to which a backbencher may be appointed is that of a Whip. On the Government side an unpaid assistant Whip can expect, if he performs his duties successfully, to become ultimately a Lord Commissioner of the Treasury; when a vacancy for a Lord Commissioner occurs it is customary to appoint the assistant Whip with the longest period of service. Opposition Whips may hope to become Lords Commissioners or receive one of the Household appointments when their party achieves office. Have Whips a chance of further promotion to a position of Departmental responsibility? The practice in this matter varies between the parties. On the basis of past experience Labour Whips have less to hope for than have their opposite numbers in the Conservative Party. However, A. Blenkinsop (Newcastle-upon-Tyne, East), C. J. Simmons (Brierley Hill) and R. M. M. Stewart (Fulham) are examples of Labour Whips who subsequently became Junior Ministers. Prospects for Conservative Whips are much brighter. Successive Chief Whips have attained Ministerial status—Captain Margesson,[2] Secretary of State for War; Captain Stuart (Moray and Nairn), Secretary of State for Scotland; P. G. Buchan-Hepburn,[3] Minister of Works. Among the Deputy Chief Conservative Whips, Sir Thomas Dugdale (Rich-

[1] They were F. Beswick (Uxbridge), W. Blyton (Houghton-le-Spring), J. P. W. Mallalieu (Huddersfield), R. Mellish (Bermondsey) and G. Rogers (Kensington, N.).

[2] Member for Upton 1922–23 and Rugby 1924–42. Now Viscount Rugby.

[3] Member for Liverpool, East Toxteth, 1931–50 and Beckenham 1950–57. Now Lord Hailes.

mond, North Riding) became Minister of Agriculture and Brigadier Mackeson (Folkestone and Hythe) became Secretary for Overseas Trade, and there are many examples of rank-and-file Conservative Whips receiving promotion. It is a matter of doubt whether the experience of a Government Whip fits him for Ministerial responsibilities, for as he must be silent in the House he is unaccustomed to the cut-and-thrust of parliamentary debate. None of the Chief Whips noted above did receive positions likely to expose them to the centre of the parliamentary battle, for even Captain Margesson's appointment occurred in the special conditions of war-time when political controversy was muted.

The greatest opportunity for Members to achieve promotion comes when a new Government is formed. If political conditions are unsettled, if the electorate favour the Opposition at each general election, the rise and fall of Ministers will be rapid. But the composition of the Cabinet when the Opposition comes to power is greatly influenced by the membership of its previous Shadow Cabinet, the alternative government, which largely consists of ex-Ministers. While a place in the Shadow Cabinet offers great hope of future Ministerial office it is also a position which a mere backbencher is unlikely to attain. The Shadow Cabinet is responsible for guiding the Opposition's policy in the Commons and from it are nominated the party's major spokesmen on the whole range of government activity.

When the Conservatives are in opposition their Shadow Cabinet, known as the 'Consultative Committee', is appointed by the party Leader with whom ultimate authority rests. The Consultative Committee is also assisted by a larger body called the 'Business Committee' which includes the leading officials of the various Subject Committees. No limitations exist upon the authority of the Leader to select his colleagues, either in or out of office, and prospects of appointment depend in great measure on the personal favour of the Leader. This was illustrated frequently in the inter-war period by the exclusion from Conservative Cabinets of ex-Ministers of great experience and undoubted ability.

The Conservative Leader is elected for an unlimited term, which ends either in death or resignation. The formal election takes place at a meeting to which are invited all Peers and Members who receive the Conservative Whip, all prospective candidates adopted by constituency associations and members of the Executive Committee of the National Union of Conservative and Unionist Associations. This is, indeed, a large body to assemble to elect a Leader, but the election is always pre-arranged and unanimous. The meeting is a demonstration rather than an electoral college. Only once in modern times has the succession to the leadership been in doubt when the Party was in opposition, and then (1911) the two strongest contenders, Austen Chamberlain and Walter Long, both stood down to avoid a contest and Bonar Law was unanimously elected. When the Conservatives are in office the electoral college has no problem. The choice falls on the politician already nominated to be Prime Minister by the Monarch, it being understood that in cases of difficulty the Monarch will first consult with elder Conservative statesmen and, if possible, the outgoing Prime Minister. This system was demonstrated fully by the appointment in 1957 of H. Macmillan[1] as Prime Minister and subsequently as Leader. Do Conservative backbenchers, therefore, play no part in this process? The answer is not clear because the relative standing of the most prominent Conservatives must owe something to their reputation among parliamentarians, and in cases like that of 1957 it cannot be known how far backbench opinion affects advice given to the Monarch. When it was rumoured that Sir Anthony Eden might resign many Conservative Members wrote to their Chief Whip to express a preference for Macmillan rather than R. A. Butler (Saffron Walden): whether this had any effect on the outcome is a matter of doubt. Nor is it certain that the letters fairly reflected Conservative opinion because Members who favoured Butler, the probable choice, may have felt it unnecessary to write.[2]

The average Labour Member has more obvious influence. An annual election is held for the posts of Leader and Deputy Leader when the Party is not in office. Since 1922 the re-election of the Leader has always been unopposed but his initial election is often a keen contest. The first Chairman,[3] Keir Hardie, obtained the position in 1906 by a majority of one: in 1922 MacDonald's majority over Clynes was five: in 1935 Attlee won a triangular fight against Morrison and Greenwood on the second ballot. When Labour is called

[1] Member for Stockton-on-Tees 1924–29, 1931–45 and Bromley since 1945.

[2] For an examination of the problems of selecting a Prime Minister when a coalition is being formed see Sir W. I. Jennings, *Cabinet Government*, Ch. 2, and Byrum E. Carter, *The Office of Prime Minister*, Ch. 2.

[3] The term Leader was not used until 1922. Cf. R. T. MacKenzie, *British Political Parties*, p. 306.

upon to form the Government, the Monarch invites the Leader to become Prime Minister and the annual elections cease. In 1945 some important Labour politicians felt that the Parliamentary Labour Party should meet to choose a Leader *before* anyone accepted the post of Prime Minister,[1] but the fact that Attlee did take office without re-election and without trouble has created a strong precedent for the future. To date, no Labour Prime Minister has died while still at Downing Street, or resigned leaving his Party with a majority in the Commons. Thus the conditions under which Macmillan followed Eden have not yet arisen for the Labour Party. After the royal nomination of Macmillan the Party issued a statement to indicate that should a Labour successor be sought for a Labour Prime Minister, the Parliamentary Labour Party would first proceed to elect a new Leader who would then be ready to accept the invitation of the Crown to take office.[2] Thus the rights of Labour Members have been safeguarded in advance. Further it is not certain that they would choose an ex-Deputy Leader or Deputy Prime Minister if one were available: the record of history quite fails to show that a Deputy Leader is expected to succeed his chief. Greenwood became Deputy Leader in 1935 although Morrison, not Greenwood, had been runner-up to Attlee in the election for the Leadership. In 1955 Morrison, then Deputy Leader, was passed over in favour of Gaitskell as the successor to Attlee, and it is highly doubtful whether the present Deputy Leader, J. Griffiths (Llanelly), has ever been considered as a possible successor to Gaitskell—quite apart from the fact of their relative ages. By both precept and custom Labour Members have full freedom of action when the Leadership is vacant.

A Labour Shadow Cabinet is composed of the Parliamentary Committee of eighteen, the Leader, Deputy Leader, Chief Whip, three Peers and twelve other Members, elected annually by all Labour Members. It does not follow that only ex-Ministers will find favour with their backbench colleagues: in 1956, two of the twelve, A. Greenwood (Rossendale) and G. Mitchison (Kettering) had not held posts in previous ministries. The Labour Leader also nominates a Shadow Government in which one or two Members are allocated a watching brief over each Department and are responsible for presenting their Party's case on cognate issues. The Shadow Government is much larger than the Parliamentary Committee and in 1955

---

[1] H. Dalton, *The Fateful Years*, pp. 467 and 473.
[2] *The Times*, 22nd January, 1957.

numbered 35; it includes all Members on the Parliamentary Committee, together with many ex-Ministers from the previous Labour Cabinet. The distribution of responsibility is entirely within the discretion of the Leader and carries no guarantee of appointment should Labour win power. It is also possible for the Leader to give a 'Shadow portfolio' to a Member who is neither an ex-Minister nor on the Parliamentary Committee, but so long as many ex-Ministers are available the chances of the mere backbencher are small. When Labour is in Opposition, therefore, a process of election helps to determine both the colour of Party policy and the selection of its spokesmen. A comparison of the voting figures at the annual elections can be used to show whether advocates of more extreme or more moderate policies are gaining in popularity, and this imposes on the Labour Leader a type of pressure unknown to a Leader of the Conservative Party.

The Prime Minister, whatever his party, has unfettered discretion in the selection of his Cabinet. He may consult with senior colleagues and the advice of the Chief Whip is often sought in filling minor posts. A Minister may make suggestions for filling the junior post(s) in his Department. There are also various political considerations which affect the choices made. A Conservative Premier will introduce Liberal Nationals into his team. A Labour Premier must allocate some senior positions to representatives of the trade union movement and the Co-operative Party. Room must be found for at least one woman in any government, if only as a Junior Minister. It will strengthen a Cabinet if it includes advocates of the major streams of opinion among its supporters, and the Secretary of State for Scotland normally comes from a Scottish constituency.[1] The Cabinet also needs adequate representation in the House of Lords and by the Ministers of the Crown Act, 1937, at least three Ministerial heads of departments and three other Ministers must sit in the Upper House.

It is also for the Prime Minister to determine the general structure

---

[1] In 1951 Sir Winston Churchill gave the Home Office special responsibility for Welsh affairs and nominated D. Llewellyn (Cardiff N.) as Under-Secretary of State. The choice was not a happy one as Llewellyn resigned after a few months. It is difficult for a Conservative Government to secure Welsh representation; since 1951 only four Members from Wales have been among their supporters. In 1957, responsibility for Welsh affairs was transferred to the Ministry of Housing and Local Government. The problem of Welsh representation was solved in the following year by the appointment of Lord Brecon, a newly-created peer, as Minister of State for Welsh Affairs.

of his government. The size and nature of the Cabinet have varied considerably in recent years and have reflected the needs of the time as interpreted by successive Prime Ministers. In war it is usual to have a small Cabinet from which many Ministers in charge of Departments are excluded; during the period 1916–18 and for a part of the last war the Cabinet consisted almost entirely of Ministers without departmental responsibilities. Even in peace-time there should be an upper limit to the size of the Cabinet if it is to be an effective body, and the formation of new Ministries since 1939 has led to the exclusion of the less important Ministers from the Cabinet. The three Service Ministers were omitted from the Cabinet in 1946 and were replaced by the Minister of Defence responsible for co-ordination of all the Armed Forces. A further development is that some departments, especially those concerned with negotiations abroad, are now allowed additional political heads at Ministerial level: there are two such Ministers of State at the Foreign Office, one at the Colonial Office and one at the Board of Trade, none of whom are members of the Cabinet. As a result of these changes a new intermediate grade of political appointment has emerged between the traditional categories of Cabinet Minister and Junior Minister. A new rung has been added to the ladder for the ambitious Member to climb, but there are also more positions available for him than there were before 1939.

The table below shows the totals of Members occupying official positions in the four most recent governments and the pre-1939 administration. As the figures exclude peers they do not show the full size of these Cabinets which were—1937 twenty-one, 1950 eighteen, 1951 sixteen, 1955 eighteen and 1957 eighteen. It will be noticed that the proportion of peers in the Churchill Cabinet, six out of sixteen, was high, indeed the highest for any government in this century.[1]

[1] Subsequent to the formation of this Government, the proportion rose to seven out of seventeen. The structure of this Cabinet was affected by the system of 'Overlords'. The 'Overlords' were Peers responsible for representing Departments in the Cabinet and for co-ordinating their work. They were, therefore, the 'Overlords' of Departmental Ministers not included in the Cabinet. Besides the Minister of Defence, who supervised the three Service Departments, there were the Lord President of the Council who had special responsibility for the Ministries of Food and Agriculture, and the Secretary of State for the Co-ordination of Transport, Fuel and Power who had a self-explanatory title. During the period of this Ministry, however, the 'Overlord' system broke down.

Date	1937	1950	1951	1955	1957
Prime Minister	Chamber-lain	Attlee	Churchill	Eden	Mac-millan
Cabinet Ministers	15	15	10	14	14
Non-Cabinet Ministers	4	13	14	11	11
Junior Ministers	18	25	26	29	29
Lords Commissioners	3	5	5	5	4
Officers of the Household	3	3	3	3	3
Law Officers	4	4	3	4	4
Others[1]	2	2	2	2	2
Totals	49	67	63	68	67

Other Members connected with the Government are the P.P.S.s and the unpaid assistant Whips. Most Ministers have a P.P.S. and exceptionally a Junior Minister may have one, especially if his chief is in the Lords. The numbers vary a little but if allowance is made for twenty-five P.P.S.s and four assistant Whips, it follows that the total of Honourable Members associated with the Government borders upon one hundred. In 1937 the corresponding figure was below seventy.

There is no fixed pattern of political promotion. Naturally when senior positions become vacant there is a tendency to appoint those who have had ministerial experience at a lower level. Yet there are many instances of a backbencher obtaining direct advancement to ministerial status, quite apart from the selection as Ministers in wartime of men who were not then in Parliament—Ernest Bevin,[2] Andrew Duncan,[3] and Oliver Lyttelton.[4] In 1945 G. Isaacs (Lab. Southwark) became Minister of Labour and A. Bevan became Minister of Health without previous experience of office. If a party achieves power after a long period in Opposition there may be an inadequate supply of previous Ministers to fill all the senior positions; when the first Labour Government was formed in 1924 it was

---

[1] The Charity Commissioner and the Church Estates Commissioner. They are not Ministers but they hold office under the Crown.

[2] Member for Central Wandsworth 1940–50 and East Woolwich 1950–51.

[3] Member for the City of London 1940–50.

[4] Now Viscount Chandos: Member for Aldershot 1940–54.

inevitable that the majority of Ministers were quite unversed in their new responsibilities. The Conservatives, however, are never short of Ministers or ex-Ministers, yet in 1952 I. Macleod (Enfield, W.) moved from the backbenches to become Minister of Health and similarly in 1955 A. Jones (Birmingham, Hall Green) was appointed Minister of Fuel and Power. These examples do indicate how carefully the activities of the rank-and-file are noted by party leaders, and how they may be the cause of rapid preferment. The careers of H. Gaitskell (Lab. Leeds, S.) and Selwyn Lloyd (Con. The Wirral) also show how Ministers thought to have unusual ability may be rapidly elevated to the highest Cabinet posts.

In normal circumstances new Members cannot expect to be asked to join the Government immediately, and for those in opposition hope must be deferred until after a general election. If their party is in office, how long must they wait? The general answer is that a Member who has sat on the Government backbenches for five years has a steadily diminishing prospect of promotion. It is probably advantageous for a Member to enter the Commons when his party is in a minority, for this allows a few years of freedom on the opposition backbenches in which to gain experience and the beginnings of a reputation. Then on the morrow of electoral victory there are many posts to be filled at a time when the flush of new Members on the winning side have not the necessary standing. But a Member first returned when his party gains power is less happily placed. After an interval he may be thought ready for office but by then the political pendulum may have swung back and installed his opponents; alternatively, if his own party remains in the ascendant, only a trickle of junior ministerial vacancies will arise for which there will be many well-placed competitors. Among exceptions to the rule that promotion comes early if at all are H. Molson[1] and H. Brooke.[2] Advancement was slower in the 1930s because of the large and stable Conservative majority. Today both parties are well aware that if the more promising of new Members are not given an early opportunity of office, a future shortage of experienced Ministers is a serious probability.

[1] Member for Doncaster 1931–35 and High Peak since 1939; appointed a Junior Minister in 1953 and Minister of Works 1957.

[2] Member for West Lewisham 1938–45 and for Hampstead since 1950; appointed a Junior Minister in 1954 and Minister of Housing and Local Government 1957.

Any attempt to compare speeds of advancement in the two major parties is beset with pitfalls. A party that is out of office for a long period is not in a position to provide ministerial experience for new Members. While Conservatives have been the more willing to give young men a chance, it is also the case that there are more Conservative Members in the lower age groups. The result of a comparison of the ages of opposing party leaders will depend on the date chosen for the inquiry; the leading figures in the Parliamentary Labour Party in 1956 were much less elderly than in the previous year. Only five of the fifteen Members on the Labour Parliamentary Committee elected in November, 1956, had sat in the House before the 1945 Election, while eleven of the fifteen Members in the contemporary Conservative Cabinet could claim at least this length of parliamentary service. Yet at any future date the position may well be reversed.

For the individual there is a significant element of luck or accident in public life, and it is a great advantage for a Member to have a seat safe enough to withstand the greatest conceivable wave of success by his adversaries. Earl Attlee is a leading example of this truth. At the 1931 Election Labour candidates were routed and a mere fifty-nine were returned; the small band of survivors included but three of the Ministers of the previous Labour administration, Lansbury, Attlee and Cripps. The latter had been a Member for little more than twelve months, so it was unsurprising that Lansbury, the most senior, became Leader with Attlee as Deputy. In 1933 Lansbury was kept away from Parliament for several months through injury sustained in an accident, and Attlee acted as Leader. Then shortly before the 1935 Election Lansbury resigned owing to differences of view with his colleagues, and Attlee again led his Party during the Election. This helped Attlee to become Leader in 1935, although many Labour politicians senior to him in 1930 had by then regained their seats. The 1931 Election, therefore, can be said to have had great influence over the future of the Labour Leadership—fortunately for Earl Attlee, unfortunately for Morrison and Greenwood.

The smile of fate and a safe seat are great aids towards achieving a ministerial career, but they are by no means sufficient conditions to ensure it. The Commons plays a decisive part in judging the fitness of those called upon to lead in our national life; a Member who is not well respected is unlikely to receive an appointment and a Minister who is not a success in the House is ill-placed to receive further promotion. Yet it is difficult to explain how the House chooses its leaders. As Harold Laski wrote 'the selective function of the House of Commons is the most mysterious of all its habits'.[1] Conditions of work in the House are sufficiently intimate for it to be acutely conscious of personalities and most Members have decided views on the qualities of other Members. Sincerity, good humour and respect for the Commons as an institution assist the construction of a favourable reputation, while Members who appear self-centred and to crave publicity rank low in the estimation of their colleagues. A Member with great achievements to his credit before he enters the House will find that his past is of little help to him, for in the House every new Member is equally a beginner. In debate, cleverness and facility with words are less important than what is felt to be the inspiration of a contribution, for hearts are judged as well as minds. But while it is possible to suggest factors that inhibit success, the aspiring Member cannot find an infallible prescription to achieve it. Every Government contains men with a wide variety of qualities, some of which may be antithetical; each period of time may require a different type of leadership. The path to high office is an incalculable journey and many of those who seek greatness with the fullest determination are among the most disappointed.

---

[1] *Parliamentary Government in England,* p. 158.

Parliamentary Privilege

At the commencement of each new Parliament Mr. Speaker goes to the Upper House to receive the royal assent to his election. It is customary then for the Speaker,

'In the name, and on behalf of the Commons, to lay claim by humble petition to their ancient and undoubted rights and privileges; particularly that their persons may be free from arrests and all molestations; that they may enjoy liberty of speech in all their debates; may have access to Her Majesty's royal person whenever occasion shall require; and that all their proceedings may receive from Her Majesty the most favourable construction.' The Lord Chancellor replies—'Her Majesty most readily confirms all the rights and privileges which have ever been granted to or conferred upon the Commons by Her Majesty or any of her royal predecessors.'

The Speaker duly reports this reply to the Commons, but the privileges of the Commons do not depend upon the will of the Crown thus expressed by the Lord Chancellor. Some of the rights of the Commons, e.g., freedom of speech,[1] have been incorporated in statutes and the House also claims that its privileges are unwritten law, to be determined by itself through reference to its own precedents. By a resolution passed in 1704, however, the House agreed that it should not extend its privileges beyond those which already existed.

Two of the rights specifically named by the Speaker are of minor significance. The desire that 'their proceedings may receive from Her Majesty the most favourable construction' is an echo of earlier centuries. The right of access to the royal person is not to be exercised individually by Members but belongs to the House as a whole which,

[1] Bill of Rights, 1689, S.9.

acting collectively, may submit an Address to the Crown through the Speaker.

Freedom from arrest does not apply to criminal cases or to detention under emergency legislation.[1] During the last war Captain Ramsay[2] was imprisoned for security reasons under Defence Regulation 18B. When a Member is arrested on a criminal charge the House expects to be informed: on 1st December, 1954, the Speaker received a letter from Mr. Justice Lynskey which informed him that Captain Baker had been sentenced to seven years imprisonment for issuing forged documents.[3] Likewise, the conviction of D. Weitzmann (Lab. Stoke Newington), for conspiracy to contravene Board of Trade regulations restricting the manufacture and supply of toilet preparations was reported to the House, as was the subsequent quashing of the conviction on appeal.[4] Privilege protects Members from arrest in relation to civil matters for the duration of the parliamentary session and forty days before and after the session. Since 1869 this has been of diminished importance, for in that year imprisonment for debt was abolished and Members are not protected from distraint on their goods. Yet the principle behind this privilege is of the highest importance. If Members are to carry out their parliamentary duties it is essential that they should enjoy physical liberty. With exceptions, the duty of Members to attend the House is expected to have priority over other official obligations. Thus, Members are exempt from jury service and they used to be able to resist subpoenas, but this aspect of privilege is now waived. In 1938, however, the House decided[5] that an order to a Member, D. Sandys,[6] who was also a Territorial Officer, to attend a military court of inquiry constituted a breach of privilege. The court was seeking to discover how he had obtained certain confidential information. Sandys had already complained in the Commons that a Minister had put pressure on him to disclose the source of this information, and the House had agreed to refer the matter to a committee. It followed that the order of the military court was an attempt to anticipate, and thereby interfere with, the proceedings of a parlia-

[1] Privileges. Committee Report; 1939–40 (164) iii.

[2] Conservative Member for Peebles 1931–45.

[3] H.C. Deb., Vol. 535, col. 145. Captain Baker was Conservative Member for Norfolk, South, 1950–54.

[4] H.C. Deb., Vol. 443, col. 1053 and Vol. 448, col. 2061.

[5] H.C. Deb., Vol. 337, col. 2237.

[6] Conservative Member for Norwood 1935–45 and for Streatham since 1950.

mentary committee. This incident led to a full examination of the application of the Official Secrets Acts to Members. A Select Committee reported that Members were not entitled to solicit the disclosure of confidential information, but Members did, in fact, sometimes obtain such information and it would affect their parliamentary duties if they did not. The extent of the immunity of Members from the Official Secrets Acts has not been precisely defined and the Committee recommended that the Official Secrets Acts should not be used to impede Members from carrying on their parliamentary activities.[1]

Associated with freedom from arrest is the right of freedom from molestation when entering or leaving the Palace of Westminster. Each session the Commons make a Sessional Order in the following terms:

'That the Commissioner of the Police of the Metropolis do take care that during the Session of Parliament the passages through the streets leading to this House be kept free and open and that no obstruction be permitted to hinder the passage of Members to and from this House, and that no disorder be allowed in Westminster Hall . . .'

This Order helps to protect Members from organized lobbying by large crowds. When Parliament reassembled in October, 1955, the British Peace Committee arranged for mass deputations to 'lobby their Members on the vital issue of peace', and the Commissioner of Police issued a warning to those taking part in this demonstration which drew their attention to the Sessional Order quoted above.

It has been noted that the fourth privilege requested by the Speaker, freedom of speech, is also guaranteed by the Bill of Rights which enacted that 'The freedom of speech and debates or proceedings in Parliament ought not to be impeached or questioned in any court or place out of Parliament'. Members are not, therefore, restrained in their speeches by fear of actions for slander.[2] Originally it was essential for the Commons to insist on this right to protect them, not from litigation, but from the King. In the days of conflict between King and Parliament, Members were fearful of royal dis-

---

[1] Official Secrets Acts. Select Committee Report; 1938–39 (101) viii.

[2] In 1957 the question arose as to whether a letter written by a Member to a Minister was a 'proceeding in Parliament' and, therefore, protected by privilege. The Committee of Privileges reported that such correspondence was thus protected but the Commons decided to reject the view of the Committee. See the Postscript *infra*, pp. 262–7.

pleasure and this explains why the Commons have insisted on the control of both the admission of strangers to debate and the publication of debates. These precautions were thought of as methods to prevent the King from discovering the opinions of individual Members. Today secret sessions are held in war-time if the House is discussing confidential defence matters, and to go into private session it is only necessary for a Member to 'spy strangers'; under Standing Order 89 the question, 'That strangers be ordered to withdraw', is put without discussion.[1]

As the struggle with the monarchy waned the Commons came to tolerate, in practice, the publication of reports of debates. By the middle of the eighteenth century their chief concern was to prevent misrepresentation of what had actually been said in the House. Since 1909 the reports of debates have been the responsibility of an official reporting staff acting under the authority of the Speaker and are sold to the public by the Stationery Office.[2] Immunity given to speeches of Members does not apply if a Member publishes his own speech apart from the rest of the debate:[3] immunity is granted if the whole of a debate is published.[4] By the Parliamentary Papers Act, 1840, papers printed by order of the House are privileged as well as faithful copies of them. This Act was passed to reverse the decision in the famous case, *Stockdale v. Hansard*,[5] where the Court held that the report of a statutory body which the House had ordered to be printed was not privileged. Members are still responsible to the House for remarks made in debate, and the House protects its own Members and the Chair from observations held to be improper.

There remain two other main items of privilege which are not mentioned by the Speaker in his supplication: they are the power of the Commons to deal with matters affecting the conduct of its own business and the power to punish for breach of privilege. Various aspects of the constitution of the House involve privilege. The House has the right to order the filling of casual vacancies. When such a

---

[1] Naturally, *Hansard* does not record what is said in secret session, but on 31st March 1943, a division took place during a secret session and the form of the question and the way in which Members voted were published. H.C. Deb., Vol. 388, cols. 200–204.

[2] For the history of the printing of parliamentary debates in the nineteenth century, see P. and G. Ford, *A Guide to Parliamentary Papers*, pp. 68–76.

[3] *R. v. Creevy* (1813) 1 M. & S., 273.

[4] *Wason v. Walter* (1868) L.R. 4 Q.B. 73.

[5] 9. A. & E. 1.

vacancy occurs the Chief Whip of the Party to which the seat belonged moves that a new writ be issued for the election of a Member. It is normal for such a motion to be unopposed, but in 1943 Sir Richard Acland objected to the issue of a writ as a protest against the condition of the electoral register, which had not been revised during the war.[1] If a vacancy occurs during the recess the Speaker may, by statute, issue the necessary writ; this power does not extend to vacancies caused by the lunacy of a Member or an appointment to the Stewardship of the Chiltern Hundreds or of the Manor of Northstead.

The House has the right to decide disputes arising from the election of Members. These may be divided into two categories: those which concern the conduct or the result of an election and those where the qualification of the person elected is a matter of doubt. The latter issue was considered in detail in Chapter 3. Disputes about election returns have been tried since 1868 by two High Court judges and the procedure is now governed by the Representation of the People Act, 1949, together with the Election Commissioners Act, 1949. The House, therefore, has surrendered this function. Before 1770 such disputes went before the whole House and between 1770 and 1868 they were dealt with by a Select Committee, but there was a considerable element of party bias in the decisions made. Election petitions are now presented to the High Court and the Commons have no part in the proceedings until the report of the two judges is notified to them.

Parliamentary privilege has led, in the past, to clashes between Parliament and the Courts. As was seen above in *Stockdale v. Hansard*, the Courts have asserted the right to define the limits of privilege. The Courts admit claims of privilege on any matter where its recognition is necessary for the efficient and dignified discharge of parliamentary functions; so they will not inquire into anything, except crime, that occurs in the Palace of Westminster. Thus when the Commons refused to let Bradlaugh, who had been duly elected for Northampton but who was an avowed atheist, take the Oath, the Queen's Bench refused to interfere on the ground that this was a matter of the internal management of the House.[2] By application

[1] H.C. Deb., Vol. 388, cols 1–5 and 61–70. Sir Richard Acland was then the leader of the Common Wealth Party which was opposing the Government at by-elections.

[2] *Bradlaugh v. Gosset* (1884) 12 Q.B.D. 271.

of the same principle Parliament is allowed to disregard the Licensing Acts. In 1934 A. P. Herbert, who had not then become an Honourable Member, challenged this disregard for the law by laying an information against the Kitchen Committee for selling liquor without a licence. But the Court of King's Bench decided that the Licensing Acts could not be applied to Parliament[1] and reference was made to the following passage from *Stockdale v. Hansard*: 'The Commons of England are not invested with more power and dignity by their legislative character than by that which they have as the grand inquest of the nation. All the privileges that can be required for the energetic discharge of the duties inherent in that high trust are conceded without a murmur or a doubt.' It seems pertinent to ask the question whether this uncontrolled consumption can be said to be required for the energetic discharge of the duties of Parliament.[2] But even with the advantage of this special privilege the Kitchen Committee is frequently in financial difficulties.

The Courts agree that Parliament may punish those guilty of contempt,[3] including both Members and other persons. A Member guilty of disorderly conduct may be named by the Speaker and, if he refuses to withdraw, he can be suspended for the remainder of the session or for some prescribed period. The House may also have recourse to other forms of punishment of varying severity. An offender may receive an admonition from the Speaker or, in more serious cases, the Speaker will issue a reprimand and the offender will appear before him in charge of the Serjeant-at-Arms. The most drastic punishment is to commit to prison, but the prisoner must be released as soon as the House is prorogued. The Commons may also decide that a person elected to the House, albeit legally qualified, is unfit to sit. All Members are Honourable Members. If, therefore, a Member has engaged in conduct that the House finds dishonourable, he may be expelled. Expulsion does not prevent a person from re-submitting himself to the electors, so that it is possible theoretically, as with John Wilkes, for a series of expulsions and re-elections to take place. There seems, however, to be little likelihood of a

---

[1] *R. v. Graham-Campbell—ex parte Herbert* (1935) 1 K.B. 594. The issue had been raised previously in *Williamson v. Norris* (1899) Q.B.7, but was not then pressed to a conclusion.

[2] A. P. Herbert, *Independent Member*, Chapter I, especially p. 17.

[3] *Burdett v. Abbot* (1811) 14 East 1, and *The Sheriff of Middlesex's Case* (1840) 11 A. & E. 809.

HONOURABLE MEMBERS

repetition of this process in the conditions of the twentieth century.

An instance of expulsion was that of Garry Allighan (Lab. Gravesend) in 1947.[1] Allighan's contempt was based on an article in the *World's Press News* in which he alleged that some Members conveyed private and confidential information to newspapers in return for financial reward, or personal publicity, described by Allighan as 'payment in kind'. He also alleged that Members betrayed information when under the influence of drink and that it was customary for newspaper representatives to purchase intoxicants for Members in the expectation of obtaining useful material. The Committee of Privileges found that some of this information was in connection with events at private meetings of the Parliamentary Labour Party; it took the view that the disclosure of such private proceedings was a gross breach of confidence, yet was not, of itself, a breach of privilege. But the Committee also ruled that the receipt of payment by a Member, in return for information obtained through his status as a Member, was a contempt of the House. This was a development of the old-established principle that a Member may not receive remuneration for professional services associated with parliamentary business: a Member may not appear as counsel before a parliamentary committee. Party affairs now share the protection against bribery previously accorded to parliamentary business. Two Members were found to have received improper payments—Allighan himself and E. Walkden.[2] Allighan's conduct was held to be a grave contempt of the House for he had made charges against others in respect of the very matter of which he was guilty himself.[3] Subsequently, the House expelled Allighan, and Walkden was reprimanded by the Speaker.

Matters of privilege take precedence over other business and are usually dealt with after question-time. Disorders are dealt with as they occur. When a Member raises a point of privilege it is for the Speaker to rule whether a *prima facie* case has been made out. If the Speaker agrees that a *prima facie* case exists the matter will then be referred to the Committee of Privileges. For the Speaker to give his assent, apart from the merits of the case, two conditions must be

[1] H.C. Deb., Vol. 443, col. 1198.

[2] Member for Doncaster: 1941–47 Labour, 1947–50 Independent.

[3] The report of the Committee of Privileges on the Allighan case is a most important document—1946–47 (138) ix.

224

observed; the matter must be raised at the earliest opportunity and, if some document is complained of, the whole of the document must be handed to the Speaker. Two publications were complained of by Colonel Lipton (Lab. Brixton) on 19th December, 1955: the Speaker would not rule that a *prima facie* case existed because the booklet concerned had been on sale for several days, and on the second item, a newspaper article, a cutting was handed to the Speaker and not the whole issue of the paper.[1] If the Speaker does not declare a *prima facie* case exists it is still open to the aggrieved Member to put a motion on the Order Paper, but there is no guarantee that time will be available to discuss it. The purpose of asking for a Speaker's ruling is to ensure priority for the proposal to refer the matter to the Committee of Privileges. Failure to obtain a ruling need not be fatal to a complaint: on 22nd March, 1955, the Commons agreed, without a division, to refer a complaint by T. Driberg to the Committee of Privileges, after the Speaker had failed to agree that Driberg had established a *prima facie* case.[2] The Privileges Committee is appointed regularly at the commencement of each session in readiness for any issue that may be referred to it. The chairman is a senior Minister; it works in a non-party spirit and in a quasi-judicial atmosphere. Normally its reports are unanimous.

A useful classification of types of breach of privilege has been given by Anson.[3] The three categories are—disrespect to a Member, as such, by a non-member: disrespect to the House collectively, committed either by a Member or a non-member: disobedience to the orders of the House, or interference with its procedure, its officers in the execution of their duty, or with witnesses appearing before committees in respect of their evidence.

It must be stressed that an action affecting a Member will not constitute a breach of privilege unless it has some direct bearing on his parliamentary duties. Thus, in 1951, a scurrilous communication about Sydney Silverman (Lab. Nelson and Colne) was held not to be a breach of privilege as it contained general abuse but did not allege misconduct in relation to any parliamentary activities.[4] The Committee of Privileges are not eager to recommend action when a

---

[1] H.C. Deb., Vol. 547, cols. 1668–70 and 1866–70.

[2] H.C. Deb., Vol. 538, cols. 2273–4 and Vol. 539, col. 165. Driberg was Member for Maldon: Independent 1942–45, Labour 1945–55.

[3] *Law and Custom of the Constitution*, 5th ed., Vol. I, p. 187.

[4] Privileges. Committee Report; 1950–51 (149) vii.

complaint is lodged on behalf of an individual Member; like mercy, privilege is not strained. Such a complaint may arise from alleged misrepresentation of what a Member has said in the House. Any report of a debate is still technically a breach of privilege but, unless the misrepresentation is thought to be serious, no action will follow.[1] A suggestion that readers of the *Sunday Graphic* should ring up W. Lewis to indicate that they disagreed with his views about sending relief to Egypt succeeded in putting Lewis's telephone out of action: this was held to constitute molestation and a breach of privilege.[2]

More important cases are those in which it is suggested that some kind of improper pressure has been put on a Member by an organization. Many Members receive payments from outside bodies, often in return for services rendered. Such arrangements inevitably admit the possibility that payments will cease if, for any reason, relations between the Member and the organization become strained. When this occurs it is but a short step to suggest that financial pressure has been exerted to affect the performance of parliamentary duties. W. A. Robinson,[3] whose candidature had been sponsored by the National Union of Distributive and Allied Workers, was called upon to resign by the Union during the last war. The Union acted in this way after receiving complaints from the St. Helens Labour Party about their Member. When Robinson refused to resign N.U.D.A.W. told him that certain payments made to him would be stopped. Thereupon the matter was raised in the Commons and referred to the Committee of Privileges. The subsequent report of the Committee argued that if an outside body gave financial assistance to a Member it 'must normally be free and entitled to withdraw it. A statement that such support would be withdrawn unless certain action was taken in Parliament ... (might be) a breach of privilege. It depends on the circumstances.'[4] In the case of Robinson it was held that no breach of privilege was involved, because the Union were generally dissatisfied with Robinson, and there had been no attempt to influence his action on particular issues.

[1] 1948–49 (261) x. This case concerned the alleged misreporting of R. Blackburn by the *Daily Worker*. Blackburn was Member for Birmingham, Kings Norton: Labour 1945–51, Independent 1951.

[2] 1956–57 (27). W. A. Lewis has been Labour Member for Upton 1945–50 and West Ham, N., since 1950.

[3] Labour Member for St. Helens, 1935–45.

[4] Para. 4; 1943–44 (85) ii.

The more recent case of W. J. Brown is of a similar kind. Brown had been the Labour Member for Wolverhampton, West, from 1929 to 1931, and in 1942 was elected as an Independent for Rugby. He was also the General Secretary of the Civil Service Clerical Association, and when elected for Rugby he was appointed as Parliamentary General Secretary of the C.S.C.A. at a salary of £1,350 p.a. plus certain other expenses and facilities. This arrangement was open to termination by Brown but not by the C.S.C.A., except in the event of grave misconduct. Brown was re-elected in 1945. In 1947 it was alleged that an atmosphere had been created which put pressure on him to alter his views, and that if he did not his position as an official of the C.S.C.A. would be rendered intolerable. The report of the Committee of Privileges on this matter suggested that no action was necessary. 'Where a Member voluntarily places himself in a contractual relationship . . . with an outside body he must in general be taken to have accepted its possible termination as a matter which would not influence him in his parliamentary duties and, therefore, must further be taken to require no protection against a *bona fide* attempt by the outside body to bring the relationship to an end.'[1] Further, if a Member entered into a voluntary agreement with an outside body it was felt to be difficult to argue that the latter was precluded from bringing the agreement to an end so long as the Member remained in the House.[2] The Committee also noted that there was no evidence that the conduct of W. J. Brown had been affected in any way by the C.S.C.A.

It remains, of course, a contempt of the House to attempt to intimidate Members by financial or other means; but to constitute a breach of privilege the threat must be reasonably specific and direct. On the other hand a Member ought not to enter into agreements which make him susceptible to sectional pressures. In the debate on the Brown case the House carried a motion which declared it

'Inconsistent with the dignity of the House, with the duties of a Member and with the maintenance of freedom of speech for any Member to enter into a contractual agreement limiting the Member's independence and freedom of action in Parliament . . . the duty of a Member being to his constituents and to the country rather than to any particular section.'[3]

[1] Para. 15; 1946–47 (118) ix.
[2] Ibid., para. 18.
[3] H.C. Deb., Vol. 440, col. 365.

The principles involved are clear: if Members receive payments from outside bodies they should either be in return for service unconnected with parliamentary work or be entirely *ex gratia*. Even so, much has to be left to the conscience of the individual Member.

The second broad category of contempts comprises disrespect for the House collectively committed by either a Member or a non-member. Allegations of improper conduct are thought to be particularly serious if they reflect upon the actions of officers of the House. An example of this kind is the speech made in 1951 by Lady Mellor to the women's branch of the Banner's Gate Ward of the Sutton Coldfield Conservative Association in which she criticized the conduct of the Deputy Speaker in refusing to permit discussion of certain amendments during the debate on the Finance Bill. She was further reported as saying that 'it seemed a particularly bad thing when a Government, with such a small majority, was in power, refused to admit full and free discussion'. Set in its context this comment carried an imputation of partiality by the Chair. The Committee of Privileges decided, by a majority, that a breach of privilege had occurred; yet, as the incident was of minor significance, no further action was taken.[1]

How far is it legitimate to exert pressure on Members to vote or to act in a particular way? This is the main problem raised by this second category of privilege issues. Clearly it is legitimate to try to persuade Members; it is not permissible to intimidate them. At what stage does political activity become an attempt to exert influence by improper means? A threat merely to withdraw political support is unobjectionable: other types of threat may be more serious. The Committee of Privileges has noted that the borderline of legitimate action is difficult to determine. The case in point was that of Mrs. Eleanora Tennant, Chairman of the Face the Facts Association, who was responsible for the production of a poster which announced that 'Names of M.P.s voting for bread rationing will be published here as public enemies and traitors'. Her offence was aggravated by the display of the poster at the entrance to New Palace Yard; as it was an attempt to intimidate, rather than persuade, a breach of privilege was held to have taken place.[2] A similar view was taken of a letter to Members containing questions about proposed legislation on blood sports: the writer intimated that if he did not hear from

[1] 1950–51 (235) vii.
[2] 1945–46 (181) viii.

Members he would feel justified in informing their constituents that they had no objection to cruel sports.[1] It is of the greatest importance that Members should be free to pursue their duties free from all forms of intimidation, and the trivial nature of these infringements is a measure of the health of our Parliamentary institutions.

Disorder in the precincts of the House is punishable as a contempt, for it may lower the dignity of the House and reduce its authority.[2] Defamatory speeches or writings about parliamentary activities are objectionable for the same reason: yet if this principle were applied too rigorously it might come to be a serious limitation on the free expression of opinion. In such cases it is common for the Committee of Privileges to find that a breach of privilege has occurred but to recommend that no action be taken. Recent examples are those of Mrs. Ford[3] and Colm Brogan. The latter case arose from comments in a broadcast, subsequently repeated in the *Daily Mail*, in which Mr. Brogan argued that future secret sessions of Parliament would be useless as Communists would betray confidential information. The *Daily Mail* report suggested that the Communists had twenty-nine secret supporters in the Commons. The report of the Committee of Privileges on these statements faced squarely the difficulties of dealing with defamation.

'Your Committee are of opinion that it is not consistent with the dignity of the House that penal proceedings for breach of privilege should be taken in the case of every defamatory statement which, strictly, may constitute a contempt of Parliament. Whilst recognizing that it is the duty of Parliament to intervene in the case of attacks which may undermine public confidence in, and support for, the institution of Parliament itself, your Committee think it important that . . . the law of Parliamentary privilege should not be administered in a way which would fetter or discourage the free expression of criticism or opinion, however prejudiced or exaggerated (it) may be.'[4] The Committee also noted that it was undesirable for the process of Parliamentary investigation to give added importance to irresponsible statements.

[1] H.C. Deb., Vol. 301, cols. 1545–7.

[2] 1946–47 (36) ix.

[3] Member for Down, North, 1953–54. Immediately after her introduction to the Commons Mrs. Ford wrote an article for the *Sunday Express* which criticized the conduct of Members at late-night sittings. See 1952–53 (171) vi.

[4] 1947–48 (112) ix.

Precisely the same issues arose from the crop of privilege cases that resulted from the re-imposition of petrol rationing in the winter of 1956–57. An article in the *Sunday Express*, a cartoon in the *Evening News*, some comments in an 'Any Questions' programme and a statement by a prospective Liberal candidate published in a local newspaper were each challenged because they complained of the allegedly over-generous petrol allowances that had been made to Members and parliamentary candidates. The *Sunday Express* article was critical of Members for failing to protest against the discrimination in their own favour; proceeding on a report from the Committee of Privileges, the House summoned the editor, Mr. John Junor, to the bar of the House where he made due apologies. No action followed in the other cases in two of which the Committee found that the criticism was directed against the petrol rationing scheme, not against the behaviour of Members, and was thereby unobjectionable. The Junor incident caused some uneasiness, inside and outside the House, about how far parliamentary privilege might be used to restrict freedom of discussion: R. H. S. Crossman (Lab. Coventry, East) suggested that much newspaper controversy over a decision to raise Members' pay might, strictly speaking, be regarded as a breach of privilege.[1]

The third class of contempts noted above consists of disobedience to the orders of the House, or interfering with its procedure, officers or witnesses. Few important instances of this kind have arisen in modern times: one notable exception was the refusal of the Editor and the Political Correspondent of the *Evening News* to answer questions put to them by the Committee of Privileges when investigating the Allighan case.[2] The tampering with witnesses is a serious offence, and includes bribery, intimidation and any attempt to persuade a witness not to give a committee a full and frank statement of opinion derived from facts known to him.[3] This rule applies only to

---

[1] H.C. Deb., Vol. 563, col. 207 *et seq.* Cf. also *The Times* article on 'Parliamentary Privilege' of 27th March, 1957. When Sir Charles Taylor (Con. Eastbourne) complained about the *Sunday Express* article the Speaker at first refused to rule that a *prima facie* case of breach of privilege had been made out on the ground that the allegations in the article were insufficiently serious. This view was subsequently over-borne by the general feeling of the House. H.C. Deb., Vol. 562, col. 938 *et seq.*

[2] 1946–47 (137) ix.

[3] Witnesses. Select Committee Report; 1934–35 (84) vi.

witnesses before committees; it does not protect a person who happens to be in communication with an individual Member.[1]

The number of cases referred to the Committee of Privileges has shown an increase in recent years. Between 1945 and 1957 twenty reports were issued by the Committee on matters submitted to it. This figure should be compared with the total of six similar reports in the inter-war period 1919–39, together with two further reports from the Select Committee on the Official Secrets Acts which were also concerned with the privilege of Members. It is not easy to account for the sharp rise in the post-1945 period. A few cases arose from the misconduct of Members: for the rest, the explanation must be either that Members became more sensitive about contempts of the House or that there was more cause for complaint than in previous years. In moments of political excitement there is a tendency among Members from both parties to invoke the high weapon of privilege in trivial matters that do not represent any threat to Parliament as an institution.[2]

The Committee of Privileges has taken every care not to extend the scope of privilege; in the majority of cases where some offence against Parliament has been committed, it has recommended that no action be taken. And it should be emphasized that a person returned to the Commons by a constituency does not acquire a superior and highly protected legal status from the mere fact of his election. 'Privileges of the House of Commons apply to individual Members only in so far as they are necessary in order that the House may freely perform its functions. Such privileges do not exalt the Member above the ordinary requirements of law which apply to his fellow citizens.'[3]

---

[1] 1954–55 (112) iii. This Report was on a complaint that the Deputy Assistant Chaplain General, Salisbury Plain District, had threatened a subordinate chaplain with a view to influencing proceedings in Parliament.

[2] A good example was the complaint by A. Manuel (Lab. Central Ayrshire, 1950–55) about a speech at a political meeting by Sir Robert Boothby (Con. East Aberdeenshire). Sir Robert had said that the tactics of the Opposition were to harass the Government, with its small majority, by keeping the Commons sitting late at night. The Speaker refused to agree that the implications of the speech constituted a *prima facie* breach of privilege. H.C. Deb., Vol. 485, cols. 1546–8.

[3] Para. 22; 1950–51 (244) vii. This Report concerned a complaint by John Lewis (Lab. Bolton, West, 1945–51), that the police obstructed him at the Victoria Gate, Hyde Park, when proceeding to the House. His complaint was rejected by the Committee of Privileges.

13

The Remuneration of Members

I

Payment of Members was the fifth of the six points incorporated in 'The People's Charter' of 1838, so this demand had a notable place in the reform movements of the nineteenth century. In common with other Chartist policies there was a considerable passage of time before the idea was accepted. The Liberal administration of Sir Henry Campbell-Bannerman supported the principle of payment, but it was not until the eve of the second general election of 1910 that the succeeding Liberal Cabinet of Asquith gave a definite pledge on the subject. Accordingly, the proposal to pay Members £400 per annum was introduced in the Budget statement to the Committee of Ways and Means in 1911,[1] and was subsequently approved by the House by 256 votes to 158, the Conservatives opposing the resolution. Presenting the case for the Government, Lloyd George, Chancellor of the Exchequer, commented:

'When we offer £400 a year as payment of Members of Parliament it is not a recognition of the magnitude of the service, it is not a remuneration, it is not a recompense, it is not even a salary, it is just an allowance, and I think the minimum allowance, to enable men to come here, men who would render incalculable service to the State . . . but who cannot be here because their means do not allow it.'[2]

In 1920 the Select Committee on Members' Expenses were impressed by evidence of financial hardship suffered by some Members, but recommended that no immediate action be taken to increase the figure of £400.[3] Apart from a temporary reduction of 10% in 1931, the salary of Members remained unchanged until 1937, when it was

[1] H.C. Deb., Vol. 25, cols. 1854–5.
[2] H.C. Deb., Vol. 29, col. 1361 *et seq.* In spite of the Chancellor's description, the payment has always been regarded as taxable remuneration.
[3] 1920 (255) vii.

increased to £600 p.a. on the motion of the Prime Minister, Neville Chamberlain.[1] A further advance to £1,000 p.a. was made in 1946, after a Select Committee had suggested both a rise to this figure and that half the £1,000 should be treated as an expenses allowance that would be free of income tax. The latter recommendation, however, was rejected by the Labour Government. Opposition to these increases was voiced in 1937[1] and 1946[2] by a small group of Conservatives; on both occasions an amendment was defeated that sought to postpone the higher pay until after the next general election.

The remorseless fall in the value of money in the post-war period has inflicted hardship on the less affluent Members, as on all persons living on fixed incomes. In 1953 a Select Committee on Members' Expenses reported that to restore to Members the purchasing power of £1,000 in 1946, salaries would have to be raised to £1,446. The Committee proposed an increase to £1,500[3] and this was approved by the Commons on a free vote (24th May, 1954) by 280 votes to 166: Labour Members formed part of the majority, while the Conservatives were hopelessly divided, with some voting for, most voting against and some deliberately abstaining. This verdict was not accepted by the Government. Instead, in July 1954, the Prime Minister (Sir Winston Churchill) announced the introduction of a sessional allowance of £2 for each sitting day from Monday to Thursday which would be free of income tax.[4] For an average session the value of this allowance was about £280. Labour Members were greatly dissatisfied with the failure to implement the views of the Select Committee and the free vote of the House and, for a short while, they refused to 'pair' with Government supporters. Within eighteen months the question of Members' pay was again a source of public discussion: Earl Attlee, soon after he had resigned the Leadership of the Labour Party, told the Cardiff Business Club that Members were grossly underpaid and some were 'walking about in the House and really dying on their feet'. In June, 1956, the Leaders of the Labour and Liberal Parties wrote to the Prime Minister (Sir Anthony Eden) urging the establishment of an independent extra-parliamentary committee to investigate Members' claims for more

[1] H.C. Deb., Vol. 325, col. 1049 *et seq.*
[2] H.C. Deb., Vol. 423, col. 1231 *et seq.*
[3] Report, para. 63; 1953–54 (72) vii.
[4] H.C. Deb., Vol. 529, col. 2347.

pay; this was turned down by the Government. A further debate the following month merely brought forth another refusal from the Treasury Bench, because of the general economic situation, to ease the hardship that it was admitted some Members were suffering.[1] The next year Members were luckier. Two months before the onset of another financial crisis the Prime Minister (Mr. Macmillan) announced salary increases for Members, and in ministerial salaries less than £5,000 p.a.[2] The sessional allowance for Members was terminated but their pay was raised to £1,750 p.a. the whole of which is taxable. According to the Prime Minister this sum should be regarded as having two parts, £1,000 as a basic salary and £750 to meet the expenses of parliamentary life. Members accepted this benefit with a minimum of comment.

Originally the payments to Members did not extend to Ministers, but from 1946 those receiving a salary of less than £5,000 p.a. have had added half (£500) of their salary as Members. The extra sum was put up to £750 in 1957 when all Ministers became entitled to receive it. This has an effect on liability for tax. Members can claim that the part of their salary which is spent 'wholly, exclusively and necessarily' in pursuance of their parliamentary duties shall be free of income tax; Ministers who received no salary in connection with their parliamentary duties could not claim relief for such expenditure, while Junior Ministers obtained relief only on the £500 they received as Members. No Member can claim for a total of expenses greater than his parliamentary salary. The average sum allowed as expenses by the Inland Revenue rose from £550 in 1946 to £750 in 1953,[3] showing clearly how they have increased. Items admitted as expenses include cost of living away from home, postage and telegrams, etc., secretarial assistance, travelling within a Member's constituency, and the hiring of rooms to meet constituents.[4] In the evidence submitted to the Select Committee of 1953 it was suggested that tax inspectors probably question Members less closely about their tax claims than is the case with other people.[5]

[1] H.C. Deb., Vol. 556, col. 611 et seq.

[2] H.C. Deb., Vol. 572, col. 1316. At the same time an expense allowance was introduced for Peers who attend the House of Lords, and pay increases were awarded to a large number of civil servants, members of a variety of public boards and holders of some judicial appointments.

[3] Members' Expenses. Select Committee Report, para. 21; 1953–54 (72) vii.

[4] Ibid., para 22.

[5] Ibid., Minutes of evidence Q. 73.

Members enjoy certain other free facilities in addition to their salaries.[1] The recommendation of the 1920 Committee on Members' Expenses that free first-class rail travel should be provided between London and a Member's constituency was adopted in 1924. Third-class sleeping berths were provided in 1932; four years later first-class berths were allowed; in 1945 free travel to the constituency embraced air and sea travel. Accident insurance for Members travelling on the business of the House was provided in 1957. Since 1911 Members have been entitled to some free stationery; the daily ration is two dozen full sheets octavo and two dozen half sheets quarto, together with the appropriate envelopes. This quantity is put out each day in bulk so Members are not restricted, in practice, to their official entitlement. The 1920 Committee proposed that Members should enjoy free postage; this has never been adopted, but Members may mark correspondence O.H.M.S. when writing to Government Departments or public corporations. They also have free local (London) phone calls from the House. To assist them with parliamentary business, Members have a free copy of every Act of Parliament, parliamentary report or paper issued during the current session.[2] At the beginning of each session a bound volume of Acts passed during the previous session is supplied on application, and a Member, also on application, will be given a copy of any parliamentary paper issued during the previous session if it is available. In addition, Members receive a subsistence allowance when travelling on official business, for example, when going abroad in a parliamentary delegation: the rate of expenses allowed is that applicable to civil servants of the rank of assistant secretary.[3]

Figures in the opening chapter showing the wide range in the social background of Honourable Members also give an indication of the great variation in their personal financial circumstances. For a few the parliamentary salary is but a minor addition to their resources; other Members are almost wholly dependent on their £1,750 p.a. It is true that Members, except for Ministers, are free to

[1] Ibid., paras 15–18.

[2] Since 1921 a considerable number of official reports have been issued as non-parliamentary papers in order to restrict free circulation. This has two unfortunate results. Non-parliamentary documents are used less widely and they are also more difficult for scholars to trace. Cf. P. and G. Ford, *A Guide to Parliamentary Papers*, pp. 16–20.

[3] H.C. Deb. Written answer, 14th Feb. 1957.

follow occupations which attract additional remuneration, but the alternative employment must not demand regular attendance at fixed hours. A miner, a factory worker, or a clerk cannot continue to follow his trade. There are five main vocations which are compatible with the performance of parliamentary duties—the law, journalism, trade union organization, company directorships and the management of private wealth.[1] Although opportunities in journalism and company direction may arise as a consequence of election to Westminster, there is no doubt that many people, who could not slip easily into one or more of the five categories noted above, are deterred from entering upon a political career. Men of high ability, engaged in a profession (other than law) and business executives, who are keenly interested in public affairs, may well shrink from the economic risks of attempting to enter the Commons. Major party candidates no longer contribute to election expenses, but the cost of 'nursing' a constituency remains; if, as is normally the case, a candidate is unsuccessful at his first attempt, the nursing expenditure is wasted. And politics is a highly uncertain walk of life. The possibility of losing a seat is always present, and Members with an insubstantial financial position must fear the prospect of unemployment. The hardship suffered by some ex-Members is discussed below.

Monetary considerations have also deterred Members, notably Conservatives, from accepting office as Junior Ministers. Up to 1957 the total pay of a Parliamentary Secretary was £2,000 p.a.—£1,500 plus £500 of his parliamentary salary: the position is now eased as the remuneration has been raised to £3,250 p.a.—£2,500 plus £750 of the parliamentary salary. But all Ministers have to surrender any position or employment that added to their earned income. In the past some Members have suffered financial loss when joining the Government in a minor post; others have accepted a reduction of income in the hope it would be temporary and lead to further political promotion or other opportunities. But the hazards of holding ministerial office are even greater than those of holding a seat in the Commons.[2]

[1] Cf. speech by Sir Frank Markham (Con. Buckingham), H.C. Deb., Vol. 556, col. 658 *et seq.*

[2] Emmanuel Shinwell has given a first-hand account, in *Conflict without Malice*, of the economic difficulties of an ex-Junior Minister who had also lost his seat in the House. Shinwell was Labour Member for Linlithgow 1922–24, 1928–31, Seaham 1935–50 and Easington since 1950.

How great are the expenses which Members incur arising out of their parliamentary activities? These depend partly on the luck of circumstances and partly on what a Member can afford. Representation of constituencies near London is normally less expensive, as there is no need to stay away from home while attending the Commons or when visiting the constituency. For a Member who already has a home in the provinces, and who is elected to represent a distant —but not a Metropolitan—division, there is a choice of moving house or of much triangular travelling and consequent hotel bills. The rise in hotel charges since the war has most greatly affected those Members least able to meet it. On clerical help Members manage as best they can with what they can afford: some have full-time secretaries that are also used for non-parliamentary work; some share a secretary; some use the services of a typing agency; others write all letters in longhand. Labour Members sponsored by a trade union may also receive clerical aid from their organization. Hospitality is an item that is also flexible. Some Members spend considerable sums on entertaining constituents and those who come to discuss public affairs with them: other Members can barely rise to a cup of tea. The 1953 Committee on Members' Expenses issued a questionnaire to all Honourable Members, except the Speaker and the Prime Minister; 377 Members replied giving details of their expenditure, and a few more wrote letters explaining their inability to reply because, for example, of only having had a brief period of membership. From the answers the Committee was able to estimate that the additional cost of accommodation for Members with a home outside London was £250 p.a.; that the cost of a full-time secretary was £7 per week and that part-time assistance cost £150 p.a.[1] It was noted above that the average sum allowed by the Inland Revenue as expenses, wholly, exclusively and necessarily incurred was given as £750 p.a. The Committee's findings on the evidence obtained from the questionnaire deserves to be quoted at length.

'A considerable number of Members have made it clear that they cannot afford the expenses which they deem necessary for carrying out their Parliamentary duties efficiently and, at the same time, maintain a reasonable standard of living for themselves and their families. Some have sold or mortgaged homes: the savings that others had made before entering Parliament are now exhausted and debts are accumulating: others have sacrificed pension rights which

[1] Report, para. 23; 1953–54 (72) vii.

they had established with a company or a firm . . . and are now at an age at which it would be difficult, if not impossible, for them to find employment when they leave the House of Commons: some have to refuse invitations to public functions which they ought to attend: in some cases, in order to supplement the family income, the wife of a Member has had to find employment: for a long time some have not been able to afford lunch or dinner in the dining-room of the House of Commons and use only the tea room.'[1]

Similar conclusions were reported after a survey of the financial position of Members was made in 1937 by the Conservative Government,[2] and a number of fainting attacks among Labour Members at this period were partially caused by under-nourishment.[3]

Why has there been such great resistance by Conservatives to any suggestion to raise Members' pay in face of manifest hardship? The answer is complex. Unpaid public service has an honourable place in our traditions and still dominates local government and the local administration of justice. The idea that an elected representative should not profit from his office has a natural attraction. That representatives should be paid, in order that no man be barred for financial reasons, is a radical principle quite absent from the development of conservative thought. Although the opposition to payment, so strongly expressed in 1911, has now died away, a number of Members still do not accept all the remuneration to which they are entitled. In 1947 and 1948 one Member drew no salary and ten more drew only part of it: in 1953 two Members drew no salary and a further two only drew part.[4] The net saving to the taxpayer resulting from this self-sacrifice cannot be estimated because of the unknown effect of tax liability. When the sessional allowance was introduced in 1954 some Members refused to take advantage of it.

It is alleged that if Members were better paid, a less desirable type of person would be attracted to the Commons whose motive would be that of personal gain rather than political principle or the desire to serve the community. Alternatively it is urged that the House would become composed of professional politicians, devoid of out-

[1] Ibid., para. 27.

[2] Cf. speech by the Prime Minister (Neville Chamberlain). H.C. Deb., Vol. 325, col. 1051.

[3] Sir Henry Morris-Jones, *Doctor in the Whips Room*, p. 110. Sir Henry, a qualified medical practitioner, was Member for Denbigh; Liberal 1929–31, Liberal National 1931–50. He was also a Government Whip 1932–37.

[4] H.C. Deb. Written answer, 27th Jan. 1954.

side interests and the wide range of experience which is now a characteristic of the Commons. These views, widely and sincerely held, are mistaken. If a Member's pay were such that a reasonable standard of living was assured without the need to seek additional income, many more men and women of high ability, seriously concerned with the public issues of our time, would come forward as potential candidates. Why should an increase in the supply of candidates cause a fall in the quality of Members or reduce the variety of the composition of the House? The outcome is likely to be the reverse, and if the less wealthy Members are freed from the prepossession that they must earn more, their range of knowledge may be broadened, not narrowed. The truth is that the Commons is not formed from a reasonable cross-section of the community, even of those holding the more responsible positions: it is increasingly restricted to those who, through inheritance or because of a particular type of occupation, can supplement their official allowance.

Higher salaries might increase the reluctance of Members to retire, even when they reached a stage at which physical infirmity or lack of mental vigour unfitted them for further parliamentary service. This is a real possibility. Constituency associations are the ultimate safeguard against such a development and it is not unknown for local supporters to replace an ageing Member at a general election; an increase in pay might well stimulate criticism of the performance of sitting Members. At present the poorest of Members may dread the financial consequence of leaving the House, and the present scale of remuneration scarcely permits much saving for old age. The only answer to the economic problems of retirement must be some form of pension scheme; the difficulties of arranging pensions to suit the peculiar conditions of parliamentary life are considered below.

An allied assertion is that more pay would lead to greater subservience to the Whips, for, if a seat in the House carried larger monetary rewards, Members would be loath to act in a way that might lead to its forfeiture. But are the impoverished more independent than those of better financial standing? In any case the argument seems divorced from reality. The number of serious revolts by backbenchers is low, and they occur when the rebels are stirred by deep feeling. Looking back over the recent cases of party indiscipline it is difficult to feel that a doubling of parliamentary pay would have had any influence on events. That a rise in ministerial salaries would have this effect is a more serious possibility: it might deter Members from those minor forays which never lead to expulsion from a party but which are not always an incitement to promotion.

In 1937 and 1946 some Conservative backbenchers urged that the increase in salary should be postponed until the next Parliament; repugnance at the idea of voting oneself more money is both natural and proper. No Act is required to alter the sums paid to Members, but a mere majority of the House cannot allot more money to themselves because a recommendation from a Minister of the Crown is a pre-requisite for any additional expenditure. Members are also embarrassed by the knowledge that many of their constituents suffer grievous hardships, especially the old age pensioners. A large number of Conservative supporters live on fixed incomes and are seriously affected by the constant monetary inflation: Conservative Members —many of whom clearly enjoy substantial means—must feel diffidence in facing their adherents after receiving an increase in their parliamentary salary. The plight of some Labour Members will not seem a very attractive argument to a Conservative audience.

Since 1953 this matter has been dominated by the national economic situation. The attitude of the Treasury to pay claims has come to be regarded as something of a barometer in the world of industrial negotiations; when the official paymasters are benevolent it may be urged that the danger of inflation must have receded and that the time has come for higher rewards for all. Consequently the Treasury has a further inducement—if one were needed—not to be benevolent. These considerations are held to apply *a fortiori* to salaries of the elected. As a result, post-war increases in the remuneration of Members have tended to lag far behind the rise in both prices and the wage-rates of any group of industrial workers. For a Conservative Government that has raised interest rates, instituted the 'credit squeeze' and made regular appeals for economic restraint of many kinds, the nettle of parliamentary salaries has been unpleasant to grasp. That the 1957 adjustment to Members' pay had to wait for a brief spell of economic optimism is a sad reminder of the financial instability of our times.

The considerations outlined above have been concerned either with the nature of the House of Commons or with political and economic tactics. Clearly the former demand prior attention, and it is on these grounds that the case against higher pay is so weak. Over a century ago the Chartists were urging that lack of means should not prevent men from representing their fellows. As election to the

Commons has often involved a drop in net income for many who work regular hours, the reason for instituting payment has not been wholly fulfilled. Members cannot give proper attention to their grave public responsibilities when they are harassed by personal financial troubles. It is admirable that so many Members are able to combine other occupations with parliamentary duties, but they ought not to be forced by necessity to seek secondary employment. Poverty is a poor inducement to probity, and may lead to undesirable associations. Fears of a House of professional politicians are often ridiculously over-drawn; there is no likelihood that an increase in pay would diminish the attractiveness of the Commons for the prevailing types of Member. On the contrary it may fairly be claimed that the business of parliament can no longer be conducted satisfactorily by prominent men who devote but a fraction of their time to its affairs. Low government majorities necessitating full attendance at divisions, the greater length of sessions, the growth of committee work and the complexity of the subject-matter of parliamentary discussion have all augmented the duties of Members. The House would not be able to function on its present basis unless some Members were available for the morning committee meetings which open a parliamentary day of twelve hours duration. And busy men have no time to reflect. Those who can devote the greater part of their energy to the study of public affairs should be better informed, and thereby better qualified, to help to guide the ship of state.

A wholly new approach is required to the question of Members' pay: the series of percentage adjustments merely designed to insulate them from the fall in the value of currency have been quite insufficient. Their remuneration should ensure financial independence and be at a level related to the responsibility of the representative function and the expenditure it involves. Writing in 1957 the appropriate sum is in the region of £2,500 p.a. A basic salary of £1,750 is within the scale paid to Principals, the lowest substantive grade in the Administrative Class of our civil service; to this should be added £750, the average sum now allowed by the Inland Revenue for expenses on the basis of Members' claims. No part of the parliamentary salary should be automatically exempt from tax, but Members should be able to claim relief on their expenses as at present. To obviate the objection that Members should not use their position to advance their own financial interests, it would be desirable for a change of this magnitude to be accepted towards the end of a

Parliament and be implemented only after a general election. No doubt, the figure of £2,500 would meet with criticism. Yet this sum is a minimum if those who hold important and secure positions in the community are not to be faced with a prospect of loss if they enter the Commons. The Mother of Parliaments treats her Members much less generously than many legislatures of far smaller importance.[1] For this the British tradition of honorary public service is responsible: the tradition may be noble but it is not democratic.

II

The introduction of payment to Members in 1911 led, as was intended, to the entry into the Commons of those without private means and who surrender their normal means of livelihood at the commencement of their parliamentary service. This new category of Members were, however, faced with the prospect of acute financial hardship when reaching the age of retirement. It is a cruel doctrine which insists that a man who has spent many years in helping to direct our national affairs should end his days at a standard of living comparable with that of the most indigent of old age pensioners. A quarter of a century after payment of Members was started the Chamberlain Government decided that some steps should be taken to relieve the distress of ex-Members: Sir Warren Fisher was appointed chairman of a small committee whose Report[2] formed the basis on which the Members' Fund was established.

Any attempt to arrange a pension scheme for elected representatives is fraught with peculiar difficulties. The continued employment of Members as Members depends upon the political temper of the voters. Many are in the Commons for the duration of a single parliament—or less: others have longer, but highly interrupted periods of service. As the least affluent of Members often come to the House fairly late in life there is no connection between the length of parliamentary service and the intensity of need for financial aid on retirement. A large number of Members leave the Commons voluntarily or otherwise, well before an age at which earning capacity is diminished; they can have no claim for a pension, but should they be

---

[1] Details of salaries and expenses paid to members of Commonwealth and Foreign legislatures are set out in the Report of the Select Committee on Members' Expenses, paras. 46–50; 1953–54 (72) vii.

[2] 1937–38 Cmd. 5624, xii.

required to contribute to the pensions of others? It is also undesirable to relate the right to a pension, or the size of a pension, to the period of parliamentary service, as this gives a powerful inducement for the ageing to cling to their seats as long as possible. Some form of superannuation scheme in which the benefits received by each individual are related to the amount of his own contributions is no solution, since to provide a worthwhile pension the annual sums payable would be extremely high as relatively few annual premiums per Member could be anticipated. Participation in such an arrangement would be quite beyond the resources of many Members.

In face of these difficulties the Fisher Committee proposed the establishment of a benevolent fund rather than a pension scheme. Until 1957 the Members' Fund was essentially a private charity, although regulated by statute as it received income from compulsory deductions from Members' salaries. The House of Commons Members' Fund Act, 1939, based on the Fisher recommendation, was passed in spite of trenchant opposition from a section of Conservative backbenchers. In a series of free votes more than a hundred Conservatives went into the 'No' lobby on three occasions.[1] Objection was taken to the principle of compulsory contributions and it was feared that the Fund would encourage the growth of a class of professional politicians, devoid of alternative interests and experience. Certainly the attitude inherent in some of the Conservative speeches in these debates is far removed from the current climate of opinion on welfare questions. Yet the Act itself was modest in character. It authorized a deduction of £1 each month from Members' salaries, and established a body of six Members to act as trustees for the Fund and supervise the distribution of benefits. The scale of payments was severely restricted: the maximum pension given to an ex-Member was £150 p.a. and was to be granted only if the total income of the recipient did not exceed £225 p.a., while for widows of Members the maximum was to be £75 p.a. and the total permitted income £125 p.a. To be eligible for pension Members had to be sixty years of age, or be incapacitated, and have served as Members for ten years. The Fund involved no cost to the public as the contributions were not free of income tax; to prevent the Fund from suffering heavy initial expenditure, the beneficiaries were restricted to those who had contributed to it, thus excluding Members who retired before September, 1939.

[1] H.C. Deb., Vol. 343, col. 418 *et seq.*; Vol. 349, col. 2509; Vol. 350, col. 1398.

Expenditure from the Fund is related to the rate at which impecunious Members leave the Commons. Retirements are naturally most frequent at general elections; as no such election occurred until the Fund had been in existence for nearly six years the initial demands on it were small. The annual income from Members' contributions was in excess of £7,000, while until 1944–45 the annual expenditure never exceeded £1,000. During the war years a very cautious policy was adopted by the Trustees who resolved that it would be unwise to improve the rates of benefit until a reserve of £50,000 had been accumulated. They have been guided in their policy by the Government Actuary and when, in 1946, a reserve of £48,000 had been created, they felt justified in proposing some increase in the rates of benefit.[1] The Members' Fund Act, 1948, accordingly authorized increases on the lines proposed by the Trustees. The maximum annual pension payable to an ex-Member became £250, and to widows £150, subject to income limits of £325 and £225 respectively. Beneficiaries were extended to include widowers of ex-Members, if they were incapable of earning a livelihood, in which case the limits relating to widows would apply, and provision was made for the children of Members who died. Section 4 of the 1948 Act also permitted the Trustees to make special grants in extreme cases of hardship to ex-Members or their dependants who would not otherwise qualify for relief. In addition, future alterations in the amount of contributions and rates of benefit were to require a resolution of the House and would not demand amending legislation. As a result of these changes, expenditure from the Fund increased from £2,254 in 1947–48 to £4,663 the following year; yet only about half of the income was being spent as the receipts of the Fund were now augmented with the interest earned by the capital reserve.

[1] House of Commons Members' Fund. Select Committee Report; 1946–47 (110) ix. The administration of a scheme of this nature is dominated by an inescapable dilemma. On the one hand it seems absurd to hoard money, that has been collected for the relief of distress among ex-Members, when it is clear that existing rates of pension no longer give the measure of relief intended owing to the fall in the value of money. Yet if the level of expenditure approaches too closely the level of income, there is no margin left to finance pensions for new claimants without encroaching on the capital reserve. Once the reserve is breached, ultimate bankruptcy is inevitable unless the existing beneficiaries die more rapidly than new claimants appear. The assessment of the contingent liabilities of a pension fund depends upon assumptions about the average expectation of life and is a highly skilled actuarial operation.

A full inquiry into the operation of the Members' Fund was under-taken by the Select Committee on Members' Expenses. In its Report[1] the Committee argued that the existing arrangements were defective in that assistance could be granted only in cases of really severe hardship: even then the scale of benefits was insufficient, but could not be improved owing to the restricted income of the Fund. At their present rate of remuneration Members could not afford the large increase in contributions that would be required to finance adequate pensions. Accordingly, the Committee proposed the introduction of a non-contributory pensions scheme. The average Member, it asserted, was unable to save for retirement and old age out of his parliamentary salary. If formerly he belonged to some form of super-annuation scheme, he normally had to leave it on entering the Commons, and he may have had to sacrifice pension rights that he had accrued. The problem was particularly grave for those Members who devoted the last years of their working life to parliamentary service. 'By comparison with employment in professions and industry therefore, Membership of Parliament is found to impose not only a current sacrifice while a Member, but continuing sacrifice after leaving the House, through its absence of pension benefits ... More-over, Members of Parliament are the servants of the public: they have a capricious employer who has the right to dismiss them temporarily or permanently.'[2]

As the scheme proposed by the Select Committee was non-contributory, its burden would have fallen squarely on the taxpayer. Apart from this aspect, it faced at least two other major difficulties. The first was whether Members should receive a pension irrespective of means: while some ex-Members are reduced to the borders of poverty, others are wealthy. The second objection was that as eligibility for a pension, and its amount, would depend on length of parliamentary service, a strong inducement might arise for ageing Members to retain their seats as long as possible. This plan was referred to the Trustees of the Members' Fund for fuller examination. The Trustees subsequently produced an alternative plan for con-tributory pensions combined with the continuation of a benevolent fund:[3] to finance these arrangements a total annual payment of £72

---

[1] Para. 35; 1953–54 (72) vii.

[2] Ibid., para. 36.

[3] House of Commons Members' Fund. Report concerning Pensions for Members; 1954–55 (105) viii.

would have been required from each Member. No action was taken on these lines, however, since many Members felt unable to afford this amount—at least on their current scale of remuneration.

The following table gives an outline of the recent history of the Members' Fund and shows the effect of a further small rise in benefit rates in November, 1955.

THE MEMBERS' FUND[1]

Year ending 30th September	Ordinary Allowances (£'s)	Special Hardship Allowances (£'s)	Size of the Fund (£'s)
1951	6,231	574	71,244
1952	6,106	474	73,604
1953	6,125	487	76,557
1954	5,666	583	79,980
1955	4,938	593	83,855
1956	6,365	653	86,116

New Grants made	To ex-Members	To Widows	Special Hardship Cases
1944–50	26	9	8
1950–55	10	12	1
Grants continuing at 30th Sept. 1955	17	21	6

It is not possible to feel wholly satisfied with the administration of the Fund which has spent, to date, considerably less than half its income, when at least a few ex-Members have lived and died in conditions of acute distress.[2] In July, 1956, while refusing to improve Members pay, the Prime Minister (Sir Anthony Eden) hinted at the willingness of the Government to make some contribution to the Fund which would finance an increase in benefit rates.[3] A contribution of £10,000 p.a. was announced in February, 1957,[4] so that

[1] Source—Annual Reports on the Members' Fund, especially for the year 1954–55; 1955–56 (167) xxi.

[2] For example the case of F. Fairhurst (Lab. Oldham 1945–50) which has been described to the Commons by L. Hale (Lab. Oldham, West). H. C. Deb., Vol. 556, cols. 635–6.

[3] H.C. Deb., Vol. 556, col. 628.

[4] Written answer 22nd Feb. 1957.

roughly half the income of the Fund is contributed by the taxpayer. Pension rates have now been brought up to respectable levels. The maximum payable to an ex-Member is £500 p.a. subject to a total income limit of £650, and the corresponding figures for both widows and widowers are £300 p.a. and £450 p.a.

The future of the Fund is impossible to foretell. Now that the principle of a state contribution has been accepted, its size may well be increased if inflation continues to depreciate the currency. Those who regret that the Fund is no longer independent of the taxpayer should recall that it is a casualty of the low level of parliamentary pay.

14

Sheep or Goats?

How important is the part played by the individual Member of the Commons in the process of government in this country? It is fashionable to reply to this question with some word like 'negligible', or even to couch an answer in derisory terms. The grounds for this attitude are formidable. At a general election, fought essentially between two giant parties, one party achieves a majority over its opponents: the leaders of the majority group form the Cabinet and exercise power until the next election decides whether they shall remain in office, or whether the leaders of the Opposition shall take over. There can be no change in the political complexion of the Cabinet between elections because of the strength of party discipline in the Commons. In this system, it is urged, the private Member becomes a voting machine whose speeches are unimportant and which, indeed, may be irritating to the leaders of his own party. Good conduct may lead to minor ministerial office, but rebellion, if persistent and serious, means the loss of the whip, repudiation by the constituency, and political oblivion after the next election. Further, the legislature is supposed to control the executive through the principle of ministerial responsibility; in practice, with the growth of the functions of government departments associated with welfare policies, the Civil Service becomes ever more influential, and Members have neither the time nor the expertise to control the actions of the bureaucracy. Even the authority to pass legislation is of diminished significance as the details of statutory provision are filled in, again by the Civil Service, through the device of delegated legislation. In these circumstances it is not surprising that Professor Keeton has written a book on the *Passing of Parliament*, or that Christopher Hollis,[1] in similar vein, has asked in a title *Can Parliament Survive?* It may appear that the

[1] Conservative Member for Devizes, 1945–55.

British Constitution works smoothly through the widespread acceptance of democratic conventions, but also because of the sheep-like
qualities of backbench Members who help to eradicate any troublesome goats that manage to enter their flock.

No complete repudiation of this indictment is possible. The harsh
facts of party discipline must be admitted and so must the frightening
range of Civil Service activities. The defence can only be that the
indictment is but a partial statement of political realities. Many of
the preceding pages have been concerned to illustrate how the backbenchers do use, in fact, the various opportunities available for them
to influence official policy. The record shows that parliamentary
criticism has a significant cautionary effect on the behaviour of
officials, and that Ministers pay much attention to the views of their
supporters in the House. To argue that the sole restriction on a
Cabinet is its fear of the next election is to simplify the political
process in this country beyond the point of distortion. Backbench
opinion can be decisive not only on matters of legislative detail but
also in times of grave crisis—witness the fall of the Chamberlain
Government in May, 1940, and the threat of forty Conservative
Members in November, 1956, to vote against the Eden Government
if hostilities in Egypt were not brought to a halt.[1] When issues are of
sufficient urgency, the party whip loses its force. And the existence
of a representative assembly is central to the maintenance of a
democratic form of rule: without backbenchers there would be no
parliament. So however imperfectly the average Member may perform his duties, however restricted and frustrated he may feel, the
role he fills in our public life is vital. A complex organism requires
nerves as well as a heart.

Those who lament the present status of the backbencher often
advocate changes in parliamentary organization. It is urged that the
Commons should streamline the established methods of conducting
business and make them more suited to modern requirements. In the
inter-war period many Left-wing Members held such views; they
feared that the traditional procedure would hinder the legislation
needed to create the socialist paradise.[2] More recently some Conservatives have become restive about the amount of time the legislature consumes. They regret that it is increasingly awkward for

[1] M. and S. Bromberger, *Secrets of Suez*, p. 147.
[2] Cf. A. H. Hansen, 'The Labour Party and House of Commons Reform',
Parliamentary Affairs, Vol. X, pp. 454–68 and Vol. XI, pp. 39–56.

Members to undertake extra-parliamentary activities, and contend that this must lead to a decline in the general quality of Members. Yet in spite of these mixed disquiets, Commons' procedure has proved remarkably resilient and the overall pattern of its routine has remained unaffected. The *status quo* has a variety of supports. Ministers, backed by the Whips, are not likely to favour schemes that would aid their critics. The House as a whole has a great respect for its own traditions, and tends to insist that changes be evolutionary rather than revolutionary. Further, most Members realize that reform of procedure is a double-edged sword: an innovation that permits policy and legislation to be considered more speedily, or by fewer people, necessarily reduces the ability of Honourable Members to intervene in its discussion. Existing procedure is a safeguard of the rights of the individual backbencher and helps to protect him from the power of the majority party. A sound knowledge of *Erskine May* is a great asset to the Member who wishes to make himself heard.

However, alterations to save time have been made, and more will surely come. Since 1945 both Labour and Conservative Governments have sponsored changes, most of which were previously recommended by Select Committees on Procedure. Another in the series of select committees was established in 1958 when the Government accepted a private member's motion by A. Oram (Lab. East Ham, S.) that this should be done. The motion had been preceded by an unusual amount of unofficial activity. Oram, J. Grimond (Lib. Orkney and Zetland), Sir R. Boothby (Con. E. Aberdeenshire), Wedgwood Benn (Lab. S.E. Bristol) and D. Price (Con. Eastleigh) sent a letter to all Members, in the nature of a 'backbench whip', urging their presence and support.[1] The debate[2] provided much evidence of the frustrations felt by Members not able to catch the Speaker's eye; unable to discuss the topics crowded out of the parliamentary timetable; dragooned by Whips to hang around the House to attend divisions on specialized matters in which they had no interest. Ameliorative measures suggested have been a time-limit on speeches, a limitation in the priority allowed to Privy Councillors, electronic voting devices and a wider use of committees. But the

[1] Interest in the work of backbenchers and doubts about its quality and effectiveness had undoubtedly been stimulated by comment and correspondence in *The Times* during the Christmas recess.

[2] H.C. Deb., Vol. 581, cols. 673–775.

basic causes of frustration must remain. Each of 630 Members cannot enjoy a place in the sun as often as they would wish. Secondly, Members are engaged in a struggle for power so the Whips must normally be on: a party that gives greater freedom to its back-benches is presenting opponents with a possible advantage. If the political struggle is to be a reality there is a limit to the extent to which the convenience of Members can be consulted.

Within these limits could means be found to give Members greater scope for self-assertion? In the past the common solution has been more committees. Various proposals on these lines have been put forward, but when closely examined the details are not always clear and the probable implications seem sometimes to have been overlooked. An early example is the scheme of F. Jowett[1] to create a series of committees, one for each Department, to which Members should be allocated. These committees would function like those in local government: each Minister would be the Chairman of the committee concerned with his Department, and all legislative and administrative matters within its scope would be examined before discussion by the whole House. Departmental documents and information should be available to these bodies. Thus fully informed, Members could make a positive contribution to the work of government.[2] A similar plan, on a rather more sophisticated level, was put forward by the distinguished constitutional lawyer (now Sir) W. Ivor Jennings in 1934.[3] This envisaged a series of standing committees to discuss the details of legislation, each specializing on the work of one department or a group of departments with cognate interests. A committee would have the right to examine civil servants, and would expect the presence of an appropriate Junior Minister. It would act as an advisory body to the Department and would also report to the House on any matter it deemed of sufficient importance. It would be, in Jennings' own phrase, 'a permanent Departmental Committee or Royal Commission'.

Arrangements of this nature would certainly tend to transform the sheep into goats, but they would also face insuperable difficulties. Could departmental committees of backbenchers avoid fouling the principle of ministerial responsibility? If a Minister were able to

---

[1] Labour Member for Bradford 1906–18, 1922–24, 1929–31.

[2] Fenner Brockway, *Socialism over Sixty Years: The Life of Jowett of Bradford*, pp. 73–74.

[3] *Parliamentary Reform*, Ch. IX.

persuade his committee of the virtues of some new policy, and the innovation proved subsequently to be a disastrous failure, it would be difficult to acquit the committee of some share of the blame. The Minister might well escape the necessity of resignation. Alternatively, a Minister who failed to obtain committee support for new proposals ought not to withdraw them merely on that account; Ministers are responsible to the Commons as a whole and not to any group of Members. In the words of Professor Wheare, there is a possibility that committees will be buffers or duffers. Further, by tending to become a focus for specialized enthusiasm, they are often quite unrepresentative of opinion as a whole. And the history of committee behaviour in the United States Congress and the French Assembly suggests that official committees of a legislature should be given closely defined terms of reference.

The second line of criticism of the Jowett and Jennings plans is that they fail to take account of party discipline; this is especially strange in the case of Jennings since he was acutely aware of the influence of the Whips on backbenchers. If the proposed bodies were to be of real value, it is inevitable that they would be a nuisance and an embarrassment to Ministers. Opposition Members could scarcely be blamed for using their authority as committeemen to attempt to unearth information about departmental actions that, if published, might cause political damage to the government. Every Ministry would be expected to go about its business with a cluster of Members metaphorically, if not literally, in its corridors every day. In reality, on contentious issues, a committee would divide on party lines, produce a government majority on all occasions and become a buffer. If ever party loyalty should fail to bring a committee to heel, Ministers could still use their majority in the House to remove recalcitrant Members, or otherwise limit its sphere of action. These plans are but an attempt to evade the implications of party discipline: they would fail because the power of a majority can always be applied to any device which seeks to challenge its authority. Jowett was clearly attempting to apply the methods of local government to central government, but the tasks of central governments are so different in scale as to be different in nature. Even in local government, where party organization is strong, the committee system tends to become another forum for political discussion which is terminated by a political vote.

In spite of all difficulties this concept of extending the committee

252

structure of the Commons has great attractions, for it would make fuller use of the energies of backbenchers and strengthen the legislature. H. R. G. Greaves has advocated departmental committees on the Jennings pattern, although he admitted they might not work smoothly because of the class division that exists between the major political parties.[1] The suggestion of H. J. Laski was more modest in scope.[2] He proposed a series of advisory committees which would meet Ministers monthly in order to keep the latter in touch with the opinions of Members on the problems facing their respective Departments. Ministers should have an 'unvariable right' to control the agenda at these meetings, and it would be clearly understood that the committees had no executive responsibility of any kind. Granted this restriction in function, the objections raised in the two preceding paragraphs do not apply to the Laski plan.

Since 1945 there has been, in fact, a great increase in committee activity by Members. Much of it has been in the form of the unofficial party gatherings, which give Ministers an added opportunity to appreciate the feelings of Members on the Government side of the House. The difference between the present arrangements and those which Laski urged is threefold. Ministers do not now control agendas; existing party groups are unofficial and are outside the formal machinery of the Commons; because of the party character of committees, Ministers do not have an equivalent opportunity of testing the views of Opposition Members. On balance, the existing system seems more likely to strengthen backbench influence, for Government supporters would not talk to Ministers so frankly with representatives of the Opposition present. In the post-war period official committees have also been more active. The Select Committee on Statutory Instruments keeps an expert vigil over the constitutional propriety of delegated legislation. The Select Committee on Estimates has also greatly extended the volume of its commentary on departmental administration, and has managed, though not without difficulty, to do so while still avoiding the forbidden field of policy. It is far too soon to judge whether the new Select Committee on Nationalized Industries will be of value, but the Public Accounts Committee continues to wield significant influence. Thus the backbenchers have vastly improved their own organization in recent years without making any great innovations in parliamentary institutions.

[1] *The British Constitution* (1938), p. 49.
[2] *Reflections on the Constitution* (1951), pp. 52–3.

It has been emphasized that Members make their major impress on public issues before official decisions are made. In general, the Whips are not concerned with this ante-natal interference; their task of persuasion cannot commence until a 'party line' has been established. For this reason the frustration caused by the Whips can easily be exaggerated, but it is still arguable that the bonds of party discipline could be relaxed with advantage. Yet should one of the chief parties allow more freedom for its Members to vote at will in the House, a great opportunity is presented to its opponents to emphasize the disunity on the benches opposite. Professor Wheare infers that party discipline on the committee stage of legislation is stronger than it need be since details only are involved, general principles having been accepted previously by the whole House.[1] This view underestimates the importance of detail; simple amendments can be expensive, introduce inconsistencies and otherwise be awkward to apply. In the interests of smooth administration there is more to be said for a free vote on whether to do X or not to do X, rather than allowing Members to decide how X should be put into practice. Administrative desiderata should not become final determinants of the form of legislation, but it is not difficult to see why Government Whips are active in committee. Free votes have a habit of creating trouble for Ministers. They are held to imply that a Cabinet cannot make up its mind, and critics urge that it is the job of the Government to govern. Certainly there are occasions, especially when procedural matters are in question, when the issue of a whip could well be avoided. Yet granted the existing pattern of our political life it is idealistic to hope that the claims of party loyalty will be much diminished.

Little has been said in the preceding pages about the national party organizations. This is because most Members play but a small role in them, apart from being asked to do some speech-making and appearing at an Annual Conference. The Conferences themselves are designed for constituency stalwarts, and Members have a limited role in the discussions: an analysis of the report of the 1956 Labour Conference shows that of the 156 persons who spoke only 43 were Members, and of these eight spoke from the platform as representing the National Executive Committee.[2] Essentially the

[1] *Government by Committee*, p. 247.
[2] Parallel information about the Conservative Party is not available.

254

task of a political organization is to stimulate support for its leaders rather than to influence immediate issues of policy. This statement will be accepted more easily by Conservatives than by Labourites, yet is basically true in both cases. The Labour Party has more vigorous and systematic debates with the tradition that a vote at the Annual Conference is the final authority on party policy. By various arts the Labour leaders in the Commons can usually defeat their opponents on these occasions: if all else fails a Labour Cabinet may be forced to ignore a decision reached against its advice, as happened over tied cottages. Conservative theory is simpler to apply. Conference resolutions are reported to the Leader of the Party for his information, but the Leader remains the supreme arbiter of policy. Consequently those elected to office in the Labour Party have a much greater sense of power. Each year there is great competition for seats on its National Executive Committee, and the seven seats filled by the votes of the local constituency parties are a particular source of interest, for they provide an impressive barometer of personal popularity. In recent years these elections have been won by advocates of more extreme policies, some of whom are backbenchers—Mrs. B. Castle (Blackburn), R. H. S. Crossman (Coventry, East), T. Driberg,[1] I. Mikardo (Reading) and S. Silverman (Nelson and Colne). In 1952 five senior Ministers in the previous Labour Cabinet were rejected—Herbert Morrison, Dr. Dalton, H. Gaitskell, A. Robens and E. Shinwell.[2] It must be an unhappy experience for eminent men to be treated in this way. Yet the effect of these results on the Labour Party itself is limited because of the moderation of the trade unions which are allocated twelve seats on the Executive, and which can also dominate the election for the five seats for women by reason of their voting strength.[3] The significant point, however, is that the Labour Party's constitution does provide three main centres for argument about policy—the Annual Conference, the National

[1] Member for Maldon: Independent 1942–45, Labour 1945–55. Driberg still remains on the Executive although he left the Commons voluntarily in 1955.

[2] Before the 1951 Election these were respectively Foreign Secretary, Minister of Housing and Local Government, Chancellor of the Exchequer, Minister of Labour and Minister of Defence. In 1952 with Labour in Opposition, Morrison was Deputy Leader of the Party in the Commons: the Party Constitution was subsequently amended to include the Deputy Leader on the Executive *ex officio*.

[3] The other members of the Executive are the Leader and Deputy-Leader in the Commons, the Party Treasurer and one representative of affiliated organizations other than trade unions.

Executive Committee and the Parliamentary Labour Party. It follows
that when the soul of the Party is troubled and opinions are divided,
there are exceptional opportunities for the main protagonists—who
may include backbenchers—to join battle. Such was the case after
the resignation of Bevan and Wilson from the Labour Cabinet in
1951 until the election of Gaitskell as Party Leader at the end of
1955.[1]

The condition of a party, both in and out of Parliament, is the
dominating factor which decides the general degree of importance
of its backbench Members. Those who belong to a majority party
in the Commons are clearly more influential than those in a minority
group. A majority that is small, as between 1950 and 1955, has a hold
on power so precarious that serious dissension within the party
would lead to the downfall of the Government. Tactical pressure to
support the party leadership in such circumstances is often overwhelming. At the other extreme, when a party has a massive majority
—e.g., the Conservatives in the nineteen-thirties—criticism can be
safely ignored because there are always sufficient of the faithful to
sustain the government even against combined attacks from both
sides of the House. Backbench opinion behind the Treasury Bench is
most effective, therefore, when Ministers have an adequate working
majority, but are not so secure that they can afford always to brush
aside their adversaries. Members of the Opposition can be most
unbridled in their public utterances when there is no immediate prospect of their party gaining power; as the hope of office grows stronger,
so also does the tendency to fall into step.

Expediency is not, however, the sole guide to political behaviour.
There are still Members who feel that the possession of power is less
important than the use that is made of it. This book has been able
to record many examples of Members who have felt obliged to cause
discomfort to their friends by saying and doing what seemed to them
to be right: when a party is confused and uneasy not all of its supporters will be placid. In the nineteen-fifties frustration in Conservative circles has been aggravated rather than assuaged by the
existence of Conservative Governments, because the latter have not
been able to satisfy the aspirations of their supporters. Britain's
decline as an imperial power has continued; the international authority of the United States has become more apparent; currency

[1] Cf. two articles in *Political Studies*, 'Policy Decision in Opposition': Saul
Rose at Vol. IV, pp. 128–38 and R. T. MacKenzie at Vol. V, pp. 176–82.

inflation and rising prices that drastically affect the value of fixed incomes have not been checked; most of the social welfare policies introduced by the Labour Party have been continued at considerable cost to the taxpayer; the greater part of the nationalized industries still remain in public ownership. These harsh realities have provided much fuel for smouldering irritation, and have provoked a record level of activity by Conservative Members which perhaps reached a peak at the time of the Suez action. The disputes in the Labour Party since 1951 were aggravated by the need to choose a successor to Attlee, but have not completely died away since the election of Gaitskell. In July, 1957, thirty-two Labour Members wrote to *Reynolds News* strongly criticizing a Party document on *Industry and Society* which embodied very modest proposals for future nationalization. The following week thirty-four of their colleagues in the Commons issued a statement in support of *Industry and Society*. It is clear, then, that Labour Members are likely to play a full part in future controversy about Party policy.

Of late the political climate has been peculiarly favourable for backbenchers to exercise initiative because of the element of storm in both the major parties. As this unsettlement produces discussion, it is also good for the vitality of our democracy.

How great is the burden of work that must be carried by an Honourable Member? A good deal depends on his constituency. It is much easier to have a safe, urban seat near Westminster than to represent a marginal and scattered rural area far from the metropolis. Above all, the extent of his duties is a matter of personal choice. A respectable division record can be maintained by limited attendance at the Commons: party meetings and committees in the House can be ignored: a constituency can be given a minimum of attention. But a Member who wished to scamp his functions to this extent would be so uninterested in public affairs as to have little desire to retain his seat. Members are active and conscientious, not in order to secure political promotion or to win a few more votes at the next election, but because they want to carry out their tasks as a representative in a creditable manner. Naturally, there are exceptions. Constituency business can be tiresome and there must be some variation in the quality of attention given to correspondence. The meticulous enthusiast can easily spend the whole of his time on public affairs. Christopher Hollis, an ex-Member, has described parliamentary life as a ceaseless round of activity which necessitates the sacrifice of home life, recreations and cultural activities. He suggests that few Members have time to read many books after their election to Parliament.[1] The increase in parliamentary pay in 1957 provoked the publication of some attractive letters in *The Times* on the topic of Members' duties. Another ex-Member, Commander Bower,[2] expressed an attitude typical of some Conservative Members of his generation when he argued that the difficulties of parliamentary life were exaggerated: a Member should be able to keep abreast of current affairs by studying the press for half an hour each day; the greater part of a Member's correspondence did not require serious personal attention; on many days there was no need to attend the Commons at all and on others only a perfunctory visit was required; 'a natural speaker will have no difficulty in making well prepared and authoritative speeches'; constituencies should be satisfied with one Saturday visit a month. This commentary produced a riposte from Captain Pilkington (Con., Poole)[3] that the experience of Commander Bower related to the 'palmy days' before 1945 when the latter lost his seat.

There is no doubt that the lot of Members has been tougher since the war. In the 1945 Parliament the pressure of legislation was severe, and between 1950 and 1955 the narrow Government majorities necessitated intense whipping. Party committees in the Commons have also proliferated during this period. Thirdly, constituents are now more demanding. It is arguable that the 'surgery' system can be abused, and that it encourages the public to regard their local Member as another breed of welfare officer. And while grievances can often be explained and disposed of more easily in an interview than by correspondence, the 'surgery' does potentially submit Members to listening to the whims of peculiar persons. The questions then emerge —does it matter if the time of a Member is wasted? Should we worry if parliament consumes all the energies of Members? A negative response on these counts must have a serious impact on the quality of those attracted to political life.

It is common in human affairs to romanticize the past and to urge that things are not so good as they used to be. Thus the calibre of Honourable Members is sometimes said to have deteriorated in the last few years because party discipline has eradicated individuality.

[1] *Can Parliament Survive?* pp. 69–70.
[2] Member for Cleveland 1931–45. In *The Times*, 24th July, 1957.
[3] Since 1951. Previously Member for Widnes 1935–45.

This is not a new idea. When Lord Morley asserted in 1923 that the private Member was a shadow of what he had been at the end of the previous century, he was reminded by Mr. Birrell that W. E. Gladstone had said the same in the 1880s when arguing that the post-1832 period constituted the Golden Age.[1] But the pessimistic view has been powerfully reinforced by the cautious pen of Lord Attlee who notes that, while the general level of ability of Members is rising, there are fewer Members of distinction from other walks of life.[2] Although the House can provide a surplus of first-class Parliamentary Secretaries, there does seem a scarcity of those who are naturally destined for high office.

Certainly, no shortage of parliamentary candidates has developed, but it is almost unknown for a man of outstanding attainments in industry, trade unionism, science or university life to come forward for selection. Even should a man of this stature be willing to stand, it is by no means certain that a constituency caucus would choose him, because of the desire to have a Member prepared to give a great deal of attention to purely local affairs. The rejection of Roy Harrod by Bournemouth Conservatives in 1952 is one such example. Traditionally the House is replete with legal talent; many of the more brilliant lawyers, and therefore the most highly paid, are now reluctant to enter the political arena for financial reasons. One or two of the ablest of trade union Members have resigned from the House in order to advance their careers in the trade union movement, while some safe Labour seats tend to be treated by the large unions as pocket boroughs and are allocated representatives with mediocre qualifications. Many Members drop out of public life because they find it impossible to combine business with their parliamentary tasks. Thus pressures making for a House of full-time politicians come from two distinct sources, the constituencies and the party demand for steady attendance at Westminster. Under a Labour Government, with a large programme of contentious and time-consuming legislation, the situation is likely to be aggravated. There is nothing dishonourable in the calling of a professional politician; it was argued in the previous chapter that some are essential and, therefore, that the parliamentary salary should be sufficient to prevent Members from urgently seeking extra sources of income. But this is not to advocate a House wholly—or even largely—composed of full-time politicians.

[1] H. J. Laski, *Reflections on the Constitution*, p. 30.
[2] *The Times*, 11th April, 1957.

Indeed, if it becomes an increasing strain to combine parliamentary duties with other activities, the House will be manifestly poorer.

Meanwhile, the Commons remains a strong magnet. Since it extracts a formidable toll from Members, this attraction requires explanation. Probably some candidates have not fully appreciated the exertions that face them should they be successful: this was true of some of the Labour Members first elected in 1945. Monetary reward is certainly not the inducement and even the chance of obtaining a ministerial salary is not very exciting. The level of pay for junior ministers has been a positive disincentive for some Conservatives. The £5,750 per annum that accompanies full ministerial rank can be far exceeded in the top ranks of management and the legal profession, and is also below the salary of the most senior civil servants. Many Members, especially Conservatives, are company directors, but it would be quite false to suggest that they normally occupy these positions as a consequence of their representative status. The motive force that supplies an abundance of potential candidates must be a combination of political enthusiasm and a genuine willingness for public service. It is significant that many Members have preliminary experience in local government and that others have a family tradition of participation in public affairs. Once a candidate is elected, these sentiments are powerfully reinforced by the fascination of being close to the centre of great events and by heightened ambition to obtain office. Members who have been in Westminster for many years without achieving prominence are still reluctant to leave. The lure of the House is strong and not easy to describe. A club-like atmosphere is retained and Members know each other by Christian names; the Smoking Room is naturally the best informed centre of political gossip in the land. A real attachment to Parliament extends beyond Members to the staff of the House and to the reporters in the Gallery. It is not restricted to any political party, and I recall the private confession of one Labour Member that he was more interested in Parliament than he was in socialism.

The charm of Parliament can be equated to enchantment with power. This view, however, is unacceptable. It has been shown in some detail that the generality of Members do not possess power; the ability to make decisions about state policy is the prerogative of Ministers, and only the inner band of senior Ministers can normally sway the destiny of nations. What Members have is influence, the strength of which depends on the political situation at any given time.

For some, influence is as attractive as power, since it does not carry the same onus of responsibility. Nor is it open to precise measurement, so there must be a penumbra of doubt over the weight of the counsel from backbenches.

Finally, Honourable Members enjoy a position of respect in the community. The popular attitude to our elected representatives varies at different levels of discussion, but the reactions of the ignorant and indifferent in this matter need not be heeded. Responsible opinion recognizes that Members perform functions central to the operation of a democratic system of government, by acting as the ultimate arbiter of the fate of Cabinets, as a channel of opinion between elections and as watchdog over the executive. Party discipline may hamper Members more than is desirable, but these tasks are carried out with a high sense of duty. Our representatives receive a real measure of public esteem for what they do, and sometimes for what it is thought they can do. This is a gratifying experience for them and a further attraction of their calling. It would be most unwise to begrudge Members this pleasure. The standing of politicians in our society is a fair measure of their quality; the higher they stand in public estimation, the better will the public be served.

Postscript

The Strauss Case

W hile this book was in the press, the Commons had an important debate on the scope of parliamentary privilege. In a free vote, and by a majority of five, it was decided to reject the report of the Committee of Privileges that a letter from G. Strauss (Lab. Vauxhall) to the Postmaster-General was a 'proceeding in Parliament', and thereby protected by parliamentary privilege. The controversy stimulated by the Strauss case is relevant to a number of matters discussed in the preceding pages. The main facts of the case and the issues involved are therefore outlined in this postscript.

In February, 1957, the Member for Vauxhall wrote to the Postmaster-General complaining about the methods used by the London Electricity Board in disposing of scrap cable. The Postmaster-General replied that this was a matter of day-to-day administration and not within his sphere of responsibility; he would, however, arrange for the views expressed to be made known to the L.E.B. There followed a meeting between the Chairman of the L.E.B. and the Member for Vauxhall which failed to produce satisfaction for either party. Subsequently the L.E.B. asked that the critical statements made in the letter to the Postmaster-General be withdrawn: when Strauss refused to withdraw, the L.E.B., through their solicitors, intimated that a writ for libel would be issued. Strauss then raised the affair in the Commons as a question of privilege and it was referred to the Committee of Privileges.[1]

In November, 1957, the Committee reported that the Member's letter was a 'proceeding in Parliament' within the meaning of the Bill of Rights, 1689; therefore the L.E.B. and their solicitors, by threatening to issue a writ were acting in breach of parliamentary privilege.[2]

[1] H.C. Deb., Vol. 568, cols. 819–22.

[2] para. 20; 1956–57 (305), Article 9 of the Bill of Rights enacts that 'the freedom of speech and debates or proceedings in Parliament ought not to be impeached or questioned in any Court or place out of Parliament'.

The Committee reached these conclusions after lengthy deliberations and with a sole dissentient, the Attorney-General, Sir R. Manningham-Buller (Con. Northants, S.). The problem is what does the word 'proceeding' cover? So far, this has never been precisely defined. In 1939 it was agreed that a draft of a parliamentary question was a 'proceeding' for this purpose, and the Attorney-General at that time said he could see 'a possible construction of "proceedings" which would extend to matters outside the precincts (of the House) if they were related to what is to happen in the House'.[1] This comment opened the way for a broad interpretation and in 1957 the majority of the Committee felt that the meaning of 'proceeding' must be related to modern conditions. As the question hour is no longer adequate for the matters Members wish to raise, the practice of writing to Ministers is accepted as an ancilliary to questions: it is thus logical to argue that letters should have the same protection as questions. But Sir R. Manningham-Buller urged that in terms of common sense as well as law the word could not cover a Member's letter, and he criticized some of the opinions cited by his predecessor in 1939.[2] Further discussion of these issues was delayed for several months by the decision to take advice from the Judicial Committee of the Privy Council on another legal problem that turned out to be a red herring.[3] Finally, in July, 1958, the Privileges Committee reaffirmed their previous views but recommended that no action be taken against the L.E.B. and their solicitors as the case was the first of its kind, and as no legal action against the Member had, in fact, been commenced.[4]

Against this background of events the Commons rejected the advice of its Committee of Privileges and freed the London Elec-

[1] Official Secrets Acts. Select Committee Report, mins. of ev. q. 121; 1938–39 (101) viii.

[2] H.C. Deb., Vol. 591, col. 253.

[3] It had been suggested to the Committee of Privileges by the Attorney-General that the Commons would be acting contrary to the Parliamentary Privilege Act, 1770, if it treated the issue of a writ against a Member as a breach of privilege. This proposition, if substantiated, would have had wide implications. It was therefore agreed to seek the opinion of the Judicial Committee of the Privy Council on this point. The Judicial Committee subsequently held that the Act of 1770 did not restrict the powers of the Commons in this way. The original issue, whether a Member's letter to a Minister was a proceeding in Parliament, was not considered by the Judicial Committee as it was outside its terms of reference.

[4] para. 5; 1957–58 (227).

tricity Board and their solicitors from any blame.[1] The successful opposition to the Committee's reports was led by H. Morrison, and his 218 supporters consisted of about ten Members of his own Party and roughly 200 Conservatives including almost all Ministers who took part in the division. Among the minority of 213 were the bulk of the Labour Members, including the Leader of the Labour Party, and some two dozen Conservatives including the Leader of the House, R. A. Butler, the Chairman of the Committee of Privileges. So although there was a cleavage of opinion in both parties, there was also a dominant view on each side of the House. There can be little doubt that the delay caused by the reference to the Judicial Committee had an important influence on the result, for during this period the idea that Members' letters to Ministers should enjoy complete protection encountered growing resistance. The suggestion that the solicitors of the L.E.B. were also guilty of a breach of privilege caused great alarm in the legal profession. How, it was asked, could solicitors advise their clients fully if so to do might lead to an assertion of breach of parliamentary privilege? As the law is heavily represented in the House, this alarm was probably decisive.

But the main reason why letters should not be privileged like questions is that the former are not public while the latter are. If a Member should make an irresponsible allegation in the Chamber, another Member will always be ready to challenge and probably rebuke him. To make damaging comments about individuals in the Chamber is widely regarded as an abuse of privilege, and Members are most careful when names are mentioned. Letters, enjoying semi-secrecy, are not subjected to the same safeguards. The document that started this controversy, complaining about the commercial practices of the L.E.B., was concerned with the commercial policy of a public body: it arose not from a constituency grievance but from the personal experience of a Member who admitted frankly that he had a slight financial interest in the outcome. It is easy to understand the initial feeling that a Member should not be threatened with legal proceedings for making criticisms of this kind, even if they were couched in vigorous language. Yet had the Strauss letter been declared privileged, what final implications would have emerged? Would any letter from a Member to a Minister have become sacrosanct? If a Member were to have sent on a constituent's letter to a

[1] H.C. Deb., Vol. 591, cols. 208–346.

Minister with a short covering note, would the privilege have extended to the constituent's letter? In issues of privilege each case is considered separately on its own merits but, had the Commons decided differently, an impressive precedent would have been established. As it is, these questions do not arise. Another danger would have been the possibility of a conflict between Parliament and the Courts. The Courts consider it their duty to decide any question of parliamentary privilege that may arise in a case that comes within their jurisdiction, and to decide it according to their own interpretation of the law. The decisions of the Court are not accepted as final by the House in matters of privilege, nor the decisions of the House by the Courts.[1] Thus the Commons cannot bar access to the Courts; they can but seek to deter actions from coming before the Courts.

The decision that the Strauss letter was not covered by privilege, however, caused many Members to re-examine their own position with anxiety. Some Members were reported to be refusing to take up constituency grievances for fear of becoming involved in libel actions. A group of Labour Members demanded an extension of question-time to accommodate business that was conducted formerly by correspondence. On both sides of the House misgivings were expressed about the position of nationalized industries, as questions cannot be put down about their day-to-day administration. All this concern seems to be a little exaggerated. The volume of correspondence between Members and Ministers has grown steadily in recent decades, but the Strauss case was the first time this correspondence has led to a threat of court action against a Member. Why had such an issue not arisen before? There are three main reasons. First, correspondence from a Member to a Government Department is not normally communicated to a third party. Second, a lawsuit is a difficult and expensive venture. Third, a prospective plaintiff would find it difficult to succeed as the defendant Member would plead qualified privilege. Qualified privilege is quite distinct from parliamentary privilege and is an established part of the law of defamation. Where a man, in performance of a legal or moral duty, publishes a defamatory statement about another, honestly believing it to be true and material to the performance of his duty, he cannot be ordered to pay damages even should the statement be shown to be untrue. The defence of qualified privilege is vitiated if the plaintiff can show to

[1] Erskine May, *Parliamentary Practice*, 16th edn., p. 172.

the satisfaction of the Court that the defendant was activated by malice—but malice is not easy to prove. Thus so long as a Member chooses language that does not cast doubts on the *bona fide* of his complaint, he appears to be protected by the existing law.[1] The Strauss case has not changed the law one iota; all these safeguards still remain. What is new is that Members are now more aware of the possibility that they may conceivably be called on to defend a libel suit—albeit with a good prospect of success. Some Members feel that they should be spared the cost and trouble of this risk, but it is a risk they share with all other persons in positions of responsibility who are called on to pass judgement on the work and character of their fellows.

How should Members act when they receive a communication from a constituent containing some allegation that is defamatory? Many grievances that Members hear about are real and deserve immediate remedial action: others are merely the products of weak or disordered intellects. Clearly, they cannot themselves institute inquiries to discover beyond doubt whether a charge is well or ill-founded. There are varying techniques for dealing with the problem. One is to pass the complaint to the Minister with the addition of a compliments slip. Another is to ask the complainant if he has any objection to disclosure to a 'wider circle'.[2] Another is to ask the complainant if he has any objection to his letter being forwarded to the person against whom the charge is made.[3] Members feel, quite properly, that they have a duty to try to aid constituents who write in distress. But where the distress involves a serious allegation against a third party, Members also have a duty to consider the interests of the third party. It is difficult to see how this latter duty is fulfilled by the automatic circulation of libellous communications to Government Departments. This, of course, is a moral judgment that has no bearing on the present legal position. Nor does it solve the problem. A

[1] However, a legal controversy broke out in the correspondence columns of *The Times* on how far malice in a constituent's letter would destroy a defence of qualified privilege if the Member had forwarded the malicious complaint to a Minister. *Inter alia*, see the issues dated 11th, 16th and 19th July, 1958. But the dominant view is that a Member would not be liable if there were no suggestion of malice in the wording of his covering letter.

[2] H.C. Deb., Vol. 525, col. 211. A suggestion by the Prime Minister (Sir W. Churchill) in 1954.

[3] Cf. letter to *The Times*, 10th July, 1958, by Sir H. Lucas-Tooth (Con. Hendon, S.).

letter like that received by J. Callaghan[1] (Lab. Cardiff, S.E.), from a lady alleging that her doctor had twice made an improper suggestion to her, does create a difficulty for the recipient Member. In future, such missives may be treated with more caution. Meanwhile, to urge the electorate that Members should not be entangled with affairs of this nature is the counsel of perfection.

The discussion on the Strauss case has raised issues far removed from its origin which should not be forgotten. The threatened action of the London Electricity Board was a shock to a wide body of parliamentary opinion: it is a reminder that a satisfactory relationship between the Commons and the nationalized industries has yet to be established. The economic and constitutional position of the nationalized industries is such that Ministers cannot escape ultimate responsibility for their good conduct. Freedom in matters of day-to-day administration should be regarded as a concession from the normal system of ministerial supervision, granted to assist managerial efficiency and flexibility. It is a freedom that demands justification by results. Certainly it should not be used to limit the very necessary interest that Members take in the work of nationalized undertakings. So long as parliamentary questions about these bodies are barred, a letter to a Minister is a natural substitute for Members to utilize. Such letters should not force Members to defend themselves in Court against a plaintiff financed by corporate funds. That there is a good defence, if the comments are found to be *bona fide*, is inadequate consolation. Whether Members should grant themselves wider protection against public boards is doubtful as real difficulties arise in defining the boundaries of this privilege. And wider protection may not be necessary. Unless the provocation is extreme, other public corporations may well think it prudent not to challenge Members in the Courts.

[1] Cf. his letter to *The Times*, 19th July, 1958.

Select Bibliography

ALLEN, Sir C. K. *Law and Orders* (2nd ed.)   Stevens 1956
ALLEN, V. L. *Power in Trade Unions*   Longmans 1954
AMERY, L. S. *My Political Life*. Vol. III   Hutchinson 1955
ANSON, Sir W. *Law and Custom of the Constitution* (5th ed.)
     O.U.P. 1922
ATTLEE, Earl. *As it Happened*   Heinemann 1954
BAGEHOT, W. *The English Constitution*   World's Classics 1928
BROCKWAY, A. F. *Inside the Left*   Allen & Unwin 1942
     Socialism over 60 Years: The Life of Jowett of Bradford
     Allen & Unwin 1946
BROMBERGER, M. & S. *Secrets of Suez*   Pan Books 1957
BROMHEAD, P. A. *Private Members' Bills in the British Parliament*
     Routledge 1956
BRYCE, Lord. *American Commonwealth*   Macmillan 1891
     Modern Democracies   Macmillan 1921
BULMER-THOMAS, I. *Party System in Great Britain*   Phoenix 1953
BURKE, E. *Speeches and Letters on American Affairs*
     Everyman 1908
BUTLER, D. E. *British General Election of 1951*   Macmillan 1952
     Electoral System in Britain 1918–1951   O.U.P. 1953
     British General Election of 1955   Macmillan 1955
CAMPION, Sir G. *Introduction to the Procedure of the House of Commons*   Macmillan 1947
CARTER, B. E. *Office of Prime Minister*   Faber 1956
CHUBB, B. *Control of Public Expenditure*   O.U.P. 1952
DALTON, H. *Call Back Yesterday*   Muller 1953
     The Fateful Years   Muller 1957
DICEY, A. V. *Law of the Constitution* (9th ed.)   Macmillan 1939
DUFF-COOPER (Lord Norwich). *Old Men Forget* Hart-Davis 1953
EAVES, J. *Emergency Powers and the Parliamentary Watchdog*
     Hansard Soc. 1957

SELECT BIBLIOGRAPHY

ERSKINE MAY. *Parliamentary Practice* (16th ed.)

Butterworth 1957

FORD, P. & G. *Guide to Parliamentary Papers* (new ed.)

Blackwell 1956

GREAVES, H. R. G. *The British Constitution* Allen & Unwin 1938

Civil Service in the Changing State Harrap 1947

HARRIS, W. *Life so Far* Cape 1954

HARROD, R. *Life of John Maynard Keynes* Macmillan 1951

HERBERT, SIR A. P. *The Ayes Have It* Methuen 1937

Independent Member Methuen 1950

HEWART, Lord. *The New Despotism* Benn 1929

HOLLIS, C. *Can Parliament Survive?* Hollis & Carter 1949

HOWARTH, P. *Questions in the House* Bodley Head 1956

JENNINGS, Sir W. I. *Parliamentary Reform* Gollancz 1934

Cabinet Government C.U.P. 1936

Parliament C.U.P. 1939

LAMBERT, J. S., and LAKEMAN, E. *Voting in Democracies*

Faber 1955

LASKI, H. J. *Parliamentary Government in England*

Allen & Unwin 1938

Reflections on the Constitution Manchester U.P. 1951

LLOYD GEORGE. *War Memoirs* Odhams 1939

MACALLUM, R. B., and READMAN, A. *British General Election of 1945* O.U.P. 1947

MACKENZIE, R. T. *British Political Parties* Heinemann 1955

MILL, J. S. *Representative Government* Everyman 1910

MILNE, R. S. & MACKENZIE, H. C. *Straight Fight*

Hansard Society 1955

MOORE-BRABAZON, J. *The Brabazon Story* Heinemann 1956

MORRIS-JONES, Sir H. *Doctor in the Whips' Room* Hale 1955

MORRISON, H. S. *Government and Parliament* O.U.P. 1954

NICHOLAS, H. G. *British General Election of 1950* Macmillan 1951

PEAR, R. *How People Vote* Routledge 1956

P.E.P. *Industrial Trade Associations* Allen & Unwin 1957

QUEEN VICTORIA, *Letters of*, 3rd Series, Vol. II Murray 1931

ROBERTS, B. C. *Trade Union Government and Administration in Great Britain* Bell 1956

ROSS, J. F. S.

Parliamentary Representation Eyre & Spottiswoode 1943

Elections and Electors Eyre & Spottiswoode 1955

270

SELECT BIBLIOGRAPHY

SHINWELL, E. *Conflict without Malice* Odhams 1955

SNOWDEN, Viscount. *Autobiography* Nicholson & Watson 1934

STOCKS, M. *Eleanor Rathbone* Gollancz 1949

TAYLOR, E. *House of Commons at Work* Penguin Books 1955

WEIR, L. MACNEILL, *The Tragedy of Ramsay MacDonald*

Secker & Warburg 1938

WHEARE, K. C. *Government by Committee* O.U.P. 1955.

WILLIAMS, F. *Dangerous Estate* Longmans 1957

WINTERTON, Earl. *Orders of the Day* Cassell 1953

WOOTTON, G. *Official History of the British Legion*

Macdonald & Evans 1956

YOUNG, G. M. *Stanley Baldwin* Hart-Davis 1952

Index of Members

273   T

General Index